THE CIVILIZATION OF THE AMERICAN INDIAN SERIES

Sitting Bull
Champion of the Sioux

Sitting Bull
CHAMPION OF THE SIOUX

A Biography

BY STANLEY VESTAL

Foreword by Raymond J. DeMallie

UNIVERSITY OF OKLAHOMA PRESS
NORMAN AND LONDON

Library of Congress Catalog Card Number: 57–5961
ISBN: 0–8061–2219–6

Sitting Bull: Champion of the Sioux is Volume 46 in *The Civilization of the American Indian Series*.

Copyright © 1932 by the Houghton Mifflin Company. Assigned 1956 to the University of Oklahoma Press. New edition copyright © 1957 by the University of Oklahoma Press, Norman, Publishing Division of the University. All rights reserved. Manufactured in the U.S.A. First printing of the new edition, February, 1957; second printing, September, 1957; third printing, 1965; fourth printing, 1969; fifth printing; 1972; sixth printing, 1976; seventh printing, 1980. First paperback printing, 1989.

10   11   12   13   14   15   16   17   18   19   20   21   22   23   24   25   26

To

LEWIS F. CRAWFORD

because he first introduced me to

SITTING BULL'S

family and friends

Contents

Part III: Captive

Illustrations

Foreword

By Raymond J. DeMallie

ORE THAN A half century has passed since Walter Stanley Campbell (who wrote under the pen name Stanley Vestal) published the first edition of *Sitting Bull*, and more than thirty years have passed since the University of Oklahoma Press brought out a revised and expanded version as Volume 46 in The Civilization of the American Indian Series.[1] The book was born of Campbell's passion for the Old West, of his sense of the larger-than-life heroes who shaped that epic time before civilization tamed the plains and transformed the frontier into civilization. His was a romantic's vision of that bygone era; for Campbell it was a world at once virile, male, and idealist—a foil for all that was wrong with modern America. Having begun his career as a historical writer with a biography of Kit Carson, whom he considered to be the preeminent white plainsman, Campbell determined to deepen his understanding of the frontier by writing a parallel biography of the greatest Plains Indian. For him the choice was obvious: Sitting Bull.[2]

Perhaps no other American Indian of the late nineteenth century experienced more notoriety than Sitting Bull, chief of the Hunkpapa division of the Teton Sioux (Lakota) people and reputed mastermind of the defeat of Lieutenant Colonel George Armstrong Custer at the Little Big Horn in 1876. Born in 1831, Sitting Bull was recognized as a leader by his

[1] Stanley Vestal, *Sitting Bull, Champion of the Sioux: A Biography* (Boston: Houghton Mifflin, 1932; new ed., Norman: University of Oklahoma Press, 1957).

[2] Stanley Vestal, *Kit Carson, The Happy Warrior of the Old West: A Biography* (Boston: Houghton Mifflin, 1928); Ray Tassin, *Stanley Vestal: Champion of the Old West* (Glendale: Arthur H. Clark, 1973), p. 131.

people based on his brave deeds in fighting enemy tribes, his successes in diplomacy, and his sacred powers derived from religious visions. When forced to resist white invaders in Sioux country, Sitting Bull led the fighting against the U.S. army. Following the Custer battle, seeking to evade further confrontation, he led his people to Canada where they attempted to continue the old buffalo-hunting way of life. But the herds diminished, and at last, in 1881, he returned to the United States and surrendered. For two years he and his band lived as prisoners of war at Fort Randall, finally being allowed to settle with the other Hunkpapas at Standing Rock Reservation in 1883. During part of 1884 and 1885 he traveled with the Wild West Show, enhancing his public image and becoming a household name. Then in 1890, as Indian-white tensions flared during the height of the Messianic Ghost Dance religion movement on the Sioux reservations, Sitting Bull was killed by the Indian police in a bungled attempt to arrest him.

For Campbell, a good part of the job of writing the story of Sitting Bull was to fill in the meaning of well-known events in the chief's life from the perspective of the Sioux themselves. Documents written by white soldiers, bureaucrats, missionaries, and adventurers could provide the outline for the story, but only living Indian people themselves could interpret Sitting Bull's deeds and assess his reputation from the perspective of Sioux cultural values and in the context of Sioux social life. Therefore, research materials for the biography would have to be collected on the Sioux reservations, and on the reservations of other tribes who knew Sitting Bull both as friend and foe. The oral testimony of Indian people would have to be accorded documentary stature and taken with the same seriousness, assessed with the same care, as more conventional documentary sources. In undertaking such field study for the writing of Indian history, Campbell was not the first. He may well have recognized that he was following in the path of George Bird Grinnell, whose masterful *The Fighting Cheyennes* was similarly fashioned from both Indian oral accounts and white written documents.[3]

[3] George Bird Grinnell, *The Fighting Cheyennes* (New York: Scribners, 1915); see Vestal's foreword to the new edition (Norman: University of Oklahoma Press, 1956).

FOREWORD

The impetus for Campbell's research on Sitting Bull may have stemmed from his attendance at the fiftieth anniversary celebration of the Battle of the Little Big Horn in 1926.[4] On that occasion Campbell met many of the survivors on both sides, army and Indian, an experience that doubtless rekindled his boyhood interest in Indian warfare. Campbell had been born in 1887 and spent his formative teenage years in Oklahoma, where he played with Cheyenne and Arapaho boys, came to know their families, and developed an abiding interest in Indian culture and history. Years spent at Oxford University as the first Rhodes Scholar from Oklahoma, in military service during World War I, and in building a career as a teacher of writing at the University of Oklahoma did not diminish his commitment to learning more about Indian peoples and the history of the West. Returning from the war, however, he found that most of the old-time warriors among the Oklahoma tribes had died, and he was told that only by going north to Sioux country could he still find men who had experienced traditional Indian life firsthand.[5]

At last, in the spring of 1928, Campbell was able to make his first research trip north, and during that summer he met One Bull, nephew of Sitting Bull, and enlisted his support for the project of recording his famous uncle's life story. One Bull himself was a recognized chief and renowned warrior, and his cooperation was critical. Slowly Campbell won the chief over, returning to spend much of the summer of 1929 with One Bull and his people. The aged Hunkpapa adopted him as a son, giving him his own father's name, Makes Room.

The next summer, 1930, Campbell continued his field study, spending the month of June on the Cheyenne River Reservation with Sitting Bull's other celebrated nephew, White Bull. The two men developed a close friendship and the material White Bull related, along with his patience to be questioned and his ability to explain, made him crucial to the success of the project. To Campbell, White Bull was especially exciting as a living exemplar of the old Sioux warrior spirit, for he was reputed to be the man who killed Custer. White Bull himself told Campbell that he could not say for sure that one of the soldiers he killed at the Little Big Horn

[4]Tassin, *Stanley Vestal*, p. 124.
[5]Ibid., p. 117.

XV

actually was Custer, but the body had been so identified by one of the Indians. Before he left, White Bull also honored Campbell by adopting him as a son, giving him the name His Name is Everywhere, suggesting that Campbell's abilities as a writer would spread White Bull's fame far and wide.

During these three summers Campbell not only interviewed Sioux people, but he traveled throughout the northern plains, interviewing Cheyennes, Nez Perces, Assiniboines, Crees, and Blackfeet. He let the old men speak for themselves, relating their memories without interruption, but he also questioned them to check and recheck details from published sources. Thus his reading in the literature throughout the school year served to guide his interviews during the summers.

Whenever possible, Campbell recorded material in the Lakota language in order to have a close check on the accuracy of translation. This included names of people and places, texts of songs and speeches by Sitting Bull as remembered and passed down by his relatives, and narratives of Sitting Bull's life by both One Bull and White Bull. In addition, he mailed detailed questions regarding specific events to be asked of One Bull, the answers to be written down in Lakota with English translation. Insistence on such documentation in the native language was a unique element in Campbell's research methodology.

In 1930, Campbell won a Guggenheim fellowship, which, with sabbatical leave, gave him fifteen months off to finish the biography of Sitting Bull—from June 30, 1930, until August 31, 1931. Following the summer's fieldwork, Campbell and his family sailed for France to join the trend of American expatriate writers. There, spending the fall and winter in Paris and the spring on the Riviera, Campbell completed the manuscript, which he delivered to the publisher in Boston before returning to Norman for the fall semester.

From his great mass of notes and interviews Campbell fashioned a biography that portrays Sitting Bull as a man born to greatness. From the portentous event of his turning over in his mother's womb, to his early visions that gave him power from the spirits of birds, to an eagle's prophecy that he would lead and protect his people, Sitting Bull is depicted as a man whose destiny for greatness was unquestionable. At the same time he is portrayed as ambitious, a man of action, who even as a boy of fourteen was a reckless warrior, ready to risk his life to achieve prominence in battle with the enemy. Campbell goes so far as to suggest that it was Sitting Bull who led his people to overrun the hunting territories of the horticultural Missouri River tribes and of the Crows, Shoshonis, and Assiniboines, seeking buffalo to the west, beyond the encroaching white frontier. And in recognition of this, in 1867 the Hunkpapas and all the others of the northern Teton Sioux conferred on Sitting Bull the unprecedented office of head war chief of his people, the leader who would protect them from the white men. At the same time, Campbell tempers his depiction of Sitting Bull with an emphasis on his human qualities of kindness and generosity, as in saving the lives of the Assiniboine boy who became his adopted brother Jumping Bull, and of Frank Grouard, the mail carrier, who ended up spending three years living with the Hunkpapas and who left a vivid account of his experiences.[6]

Campbell's biography is purely narrative in form, using context and drama to build up an understanding of Sitting Bull's world. Ethnographic detail is fitted into the narrative effortlessly but relentlessly, attempting to make plain to the reader the outward ways and inner values of Sioux culture. While today his comparisons with classic Greece and Rome tell us more of Campbell's own romanticism than they do about the Sioux, his portrayal of the fundamental beliefs of Sioux culture is more insightful. Notable is the matter-of-fact manner in which he manages to integrate sacred vision experiences into daily life as fundamental premises. His brief but masterful discussion of the Sioux ideal of "imitating" the buffalo in comparison to the modern ideal of "imitating" a machine (pp. 14–15) epitomizes Campbell's attitude toward reconstructing historical Sioux culture. He portrays Sioux men as not being obsessed with hunger or sex, but decides instead that "love of prestige was the fire which consumed their hearts" (p. 6). The sentiment fits well with his depiction of Plains Indian warfare as "sport," "a gorgeous mounted game of tag" (p. 11), and doubtlessly accurately reflected the memories of the old men

[6] Joe DeBarthe, *The Life and Adventures of Frank Grouard* (St. Joseph, Mo.: Combe Printing, 1894; new ed., Edgar I. Stewart, ed., Norman: University of Oklahoma Press, 1958).

who looked fondly back on the brave deeds of their youth. Yet dispassion-
ate assessment of the record of Plains Indian warfare and of famines, both
of which resulted in enormous loss of life, do not support Campbell's
interpretation. As for sex, the pervasive theme of jealousy over women,
which *Sitting Bull* documents so well, attests to its central place in the
Sioux man's ethos. Yet, no other historical work presents such a thorough
and consistent interpretation of nineteenth-century Sioux culture. In this
sense, Campbell's work lays a foundation for future reinterpretation.

Importantly, even though Campbell idealized Sitting Bull as a heroic
figure in the classic mold, his reconstruction of the Sioux past added a new
dimension to the historiography of the Sioux—a native point of view. It is
only obvious that having worked most closely with Sitting Bull's relatives,
the interpretation that Campbell developed reflected their point of view.
Campbell's narrative thus presents very much of a subjective, insider's
perspective, not a detached, objective analysis.

Not content to walk away from the Sioux having used only a small
portion of his interview material, Campbell returned to South Dakota in
the summer of 1932 to continue his interviews with White Bull. He had
contracted with his publisher to write White Bull's biography as well, not
only to supplement his reconstruction of historical Sioux life, but to bring
the story down to the present. In 1934 he published White Bull's life
story under the title *Warpath*, and that same year brought out a source
book that gathered together important documentary material from both
whites and Indians that would have lasting value for other scholars working in the same area. Together, this trilogy of books—and the manu-
scripts and notes on which they are based, now housed at the University of
Oklahoma—forms a major contribution to our historical understanding
of the Sioux people.[7]

Campbell's *Sitting Bull* enjoyed considerable popularity and eventually,
in the mid-1950s, long after it had gone out of print, the University of

[7] Stanley Vestal, *Warpath: The True Story of the Fighting Sioux Told in a Biography of
Chief White Bull* (Boston: Houghton Mifflin, 1934; new ed., with a foreword by Ray-
mond J. DeMallie, Lincoln: University of Nebraska Press, 1984); Stanley Vestal, *New
Sources of Indian History* (Norman: University of Oklahoma Press, 1934); Campbell
Collection, Western History Collections, University of Oklahoma Library.

Oklahoma Press decided to publish a new edition. In the years that had passed, Campbell had continued his interest in northern Plains history and both read and contributed to the burgeoning literature. He wanted to correct errors, add new material, and update the book before reprinting it, so working from a set of the original galley proofs, he edited them and inserted a considerable amount of additional typewritten material. In the end he declared the new edition to be far better than the original, and had the satisfaction of seeing his work disseminated to a new and even more eager generation of readers.

Campbell decided that the new edition should reveal White Bull as Custer's slayer. Both One Bull and White Bull had died in 1947; all the old Indians who might suffer repercussions from such a revelation were long dead, and Campbell apparently thought that the new edition of *Sitting Bull* would be the best vehicle for setting the record straight. In 1954 he had written to Savoie Lottinville, director of the University of Oklahoma Press, suggesting that the new edition "could include the story of how Custer died and who killed him which has never been published. This might help sales."[8] According to Campbell, White Bull had not wanted the story printed because it was hearsay; White Bull had never seen Custer alive, and it was only the word of his cousin, Bad Soup, that the man whom he had killed was actually Custer. For this reason, and for fear that some harm might come to the old man were he known as Custer's slayer, Campbell had suppressed the story from his earlier writings. Before Campbell completed his revision of *Sitting Bull* in 1956, however, a magazine article by his friend Reginald Laubin beat him to the punch, putting the story in print at last, much as Campbell himself understood it.[9] Subsequently, Campbell incorporated it into the revision of *Sitting Bull*, and its popular appeal was reflected in the decision by *American Heritage* to print the story of White Bull's slaying of Custer as an article, prior to publication of the book. The historical accuracy of the tale will remain forever in doubt, and the publicity Campbell received as a result

[8] Campbell to Lottinville, December 13, 1954 (Campbell Collection, Western History Collections).

[9] Reginald K. Laubin, "Who Killed Custer?" *Adventure Magazine*, September, 1955:27–29, 43–44.

of it led him to comment, "You would think I was the killer of Custer." [10]
Less than a year after the new edition appeared, Campbell himself died,
on Christmas Day, 1957.

Republication of *Sitting Bull*, for the first time in paperback, signals a
new life for an old classic. Subsequent historical work has suggested re-
finements in interpretation and corrected errors of fact; this is the normal
course of scholarship. But Campbell's biography of Sitting Bull will stand
as an important interpretation of a man in his time and place, not far
removed from us in time or place but greatly distant in culture—the old
culture of the Sioux in the days before the reservations, when buffalo still
provided the staff of life and a man's honor was built on the coups he
counted in war. No one has told the story better than "Stanley Vestal,"
adopted son of One Bull and White Bull, preeminent interpreter of the
Old West.

---

[10] Stanley Vestal, "The Man Who Killed Custer," *American Heritage* 8 (1957):4–9,
90–91; Tassin, *Stanley Vestal*, p. 269.

Introduction

WHEN THE FIRST edition of this book appeared, Stanley Walker in his review in *Books* declared, "This is a splendid biography."

The book had, at any rate, the distinction of being the first biography of a great American Indian soldier and statesman in which his character and achievements were presented with the same care and seriousness they would have received had he been of European ancestry. It was, moreover, unique in being the fruit of prolonged first-hand research among Plains Indians, with whom the author has been closely associated since boyhood.

Yet the book is a straight-forward narrative, not cluttered up with the documents and eye-witness accounts on which it was based; for these were separately published as *New Sources of Indian History*,[1] a source book extending to some 350 pages.

So now the publishers, having noted an insistent demand for the book, offer this new edition, updated and revised in the light of fresh evidence. And since the Indians who knew Sitting Bull are gone now and can give us no more information, this edition may well prove definitive. It is my hope that it will bring as much pleasure to the reader as the research and writing of it brought to me.

What great man born on American soil has been most misrepresented? We can think at once of several strong candidates. Mine is Sitting Bull.

[1] *New Sources of Indian History 1850–1891. The Ghost Dance—The Prairie Sioux, A Miscellany*, by Stanley Vestal (Norman, University of Oklahoma Press, 1934).

It is true that Abraham Lincoln's name trails after it more legends than any other. But after all, the Lincoln legends generally have some shred of truth about them, whereas the Sitting Bull legends seem to be made out of whole cloth, and have no relation to the facts at all. They are in general mere fabrications, many of which were concocted by war correspondents, and were afterward embodied in a book written by the Indian agent during whose term of office Sitting Bull was put out of the way. And the worst of it is, these yarns are not artistic— not half so colorful and interesting as the truth turns out to be.

For example, they said that Sitting Bull was not a warrior, though the pictorial record of some forty of his exploits (verified repeatedly during his lifetime) has lain in the Museum at Washington, D.C., for two generations. They said he was not a chief, though scores of men I knew saw him inaugurated as head chief of all the non-agency Sioux. They said he was a coward, though no one who has the slightest knowledge of Plains Indians can believe for a moment that a coward could for years have been leader of the warlike Sioux and Cheyennes. They called him a hostile because he went as far away from white men as it was possible to go. They called him a beggar and a coffee-cooler, when everyone knows that he was the very last Indian to give up his hunting and ask for rations at an agency. They accused him of opposing civilization because he resisted the hasty policy of land-hungry politicians— a policy resulting in these disgraceful conditions which the reformed Indian Bureau is now trying to remedy. Finally, they said he was crazy and killed him because he dared hope for the second coming of Christ.

It was a plain case of "give a dog a bad name, and then hang him." Like all his race, he has been misunderstood and misrepresented. Yet in this Sitting Bull has been most unlucky of all Indians, for the popular legend of his life was largely the creation of personal enemies. From the date of his birth to the manner of his death, it is a tissue of error and falsehood.

His first biographer, W. Fletcher Johnson, was well aware of the unsatisfactory nature of the materials at his disposal; his preface says as much: "In years to come, when some metempsychosis shall have translated passion into philosophy, a more discerning judgment may record in other terms these same events."

When Sitting Bull was dragged naked and unarmed from his bed and shot in the back, there were not lacking those who openly accused the Indian agent, Major James McLaughlin, of having murdered the chief. Later, McLaughlin published his interesting book, *My Friend the Indian*, a veiled defense against his outspoken critics. McLaughlin was an able man, quite superior to the run of Indian agents in his day, and in many respects his book is fine and sound. But it must not be forgotten that he was an official of the Indian Bureau at a time when that Bureau was even less enlightened than it has been since, and it was impossible for him to regard Sitting Bull with detachment. No man can rightfully claim the rôles of accuser, advocate, and judge in such a case—and then write the obituary.

Moreover, writers in the past were under terrific handicaps. For the plain fact is that until Sitting Bull surrendered, at the age of fifty, few white men had had even casual contact with him. One captive, Frank Grouard, who lived in the chief's household for some years, has left a record of his impressions which tally closely with those of my Indian informants. The rest is silence—or propaganda. But I shall make no apologies for ignoring the guesswork of men who can have had no opportunity to know the man of whom they write so glibly.

For many years the Indians who had known Sitting Bull well were unwilling to talk, and in my research I sometimes found an old man who was afraid to talk of the Custer fight, lest the soldiers come and hang him! In early days such fears tied all tongues but double ones. Indians who talked at all took care to say what their agents wished them to say. If they did not, the official interpreter usually arranged matters for them!

Now times have changed. The wall is down that parted our fathers; we have buried the hatchet. And Sitting Bull, like other famous Indians, is becoming better known. It is only a matter of time until the state of South Dakota will erect a fitting memorial to her great son; he is by all odds the most famous man ever born within her borders.

He is, besides, much the most interesting. No one can ignore so many-sided a man. His strong positive qualities, his world-wide fame; his early achievements as soldier, diplomat, organizer of the most unstable elements; his later rôles of patriot, statesman, and prophet; the crushing defeats inflicted by his warriors upon hostile Indian nations and the armies of the United States—all these afford ample scope to any lover of heroics. And the stubborn persistence of the man in the face of conquest, exile, starvation, treason, and death cannot fail to win the hearts of all who care for lost causes and forsaken beliefs and impossible loyalties.

Who can look with indifference upon this champion of that old, virile, Stone Age culture, where nothing counted but personal qualities, that culture which has been supplanted by a more effeminate and material-minded age? Certainly no male heart but must beat the faster at his story, now that it can all be told.

For the first forty-five years of Sitting Bull's life there is only one reliable source—the memories of old Indians of high reputation. To these I owe whatever is fresh in my presentation of the man's life and character. They have given unselfishly of their time and effort to make my study a success, and some of them I shall always count among the dearest of my friends—real men, from moccasin to scalplock. They were happy in their past, and proud of it. They liked to relive it, and for decades had thought of little else. Very few of those old-timers could be induced to repeat hearsay; I was often compelled to drive half a day to visit some eye-witness to an event with which my first informant was perfectly familiar, but of which he would not speak because he had not first-hand knowledge. And in all matters of warfare, old warriors generally insist on having two witnesses present to attest their statements, so important are battles in their eyes.

Such data suffer very little from the verification which historical research demands. If the ordinary book historian were one half so guarded in his statements as those old Indians, he would have to discard half his work. Educated as we have been upon books, we are altogether too apt to allow more authority to the printed page than it deserves. In an interview one has many opportunities to test the honesty, capacity, and knowledge of an informant. But when we read, we listen in the dark.

My study was pursued not merely among the members of Sitting Bull's own family, band, tribe, and nation, but among all other Indian nations with which he had contact, both in this country and in Canada. For the opportunity to carry through my research among the Indians and archives of the Dominion, and for the leisure to write this book, I am indebted to the John Simon Guggenheim Memorial Foundation.

It is impossible in a single volume to narrate even the chief events in the crowded life of so many-sided a man, and at the same time document in detail the innumerable statements which run counter to a legend almost wholly false. It is inevitable, therefore, that such a compressed narrative should at times appear to be a work of mere imagination. I assure the reader that such an impression is unwarranted. The events of this story are real events. The scenes described—many of which I have visited—are real scenes. I have invented no dialogue; the words put into the mouth of Sitting Bull are his own, and for many of his utterances I have the Sioux text. The man's psychology, where indicated, is that suggested by Indians who knew him, not by myself. And I have scrupulously tried to mark off clearly all matters of opinion or inference from matters of fact. Where legend intrudes, it is labeled.

For, when all is said, the first qualification of a biographer is doubt, a steady determination to verify everything; his second, readability. Good biography, like the good life, is based upon knowledge and inspired by human sympathy.

Of the Indian informants who assisted me, special mention is due to Moses Old Bull, the Hunkpapa historian, and to Chief Joseph White Bull and Chief Henry Oscar One Bull, both nephews of Sitting Bull. The one fought beside his famous uncle in fifteen battles; the other was adopted by the chief when four years old, and grew up in his tipi. We passed many long days together.

One afternoon, as I sat in the lodge with One Bull, checking over one item after another in the printed records for his comment, the vigorous old man suddenly turned to me and said earnestly in his native language, "My friend, I do not care to hear the lies that white men have made about Sitting Bull. I will tell you the truth!"

In this matter, the old man and I have but one heart.

STANLEY VESTAL

Norman, Oklahoma

Acknowledgments

AMONG THOSE who aided my work in Canada, special thanks are due to Colonel Cortlandt Starnes, Commissioner, Royal Canadian Mounted Police; to Francis J. Audet, Chief of the Information, Public Archives of Canada; to Mr. W. M. Graham, Commissioner, Department of Indian Affairs; and to the Librarian, Provincial Legislative Library, Regina, Saskatchewan: these, and their efficient staffs, gave most courteous and invaluable assistance.

Of those who aided my study of records in the States, I wish to mention here Lieutenant-Colonel George P. Ahern, U.S.A., Retired, Recorder of the Order of Indian Wars of the United States; the Honorable C. J. Rhoads, Commissioner of Indian Affairs; Mr. M. W. Stirling, Chief of the Bureau of American Ethnology; Mr. Tyler Dennet, Historical Adviser in the Department of State; and all those in charge of the archives of the War Department, the Library of Congress, and the Historical Collections of the States of North and South Dakota, Nebraska, Oklahoma, Minnesota, Wyoming, and Montana. For access to unpublished official records and private papers which throw an entirely new light upon Sitting Bull's last years most hearty thanks are due to Mrs. Sibley McLaughlin, Mrs. Irene Beaulieu, Judge Frank Zahn, the Reverend Father G. J. Garraghan, S.J., Mr. and Mrs. J. F. Waggoner, Mr. Francis B. Bullhead, and Mr. A. B. Welch. In addition to the informants mentioned in the Introduction and text in connection with the events they witnessed, I wish here to mention the following who have helped me with personal recollections, or in other ways.

1. *Indian Informants:*

In joint conference on Sitting Bull's War Record: (Sioux) Circling Hawk, Old Bull, One Elk, John Fine Weather, Bear-Comes-Out, Little Eagle, Eagle Boy, Owns-Medicine, Brought, Crazy Bear. Also on another occasion: Bear's Ghost, Gray Whirlwind, Many Horses, Medicine Bear, Black-Prairie-Dog. Yet another, Callous Leg and White Bird. Nez Percé: George Peo-peo-tah-likt, John Moses, Philip Andrews, Charley Kow-to-likt, Charley Stevens, Daniel Jefferson, Johnson Hayt. Cheyenne: Bob-Tail-Horse, young Two Moon, Willis Rowland, Hump (son of Chief Black Kettle). Crows: Plenty Coups, Bell Rock, John Frost, W. H. White, Mary E. Watt, Russell White Bear. (Canadian Indians) (1) Sioux: Julius Standing Buffalo, John Sioux. (2) Cree and Saulteaux (joint conference): Otterskin, Day Walker, Buffalo Bull, Wapoose, Yellow Bird, Chief Feather, Kiswish, Rabbit. (3) Assiniboin (Hohe): Silas Adam, Big Darkness, Two Bull. (4) Blood: Chief Buffalo Child Long Lance. (5) Blackfoot: High Eagle.

Individual informants among the Sioux: Chief Standing Bear, No Flesh, Putinhin, Eagle Thunder, Dog Eagle, Bear Soldier, Red Horse, Turning Hawk, Makes Trouble, Iron Dog, Ben White, Antoine DeRockbraine, Reverend Herbert Welsh, Jr., and Sitting Bull's grand-niece, Mrs. Cecelia One Bull Brown, to whom I am indebted for a thousand details and endless trouble in helping me gather information. Mr. Robert P. Higheagle spent some weeks in going over all my data, and assisted in collecting and transcribing twenty-five of Sitting Bull's songs, besides a great number of anecdotes. Finally I am indebted to Mrs. Gertrude Bonnin.

2. *White Informants:*

Mr. J. D. Allen, of Mandan, N. D.; Mr. Johnny Baker; Colonel Charles Francis Bates, U.S.A., Retired; Captain L. P. Baker; Mr. A. McG. Beede; Captain J. M. Belk; Colonel G. S. Bingham, U.S.A., Retired; Mr. Norman Fergus Black; General William C. Brown, U.S.A., Retired; Mr. A. L. Bloomer; Mr. Charles M. Bocker; Mr.

ACKNOWLEDGMENTS

A. E. Brininstool; Mr. John P. Carignan; Mr. C. Christensen; Mr. Lewis F. Crawford; Mr. Chip Creighton; General E. H. Crowder; Captain James H. Cook; Mr. Joseph Dietrich; Miss Frances Densmore; Mr. Nelson G. Edwards; Mr. and Mrs. W. A. Falconer; Mr. F. B. Fiske; Mr. Grant Foreman; Mr. T. J. Gatchell; Mr. Melvin R. Gilmore; Mr. E. A. Garlington; Mr. Frank C. Goings; Mr. George H. Gooderham; Mr. Arthur H. N. Gore; Mr. George Bird Grinnell; Miss Grace Raymond Hebard; Mr. Dave Hilger; Mr. W. T. Hornaday; Mr. F. W. Hodge; Professor R. T. House; Mrs. E. Jacobsen; Mr. Vernon La Chance; Major G. W. "Pawnee Bill" Lillie; Professor O. G. Libby; Mr. Frank B. Linderman; Mr. Bull Marshall; Dr. R. G. Macbeth; Dr. V. T. McGillycuddy; Mr. J. G. Masters; Mrs. Tilla Sielke McIntosh; Mr. Henry McKay; Mr. William McNider; Mr. Henry F. Meyer; Mr. Harvey K. Meyer; Mr. Warren King Moorehead; Mr. W. H. Nesbitt; Mrs. Margaret M. Nice; Captain Luther H. North; Reverend George Waldo Reed; Colonel Hugh T. Reed; Reverend T. L. Riggs; Mr. Doane Robinson; Mr. Marion P. Satterlee; Mr. Willard Schultz; Professor Robert Scoon; General Hugh Lenox Scott; The late Professor Maurice G. Smith; the Reverend Father Bernard Strassmeier, O.S.B.; Mr. Richard "Diamond Dick" Tanner; Mr. Chauncey Thomas; Mr. H. C. Thompson; Mr. T. J. Thompson; Mr. O. S. Upchurch; Colonel Chas. A. Varnum; Colonel S. C. Vestal, U.S.A.; Mr. W. D. Wallis; Mr. Richard J. Walsh; Mrs. Mamie L. (Wade) Weeden; Mr. Frederick Weygold; Mr. E. C. Witzleben; Mr. William Allen White; Mr. Gilbert L. Wilson; Mr. Charles Erskine Scott Wood; Mr. William Presley Zahn. I wish also to thank my cousin, Mr. J. Dallas McCoid, Jr., who was my companion and secretary in the field throughout my study.

I. Warrior

I. The Boy Volunteer

SITTING BULL came of a family of fighters. He was the only son of his parents, and since the Sioux believe that a son is the greatest and best gift of all, Sitting Bull was doubly welcome at his birth. He was born on the south bank of Ree River, now called Grand River, at a place named Many-Caches because of the many old storage pits there, a few miles below the present town of Bullhead, South Dakota. This happened during the Winter-when-Yellow-Eyes-Played-in-the-Snow, March, 1831.

At that time, however, no one could foresee his later fame and power, and he began life with no better title than the nickname "Slow." Apparently, he deserved it, for they say that, even as an infant, he was deliberate. When a bit of food or any other object was put into his baby hand, he did not immediately stick it into his mouth, like other children, but held it in his hand, turning it over and looking at it, until he had made up his mind. Once he accepted it, however, he never let go.

This deliberation, and a certain awkwardness with which he moved his sturdy body, earned him the nickname by which his world knew him for fourteen years.

That world was one in which Achilles or Odysseus would have felt at home. In those days the Sioux warrior had a dignified self-reliance which some of his unlucky descendants seem to have lost. "They are all gentlemen," wrote the Jesuit Father, and so they were. Gentlemen of the Epic, not the Romantic, mould. Aristocrats without the modern aristocrats' softness. Unafraid as a peasant of the hard labor of their hunter's life, yet without the peasant's subservience. Their camps con-

3

tained no sordid vassals. And their chiefs were neither idle nor ostentatious, but shared the work and dangers of their people, and maintained their rank by sheer personal superiority.

"Slow" was a strong, lively lad, and found this world greatly to his liking. What wonder? Was not the Sioux or Dakota nation the greatest in the world, so far as he knew? Were not the Tetons, or Prairie Sioux, the most numerous and powerful division of that great nation?

Were not the Hunkpapa, his own tribe, the bravest and most warlike of all the Tetons? Their warriors were victorious on every frontier; their hunting grounds were in the very heart of the buffalo plains and teemed with every kind of game; their camps were full of fast horses; their territory contained every sort of country—timber, prairie, and river bottom, badlands, and mountaintops. So vast it was that his people were constantly on the move, traveling in their easygoing fashion from river to river and range to range, following their buffalo, and patrolling that rich domain to keep out the enemies who hovered on their frontiers, where—as yet—no shadow of the white invader had fallen.

While "Slow" was still strapped to his baby-board, he rode slung from the horn of his mother's rawhide saddle, peering out from under the decorated hood at the ever changing panorama of the ample plains. When somewhat older, he surveyed the world from the snug folds of a shaggy buffalo robe upon his mother's shoulders. Later, she put him in a basket slung between two lodgepoles crossed above her pony's withers, and there he sat, jouncing along under the horse's tail, watching the grass slide by beneath him, holding fast with small brown hands when the going was rough, or closing his eyes tight against the splashing water when the old nag forded a stream. By the time he was five, he was riding behind his mother, chubby legs outspread, clinging to her belt. Before he was ten, he rode a pony of his own, shaping his plastic legs to the curve of the animal's barrel—a curve which would make him slightly bowlegged as long as he lived.

With the possession of that pony, "Slow" entered upon the carefree, active, interesting life of the Indian boy, upon whom no restraints were laid other than the duty of rising early, hunting small game with bow and arrows, and perhaps herding the family stock through long, lazy days on the prairie. A life all games and sports: foot races, pony races, follow-my-leader up and down the bluffs, swimming all day long in the river, or wrestling with the Cheyenne neighbor boys in the intimate Cheyenne manner. And when boyish sports palled, hanging about to watch the endlessly changing activities of their elders, whom they mimicked in private. "Slow" liked it all.

How agreeable that constant traveling! The gray mornings when he rounded up the family ponies, while his mother furled the white tent, lashed the tent poles to the saddle of her pack horse, and rode away atop a mountain of baggage, leaving behind only a feeble column of smoke rising from between the flattened rectangles of grass where the beds had been. How jolly to ride with his boy companions on the edges of that great crawling ruck of equipage, watching the snarling, wolflike dogs trotting under their packs, their long red tongues lolling across their white fangs; watching the plodding pack-mules, the loose horses, the stray colts plunging about, the scolding of exasperated women. How amusing the loud, impatient harangues of old men, the shouted, broad jests of heralds, the singing—the endless singing—of warriors parading on the flanks in all the glory of eagle plumes, paint, fine horses, and lances tossing athwart the sky. And there was always the chance of flushing game along the line of march, the pursuits, the pony-races, the boyish brags, the feats of horsemanship before the eyes of the girls.

And when the final halt was made, and the great circle of conical tipis mushroomed on the plain, each tent in its appointed order, band by band and family by family, how good the smell of wood-smoke and meat cooking, how savory the steaming soup in the kettle, the big wooden bowls of crisp white tipsin! How filling the brown pemmican larded with buffalo tallow, how tart and spicy the wild choke-cherries! And when the warriors had made a hunt, how satisfying to spend the night going over the huge stacks of fresh meat, searching out choice tidbits—of buffalo hump, or bear's ribs, or haunch of good fat venison!

And always, at night, when he had eaten all that a small pot-belly could hold, how jolly to sit by the brisk little fire in the family tent, and be put to sleep with innumerable myths of Iktomi, trickster and fool, with legends of animals which spoke to men, giving good advice, with hero tales of his people, of their far travels, their great bravery, and of the cowardly, sneaking enemies who skulked about their camps at night, and never dared show their faces in the daytime!

Then he would hear how the Sioux first met the Iroquois, long ago, and how the Iroquois haughtily demanded, "Who are you?"

"Sioux" came the answer. "And who are you?"

"Iroquois. Where are you going?"

"We are hunting for buffalo," the Sioux replied. "And you?"

"We are looking for *men*," had come the haughty answer.

"Well, we are men," said the Sioux. "You need look no farther."

Whereupon the fight began, and when it was over, the Sioux had killed or captured all those Iroquois. They slit the noses of their captives (the punishment inflicted upon unfaithful wives), and let them go. "Tell your chiefs," they said, "to send no more *women* looking for *men*!"

And when he heard that, the boy "Slow" would sway restlessly on his haunches, arms folded about his knees, and long for the day when he himself could share such brave adventures. He was proud of his nation.

"Slow's" mind was not obsessed by thoughts of sex or hunger. Among his people, women were plenty, celibacy unknown, and a marriage could be formed or dissolved at will. All material comforts were homemade, and the woman could provide them readily—if only her man was a passable hunter. No, it was not love of woman or lust for wealth that haunted the dreams of the Sioux. Their country supplied all their needs, and they took sex in their stride. Love of prestige was the fire which consumed their hearts, and upon this passion all their institutions were erected. To them prestige was all-important, and it was to be won on the warpath. "Slow" envied the warriors. Though born a male, he as yet rated no better than a woman.

Those mighty men rode away to die or conquer, and came home again in loud triumph, bringing new horses, bringing hair and captured weapons, bringing strange foreign women to be adopted into the tribe. How they sang and boasted of their exploits, how grandly they paraded around the camp circle, how they stamped and postured in the unbroken series of dances in the sociable camps! What privileges they enjoyed, what dignity, what perquisites! No feast, no dance, no ceremony was complete without a war-story narrated by its hero. What boy could fail to long for equal honor? Not "Slow." His heart was full of war. . . .

It is better to lie naked than to rot on a scaffold.

That old proverb rang in his head, as he rode idly about the summer camp of his people, reining in his gray pony now and then to watch some man straightening arrows or repairing a saddle, to watch some woman—perhaps in tears—swiftly plying her bright awl as she made new moccasins, pair after pair, and stuffed them full of good fat pemmican for the war party which was about to start.

To "Slow," war was no remote matter of hearsay. He had been born and reared in the midst of it. When he was little, his mother had often dressed his baby feet in tiny moccasins before she went to sleep at night, because they might have to run out of the tent and hide if an enemy attacked. He had learned to fear the hoot of the owl, which might really be the signal of prowling foes—perhaps Crow Indians— who would cut a small boy to pieces if they caught him. Wounds, and tears, and wild rejoicings, war dances, victory dances, with all their lively pantomime of battle, ambush, and sudden death, were part of his daily life. Only a few moons before, his uncle, Four Horns, had been left for dead on the battlefield.

"Slow" knew that on the frontiers of his nation were the bones of many heroes, who lay as they had fallen, stripped for battle, fighting his enemies. And when the wind was right, the boy did not need to turn his eyes toward the near-by hills in order to sense the gaunt burial scaffolds, which carried the carcasses of men who had died ingloriously in their beds—of sickness, of old age. He had often heard old men shouting their complaints among the tents: how they suffered from toothache, sore bones, from cold, from neglect.

"Slow" himself was young and strong, with a deep chest and broad shoulders, though of no great height for his years. Four winters back

7

he had killed his first buffalo calf, and already he was beginning to feel himself a man. He longed to prove it. Yes, it was true. It is better to lie naked on the field of honor than to rot on a burial scaffold. . . .

Members of the war party were already mounted and jogging out of camp, leading their best horses, going quietly away by twos and threes, to meet at the appointed rendezvous and start off against the Crows or the Ho'he, looking for glory, scalps, and horses. For two days the camp had been humming with excitement over the departure of the warriors. Now the men were leaving.

There was no parade, no crowd out to see them off. The Teton Sioux reserved their cheers for successful fighters. Anyone could go to war. The question was, What would he do when he got there?

"Slow" watched the men ride away, deliberating. But not for long. His mind was made up. He decided to go too.

He did not inform his family of this intention. His mother, a strong-minded, serious woman, full of common sense, might raise objection, and "Slow" always listened to her. Then again, his two sisters might cry and beg him to stay at home, and remind him that he was just a boy, only fourteen years old. That would be unpleasant; and besides, it was very awkward, almost impossible, to refuse the request of a close relative. And of course it was *not* the part of a man to consult a woman about war! "Slow" turned his pony's nose away from the camp and followed the last of the warriors.

When "Slow" reached the rendezvous of the war party, he found twenty men assembled, and among them his own father. They stared in silence at this uninvited volunteer, at his barebacked gray pony, his boyish calfskin robe, his small quiver full of blunt-headed arrows, good only for shooting small birds! All at once the boy felt the silent disapproval of these men, felt that perhaps he might be unwelcome. He rode up to his father, who waited to hear his son explain himself. The pony seemed to be "Slow's" best, perhaps his only, friend just then. Slipping from its back and throwing one arm over its neck, he declared, "We are going too."

The father listened to that simple statement, and his heart was big with pride. The family had always taken care never to thwart the boy

8

or break his spirit, and now it was too late to begin. It was no good attempting to budge "Slow," once he had made up his mind. His father did not try.

Four years back, the boy had killed his first buffalo. And more recently, when a prowling enemy was killed close by the tents, the boy had shown his courage. For when the men dragged the slain man into the circle of tipis, and egged on the boys to go up and touch that strange, bloody image of death, "Slow" had been the first to go. That day he showed more bravery than any boy in camp. . . .

"You have a good running horse," said his father. "Try to do something brave. That man is most successful who is foremost. And in hunting or in war, that man is foremost who has the fastest horse."

"Slow's" father gave him a *coup*-stick—a long, peeled wand with a feather tied at the small end—a stick to be used in striking the enemy. The boy had brought no weapons, and perhaps his father thought him too young to use them to advantage. Perhaps he thought it braver to go into the fight without weapons, to strike the enemy with a harmless stick.

When the necessary ceremonies had been performed and the leader had given his orders, the young men set out. Good-Voiced-Elk was leader.

They started. Then it was riding, riding, riding, riding away to the north and west, toward the place where Red Water empties into Muddy Water, the Missouri River. There they hoped to encounter enemies.

Plains Indian warfare, as practiced in those days, was probably the finest sport ever known in this world. No man who loves horseflesh and the bright face of danger but must long to have shared its thrilling chances. It had all the dash and speed of polo, the informality of a fox hunt, the sporting chance of sudden wealth afforded by the modern horse race, and danger enough to satisfy the most reckless. And it was no game for weaklings, for the Plains Indian seldom gave, and never expected, quarter.

Yet its prime object was not bloodshed or manslaughter. The warrior, unless he was out for loot or revenge for recent injuries, or fighting in defense of his family, made war a grandstand play. He fought, not so much to damage his enemy as to distinguish himself. In very early times the Sioux warrior had fought at close quarters simply because he had no long-range weapons. Later, when he had obtained these, he still regarded hand-to-hand combat as the only manly form of battle. He still felt that a brave man would grapple with his foe. On this conviction he erected his elaborate system of military honors, citations, and insignia of rank. He still desired, above everything, to strike his enemy with his hand or with something held in his hand. And to accomplish this, he was often willing to take dreadful risks.

This touching or striking the enemy—alive or dead—was the goal of every warrior. It is known as the *coup*, a term borrowed from the French frontiersmen. As a war honor, it ranked far above the mere killing of an enemy. Rescues, wounds, and captured horses or weapons also counted for honors: but the *coup* was the great prize. And so it was the object of every man to win as many *coups* as possible, for all social privileges and perquisites depended upon this achievement.

Four men could count *coup* upon the same enemy in the same fight, and on that occasion were rated in the order of their touching him. For that reason, many spirited races were run to win the coveted honor of the first *coup*, and the man who won it could afford to let laggards kill and scalp his enemy. When a man struck his foe, he yelled his own name aloud, adding, "I have overcome this one," so that he might have witnesses to his deed. And as soon as the fight was over, the warriors got together, and each one put in a claim for the honors to which he was entitled. If he could produce witnesses to these, they were formally awarded to him. Thereafter, the winner was entitled to narrate his deed at any public gathering. In fact, he was compelled to do so, for such a war story formed the invariable credentials of a man performing any public action. Unless a man had the right to tell such a story, he was automatically barred from participation in tribal or ceremonial affairs. He was, in effect, disfranchised and disqualified. He could not even name his child.

Naturally, his comrades took good care to see that he did not claim anything he was not entitled to, and every warrior's handicap was well

SITTING BULL WEARING CRUCIFIX GIVEN HIM BY
FATHER DE SMET.

(Bureau of American Ethnology)

PAINTING OF SITTING BULL BY MRS. CATHERINE
WELDON.

Damaged at the time of Sitting Bull's arrest.

understood by the whole camp. In those small communities, rivalry was keen, and the concentration of all desires upon the one goal—prestige—inspired an almost insane love of public honor. There were no books to hand down the deeds of great men of old times, no great population in which the individual felt lost. The Sioux was as avid of praise an an actor, and thought in terms of "me, here, now." He did his works to be seen of men, and had his reward in this world.

In short, Indian warfare on the Plains was simply a gorgeous mounted game of tag. Public honor, social privilege, wealth, and the love of women were its glittering prizes: its forfeit, death.

When "Slow" and his comrades reached the Red Water, they sent out a scout to look for "sign" of enemies. The scout soon returned, saying that enemies were coming right toward them. Good-Voiced-Elk and the others remained hidden behind a small hill, while the scout kept watch.

Before long they could see enemies coming, still quite a way off. It was a mounted party, of about the same strength as their own. Hastily the men made preparations for battle, stripping for action, uncovering their shields. They planned to lie low until the enemies came close, and then to jump them suddenly. When all was ready, the men mounted and sat waiting for the leader's signal.

Just then they noticed a boy off at one side. He was mounting a gray horse almost covered with red paint. The boy himself was naked except for moccasins, breech-cloth, and beads, and his entire body was painted a bright yellow. It was "Slow," and already he was on his war horse, starting toward the enemy, coup-stick in hand, unable to hold back any longer. He wanted his chance. The gray horse was off like an arrow.

In a flash, the others, not to be left behind, also charged. But the boy's horse had the start, it was a fast one, and he remained in the lead.

The startled enemies, seeing the Sioux pouring from behind their hill, drew rein. They did not know how many Sioux might be hidden behind that hill. Whirling in their tracks, they turned tail and galloped away, hard as they could quirt their ponies. Within a few min-

utes, those on fast horses were far ahead, while those with slow mounts
lagged behind, lashing their ponies, with the yells and thunder of the
frantic pursuit loud in their frightened ears.

Before long, "Slow" was getting close to the hindmost. The man
must have heard those pounding hooves behind him, gaining, gaining.
Perhaps he saw that he could not hope to escape, and determined to
sell his life dearly. He threw himself from his horse and turned back.
"Slow" found himself facing a man on foot with an arrow on his
bow-string.

Men who have fought Indians all agree that by far the most desperate warriors among them were the boys. In this, "Slow" was no
exception to the rule. At such a moment a seasoned warrior would
have flung himself on one side of his racing horse and wheeled away
from that deadly shaft. But the boy "Slow," full of fight, reckless of
danger as boys will be, never swerved from his headlong course. He
was too hot to win that honor, to count his first *coup*, to be foremost in
his first battle. There, just ahead, was glory, manhood, girls, all that
he desired in life. He sped straight on, leaning forward with out-
stretched *coup*-stick.

Crack! He struck the enemy smartly across his forearm, spoiled his
aim. The arrow never found its mark. *"On-hey!"* yelled the boy. "I,
'Slow,' have conquered him!" The plunging gray knocked the enemy
flat, and the Sioux warriors who followed killed him before he could
recover his feet.

When that running fight was over, the Sioux gathered up their
trophies—the horses, weapons, and scalps they had taken, and set out
for home. On nearing their camp, they concealed themselves until
dawn. Then, with a rush of plunging hooves, wild yells of triumph,
and much shooting, they charged in among the smoke-browned tents
of their people, and, forming a column, paraded around the camp
circle, singing, and announcing in loud voices the exploits which each
man had added to his record.

"Slow's" father put the boy on a fine bay horse and led him around
the circle of tents with the others. In a loud, proud voice he called the
people to observe his son, mounted upon the bay horse, and covered

from top to toe with the black paint of victory. "My son has struck the enemy!" he shouted. "He is brave! I dub him *Ta-tan'-ka I-yo-ta'- ke,* Sitting Bull!"

"Slow" sat upon the bay horse, his bare legs dangling, well content. He was fully conscious of the awe of his former playmates, the applause of the warriors, the bright eyes of the girls, the shrill ululations of the women of the camp. He frankly enjoyed himself, without a trace of false modesty. His people did not regard shyness as any virtue in a man. And then his father, in order to show appreciation of his son's distinction, gave away four good horses to poor men.

That night, in the victory dance, a new warrior showed himself, stooping and rearing and stamping with the best. For he had not only suddenly raised himself to man's estate at the age of fourteen winters. He had actually been the first to strike the enemy: he was the hero of the occasion. His heart was big that night, and as he pranced and postured to the pounding of the drums, the perfect rhythms of that wild music, he was well aware of that great throng of people singing and swaying as one in the exultation of his victory; well aware of his mother's pride, his sisters' new respect, the applause of his innumerable relatives, the perfumed bodies of the girls in the ring. That was a heady and intoxicating night for the boy who had now become a man.

A new figure had stepped upon the stage of history.

2. The Pattern of Manhood

THE STORY of Sitting Bull's first *coup* has been told often. Sitting Bull himself was never tired of repeating it: he loved the memory of that deed. And although his later exploits were many and remarkable, it is noteworthy that he never threw away the name he won that day.

Yet he had a better reason for retaining the name. It was of sacred or mysterious origin, and he was always a religious man. After he became famous, many legends arose to account for his being called Sitting Bull, not a few of which have been printed. But the truth has never been told until now.

In order to get the full significance of this story, certain facts must be kept in mind. . . .

In the first place, the Sioux were buffalo hunters. The buffalo's flesh was their chief food; its hide supplied them with clothing, bedding, tents, with the bags in which they packed their personal belongings, with the horse gear used in their hunts, with the bull-boats or coracles used in crossing their rivers. Its bones were made into many implements; its hooves gave them glue; its sinews were their bow-strings, their thread; its blood was used for paint; its horns were shaped into spoons and cups and ornaments and weapons; its hair stuffed their pillows, their saddle-pads; its tallow, mixed with ochre, anointed their faces, its very dung was used for fuel.

Sitting Bull's people lived by the buffalo: without it they were helpless. Just as, in our time, civilization rests upon millions of machines, so in those days the civilization of the Sioux rested squarely upon the humped shoulders of millions of wild, shaggy cattle.

Today, we tend to take the machine as the standard for everything. Among us, the most admired, the most successful, the most envied men are those who are most like machines: men who are efficient, punctual, serene, standardized, men who can produce work of a given quality in huge quantities, who can harness the powers of nature and turn raw materials into wealth. We think like the Sioux, only we think about different things. We imitate the machine: he imitated the buffalo. This being true, the manner in which Sitting Bull's name originated explains why he never changed it, as the following story will show.

One summer evening, some time before Sitting Bull's first exploit, four Sioux hunters sat around a small fire of buffalo chips, roasting the juicy ribs of a buffalo which they had just killed. The sun had set, but dusk had not yet come. The sky was cloudless, and everything was bright and distinct in that dry, clear air. The bare prairie sloped away toward Smoky Butte. There was no sign of life anywhere.

The small fire pushed its thin pale column of smoke up endlessly into the quiet sky, the four weary ponies stood with drooping heads, while the hunters waited for the meat to cook. They said little, for they were tired and hungry. It was the season when the bulls groan and bellow together, and at intervals, in the silence, the men could hear the dull, confused, murmuring sound of their roaring, though the herds were miles away.

All at once, they heard somebody coming, talking. Instantly they sprang up, alert, for in those days strangers were likely to be enemies. But as this stranger approached, the men saw that it was a great buffalo bull, swinging leisurely along down the narrow trail, head hung low and beard sweeping the ground, muttering and talking to himself.

One of these hunters was named Returns-Again. He was a doctor of some repute, and well versed in the sacred traditions of his people. He knew at once that a buffalo talking in this manner was a marvelous thing.

The Buffalo God was one of the great gods of the Sioux nation, even being identified with the Sun himself. The Buffalo God looked after virgins and old people. He was the patron of both sexes, of generosity, fecundity, industry, and ceremonies. As the comrade or double of the Sun, he was worshiped in the Sun Dance, and so the skull of a buffalo was always upon the altar in the Medicine Lodge. And of course this god controlled the hunt, and therefore all hunters revered him.

Returns-Again knew that this god walked the earth in the form of a great bull, and might speak to men. Also, Returns-Again was one of those gifted persons who can sometimes understand the speech of animals. And so, while his frightened companions stood there, frozen with awe, he was all ears. The bull was coming quite close now: his mutterings were audible, intelligible.

These are the words heard by Returns-Again: "Sitting Bull, Jumping Bull, Bull-Standing-with-Cow, Lone Bull."[1] This ancient Sioux formula expressed in terms of the buffalo the four ages or "divides" of life: Infancy, Youth, Maturity, and Old Age.

The four hunters stood rigid, hands over mouths. They were filled with awe, amazement, and reverence, as they watched the big bull shoulder its slow way across the prairie, until it disappeared behind a neighboring swell. They had just witnessed a remarkable thing, something very wonderful, sacred, *wa-kan'*. Four was the lucky, holy number among the Sioux, and the bull had given Returns-Again *four* names! For, since the other three hunters had not been able to interpret the sounds made by the bull, Returns-Again considered that the bull had spoken to him alone. The four names were his own, to use or to bestow.

Returns-Again already bore a warrior's name, a title of honor, earned on the warpath. It belonged to a man who, while on his way back from a successful raid, *returns again*, and strikes the enemy a second time before going home. It has sometimes been translated Forsakes-his-Home. An honorable name. Yet, after this marvelous evidence of divine favor, Returns-Again threw it away and called himself Sitting Bull.

And somewhat later, when his son "Slow" had distinguished him-

[1] "Tatan'ka Iyota'ke, Tatan'ka Psi'ca, Tatan'ka Winyu'ha Najin', Tatan'ka Wanji'la."

self (as we have seen), he called the boy Sitting Bull, and himself took the second of the four names, Jumping Bull. By this he was known to the day of his death. The fact that he gave the first name to his son is proof of his love for the boy.

Jumping Bull bestowed the other two names upon the two sons of his eldest daughter, Wiyáka-wastéwin or Good Feather Woman. Her sons are the "famous fighting nephews" of Sitting Bull, so often mentioned in old records. Both were living when this book was written. The elder, however, discarded the name Bull-Standing-with-Cow given him by his grandfather when, in 1866, he was honored by a new title—Big-in-the-Center—after the Fort Phil Kearny battle. He was a grand old man, of great intelligence and virile character, a famous warrior, and in later years was known as Chief Joseph White Bull.[2]

The younger nephew retained the name Lone Bull given him by his grandfather. It was given him because, though the smallest of the family, he was brave and not backward. Sitting Bull adopted him at the age of four years, and reared him as his own son. He was extremely well versed in the sacred lore of his people, and was associated intimately with his uncle for many years. He distinguished himself in the fight on the Little Big Horn, in 1876, in which Major M. A. Reno was put to flight. In old records his name usually appears as Lone Bull, but he was enrolled as Chief Henry Oscar One Bull.

In gathering the materials for this book, I tried to find out, if possible, what man or men were most admired by the youth Sitting Bull. But none of the old men had anything to tell me on this point. And at last one of them, somewhat indignantly, declared, "Sitting Bull did not imitate any *man;* he imitated the buffalo. There was nothing second-hand about Sitting Bull!"

When we consider where he got his name, this is not surprising. Indeed, his whole family seems to have felt a peculiar affinity for the creature which had so signally honored them.

And certainly Sitting Bull had plenty of opportunity to study and observe the buffalo under all conditions: in spring, when the ruddy calves frisked about their mothers; in summer, when the bulls, fat

[2] *Pte San' Hunka.*

and lusty from their feeding, pawed up the dust and fought together, with lowered heads and swinging horns and straining sinews; in autumn, when vast herds migrated down the range, covering the whole earth as with one great robe; in winter, when—on frosty mornings—he could spy out the herd from afar by the cloud of frozen buffalo breath floating above them, and watch them root with bleeding noses for the grass beneath the snow. He watched them eagerly, patiently, to learn their secrets.

It was not, of course, any particular buffalo that the young men imitated. Rather, it was the *idea* of the buffalo, the idealized or conventionalized figure—a figure having certain qualities widely recognized by the Sioux.

Thus, everyone knew that the buffalo was a headstrong, stubborn creature, afraid of nothing. It never turned back, never gave up, no matter what the obstacle, but always kept on going ahead, whatever the danger, whatever the weather. In winter, it moved against the wind, even in the bitterest blizzard, seeming to welcome opposition. Once it started in a given direction, nobody could head it off. It was all endurance, headstrong courage, persistence, and strength. Considering how amply Sitting Bull displayed these qualities in his after life, it is clear that the lesson of the buffalo was not lost upon him.

And, indeed, how could it be? When, every spring, he saw the Missouri River choked with the carcasses of bulls which would not turn aside from danger, but marched across the cracking ice, straight into the holes where their drowning comrades floundered by the hundred. When, every summer, he saw the desperate bulls battle to the death over the cows. Some bull would choose a fine three- or four-year-old cow without calf, cut her out of the herd, and hurry her away. Then another bull would follow and try to get between the cow and her lord and master. Immediately they would charge each other, with a mighty impact of broad foreheads, the clash of tough black horns, and then stand straining, pressing their heads tight together, thrusting hard. Thus they would strain and shove back and forth with cracking sinews and foaming jaws, their small eyes rolling in their stubborn heads, until one of them, pushed back on his haunches, found himself across the other's horns, ripped open, while the dust rose in clouds and the ground looked like a plowed field where that titanic struggle had taken place.

It was these fighting qualities of the buffalo which appealed to the Teton Sioux. Courage was the most necessary virtue of their adventurous lives, and the absolutely heedless courage of the bulls struck their imaginations with tremendous force. Such were the models held up before the youthful Sitting Bull. In following their pattern, he was stepping right in the tracks of his grandfathers.

With such a name and such a brilliant beginning, the lad was expected to go far. But his father and mother spared no pains to arm him well with lance and shield for that career which was to make him the most famous of American Indians.

3. The Yellowhammer and the Bear

ONE DAY, while hunting near Teat Buttes, Sitting Bull became very tired. He went down the bluffs into the broad bottoms of Grand River, and, entering the shady timber, lay down to rest. As he dozed off, he was aware of a yellowhammer's bright eyes peering at him from behind a tree trunk, but thought nothing of it. As he slept, he dreamed. In his dream he heard something coming, prowling through the timber. It was a grizzly bear, and the boy was frightened.

In those days the grizzly still roamed along the Missouri River—a terrible adversary for a man armed only with a bow. It was seldom that an arrow could reach its vitals, having to pierce that shaggy coat of hair, that tough skin, the thick layer of fat beneath, those iron muscles. The Sioux counted *coup* upon grizzlies as though they had been human enemies, and the man lucky enough to kill one wore the claws around his neck with pride.

No wonder the boy was frightened. While he lay there, between sleep and waking, unable to stir, he heard the yellowhammer knock twice against the tree-trunk. Then it seemed to speak: "Lie still! Lie still!"

The next moment, Sitting Bull wakened to find his dream come true. Looming over him was the huge bulk of that dangerous animal. Its long hair brushed his bare body, its strong odor choked him, its hot, rank breath flooded over his neck and face. Taking a firm grip on his courage, he obeyed the bird, and, closing his eyes, lay perfectly still.

As is well known, a grizzly—unless wounded or startled—will seldom injure a man who plays 'possum. And so, after what seemed hours, the bear moved away. Sitting Bull opened his eyes cautiously and watched that great hulk roll off into the timber. Then he got to his feet, shaking with relief.

He looked around. Sure enough, his dream had not deceived him. There on the tree trunk perched the brisk yellow bird, with its bright, alert eyes and sharp beak, watching him, unafraid. Sitting Bull's heart was filled with gratitude for this creature which had saved his life. Raising his hands toward it in the Indian gesture of blessing, he composed and sang a new song on the spot—the spontaneous overflow of powerful feelings:

> *Pretty bird, you saw me and took pity on me;*
> *You wish me to survive among the people.*
> *O Bird People, from this day always you shall be my relatives!*

Sitting Bull never forgot how the yellow bird had saved his life. From that day he was a close student of birds and their ways. His speeches are full of references to birds, and he was fond of telling stories about the Bird People. He learned to understand the speech of birds, particularly the magpie and Western meadowlark. Repeatedly, such birds gave him timely warning.

Of course, this ability to understand what birds are saying is by no means uncommon. A number of my old friends now living have this skill. The meadowlark, in particular, speaks such good Sioux that it is known as the Sioux bird. How many songs it has, who can tell? Twenty-six have been recorded, and it can imitate the songs of other birds as well. Even white people put words to the varied repertory of the meadowlark. It always tells the truth, too, and is therefore regarded as an oracle.

When Sitting Bull adopted the Bird People, he paid them the compliment of imitating their ways. Birds are good singers, and he took care to cultivate his talents as composer and musician. He had a high, resonant, melodious voice, and was always in demand as a singer at social or ceremonial gatherings. He made many songs, of which enough have been collected to form a small volume. Some of these are considered so excellent of their kind that they are still sung on appropriate occasions.[1] In fact, he was so famous as a maker of songs that he was sometimes requested to compose a new one for some special occasion—as, for example, a song praying for fine weather during the Sun Dance. This skill played a great part in making him a leader of his nation.

The Sioux do not talk unless they have something to say. But they are always singing. They have songs for every situation in which a man can find himself: for courting, for feasting, for thanksgiving and mourning, for peace and for war, for welcome and farewell, for victory and defeat—even for the moment of death. Long ago they worked out the correct response to every emergency, and there was a theme-song appropriate to every occasion. To have any social influence, a man must be able to sing the right song at the right moment. If he could do so, he might sway the people and lead them as he wished. "Let me make the songs of a nation, and I care not who makes its laws," runs the saying. Sitting Bull applied that saying to affairs. In every crisis he was always ready with a song which swept his hearers into line.

His singing also had much to do with his great popularity with women, who far outnumbered men in Sioux camps. Though well built, he was not a handsome man, and was always notoriously careless about his clothes. When Sitting Bull became chief, he found it an effort to dress the part, as he had to do on state occasions, and in manner he was singularly unpretentious. Children did not stop playing when he passed by, and young folks were seldom in awe of him. His smile was very charming, he laughed easily, and was generally in good humor until he fell upon evil days after the Custer fight. Even then, Mary Collins, the missionary, who knew him better than almost any other white person at the agency, found him "pleasant to meet," a "winning personality," and says he "was always so tender, gracious, and invariably sweet." She adds, "He had some indefinable power which could not be resisted by his people, or even others who came in contact with him."

[1] See my *Professional Writing* (New York, 1938), 168–81.

With women, he was successful in four directions. It was a recognized custom among members of the Warrior Societies to attempt to "steal" other men's wives. This sport was regarded as both pleasant and good for the tribe. Some say this dangerous sport was limited by custom, and that a man was not supposed to meddle with the wives of members of his own society. But Bull-Standing-with-Cow, who had fourteen wives, and ought to know, told me he never heard of any such rule. Sitting Bull appears to have taken his share in these pastimes. He is known to have stolen the wife of a man named Card while he was one of the Strong Hearts, yet, although he was married nine times during his life, no one was ever successful in stealing one of his women.

He was no ascetic; he thought happiness the most natural goal. He always encouraged young lovers, and, when his own daughter married, gave away horses in honor of the event. Otter Robe remembers how once, when he was a bashful boy, dancing between two girls, Sitting Bull saw his difficulty and told him what to do. Sitting Bull put the boy's arms around the necks of the girls, saying, "You'll have more fun if you dance that way."

Sitting Bull was a good husband, a good father, a good provider. Women liked him because, as they say, he "was kind to the family," and often used his influence and wealth to patch up domestic quarrels for them. They say he was like a bull elk, amorous and brave, always helping the women.

There is a story told by Red Hail (now dead) which, if true, is an interesting example of Sitting Bull's consideration for women, even of the most degraded sort.

It must be remembered that the Sioux women were remarkable among those of the prairie nations. "It is acknowledged by all that the Sioux women are better treated and handsomer than those of all other tribes," says Finerty. "They are also more virtuous, and the gayest white Adonises confess that the girls of that race seldom yield to the seducer." Boller lays the superiority of the Sioux women to the fact that they have no cornfields to hoe, and so "are generally tall and straight, without the thick ankles, the ungainly walk, and the stooping

23

shoulders of their less favored sisters. Taking them altogether, the wild, prairie Sioux have no superiors among the Indians in appearance and domestic virtues." And General Sully, who rarely had a good word for Indians, officially stated that "the females of the *wild* bands of Sioux, called the Teton Sioux, set an example of virtue worthy of being copied by any civilized nation." What wonder that, in a society where divorce was easy and celibacy unknown, the Sioux abhorred harlots? When a harlot fell into the hands of those virtuous dames, it went hard with her.

Now for the story. It seems that a war party was just back from a raid on the Crows, bringing scalps and other trophies, and a victory dance was going on. The souvenirs brought back by the Sioux included the bloodless hand of a Crow warrior, tied to a stick by the thumb, a pair of human ears, and a limp set of genitals. The Sioux were not especially interested in scalps; any outlying portion of the anatomy would serve as a trophy equally well. The ears and other exhibits were hung about the necks of war horses.

As the women danced, those who had lost relatives in wars with the Crows were allowed to approach the trophies and tap them with sticks, uttering taunting and insulting phrases. One might tap the ears and cry out, "Ah-ha, if you had been listening, you would not have been killed!" Another might tap the hand, and call out, "Ah-ha, you will never fondle anyone again!" And yet another might tap the third trophy, and shout, "And you will never enjoy another woman!" They were bitter and savage that evening. How many there had lost brothers and husbands and sons, cut to pieces by the Crows? Who can tell?

Among the souvenirs of this raid was a captive—a Crow woman. According to custom, she was slated to be adopted into the tribe. But in the midst of that wild festival, while the Sioux women, with tears streaming down their cheeks, were taunting and insulting the trophies taken from their hated enemies, it was discovered that the Crow captive was no better than she should be—in short, a *wit'ko-win*, a foolish or crazy woman; that is to say, a whore. Immediately, the hysterical Sioux women seized the unfortunate creature, tore off her clothing, lashed her to a pine tree, and piled dry brush about her, intending to burn her alive.

At that time Sitting Bull was only a boy, seventeen years old. He had no authority to interfere. Yet he was a very brave young man, and courage and cruelty seldom go together. He was very unhappy as he saw what was going forward. He walked up and down, up and down, clutching his bow in intense agitation. At last he saw them applying the flames to the dry brush. At once, without saying a word, he strung his bow, and, fitting an arrow to the string, let fly. The arrow pierced the screaming captive's heart and saved her from the flames.

4. Single Combat

He not only pointed out the way, but led the way. . . . His hand-to-hand encounter with a foe in his youth on the Porcupine settled for once and always the question of his personal bravery. —FRANK GROUARD.

IT WAS autumn of the Winter-when-the-War-Bonnet-was-Torn, 1856. The Hunkpapa needed horses. The best mounts came from Texas and Mexico, stolen by the Comanches and passed northward by way of their relatives, the Utes and Shoshoni, or other tribes nearer the Rockies. There were no horses worth mentioning east of the Missouri River, for that river was too great a barrier to fleeing horse thieves. Of course, the Sioux raised few horses: their winters were too severe. The best way to get them was to trade for them or steal them from enemies. Stealing them was a better bargain, as glory was thrown in. Accordingly, that winter the Hunkpapa decided to go west and try to take horses from the Crows. The best horses were always to the west and south.

Nearly a hundred Hunkpapa went on this warpath. The camp was then on a small stream, a tributary of the Yellowstone, between the Box Elder and Powder River. Moving up the Yellowstone, they kept looking for enemy camps where they might take horses. Most of the party was on foot, carrying lariats and empty saddle-pads, which could be stuffed with grass when they had captured ponies. When they reached the Crow country, they asked Sun-Dreamer, their shaman, to prophesy.

Sun-Dreamer was the greatest shaman ever known to the Hunk-

26

CROW FOOT, SITTING BULL'S SON, KILLED AT THE
TIME OF HIS FATHER'S ARREST.

(National Archives)

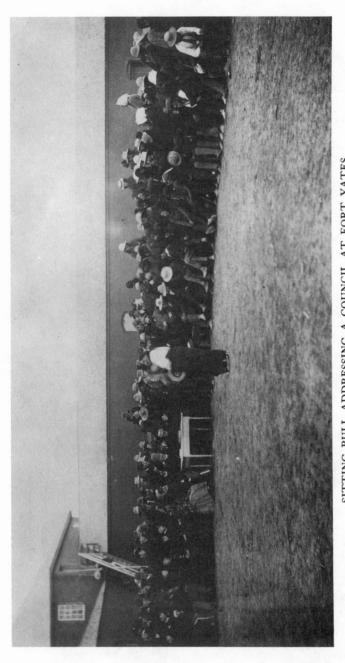

SITTING BULL ADDRESSING A COUNCIL AT FORT YATES.

The military are at the left of the table, Agent McLaughlin and his Santee Sioux wife are at the right.

(Courtesy E. A. Brininstool)

papa. Many stories are told of his wonderful power to foretell the future, or bring buffalo. He could do anything; his power was marvelous. When the Hunkpapa leaders asked him to try and divine what luck they were going to have, he agreed. He smoked and sang, and when he was through making mystery, found that the palm of his hand had turned black. This he interpreted to mean that they would meet enemies within one day.

Soon after, the scouts brought news of the Crow village, which was nearby, on Porcupine Creek, north of the Yellowstone. The Hunkpapa immediately made preparations for a fight, but kept hidden until night.

Sitting Bull had recently been promoted to be one of the two sash-wearers of the Strong Hearts. These sash-wearers were entitled to wear a close-fitting cap or bonnet covered thickly with crow feathers clipped short, and having two black buffalo horns, shaved thin as paper-knives, one over each ear. From between these horns, a lot of ermine streamers trailed down the wearer's back. Sitting Bull also wore the picket rope, or sash, of his office. That was a strip of scarlet woolen cloth about a foot wide, slit to pass over his shoulder near one end, and long enough to drag on the ground. It was decorated with feathers. The sash-wearers were supposed to stake themselves to the ground by sticking a lance or a picket pin through the tail of their sashes, so that they could not leave their post. Only a comrade could release them. They were under a vow never to retreat, once they had taken their stand, until they had been victorious.

Sitting Bull carried his shield, and, instead of his trusty lance or bow, was armed with a new and prized weapon, a muzzle-loading smoothbore gun, bought from the traders. He rode a fast black horse with white face and stockings, a present from his brother-in-law, Makes-Room. Its bridle was adorned with a "scalp" made of a horse-tail, and painted red and black, a badge showing that this horse had been used to run down an enemy.

Having put on this regalia and taken his shield from its case, Sitting Bull was ready to go with his comrades into the Crow camp and run off the horses. Certain men were chosen to do this, and after a long time they came back driving a great herd of horses through the darkness. These were divided among the young men. Some got one horse, some two. They got the horses away from the camp without a fight and struck out for home, pushing the herd ahead of them. Some of the men rode point on the herd, others on the flanks, while the main body followed behind, prepared to fight off their pursuers. It was pretty certain that they would be pursued, for the Crows had a big camp and plenty of horses left in it.

Just after sunrise, here they came, lickety-split, up the valley, a great horde of enemies, charging on the trail of the running Hunkpapa. The Hunkpapa were hampered by their captured herd and could not run away. The Crows were gaining, and, though the Hunkpapa rode hard, they could not avoid a battle. The leader ordered some of the young men to bunch the herd and hold it, while the rest of them stood off the Crows. They had not long to wait. The enemy was just over the next rise.

All at once the skyline sprouted lances, tossing like long grass blades against the sky, then black-and-white war bonnets, the heads of horses, naked, painted warriors. They rushed over the brow of the hill like water through a spillway. The charge was on. Here they came, slapping their open mouths to make the pulsating terrible war cry. "Yip, yip, yi-ip!" they yelled. And puffed through loosely closed lips, like an angry buffalo: "Ploo! Ploo!"

But when they saw the Hunkpapa line up to receive their charge, the main body slowed down, halted. Only the leaders, three brave men, came on, spread out wide, full of fight, making for the Hunkpapa line. One of these charged right in among the Sioux, counted two *coups*, and turned to make his getaway. But Loud Bear snatched the man's war bonnet by its long tail, which came away in his hand. This unusual occurrence gave its name to the year in the Hunkpapa Picture Calendar or Winter Count.

The second Crow charged and killed a Hunkpapa, Paints Brown. Sitting Bull rode forward to confront the third.

When he was well out in front of his own line, Sitting Bull jumped off his horse, gave it a slap on the rump that started it back to the

28

Hunkpapa, and turned to face the enemy. "Come on!" he yelled. "I'll fight you. I am Sitting Bull!"

The Crow did not wait for a second invitation. He ran forward afoot, and Sitting Bull ran to meet him. He did not stop to stake himself to the ground. There would be time for that when he had reached his objective. As he ran forward, he saw that the Crow wore a red shirt trimmed with ermine—the insignia of a chief. The Crow carried a powder-horn and a flintlock gun. Both men had knives in their belts.

But as the Crow saw Sitting Bull coming with his gun in hand and his shield before him, saw that trailing sash and that horned bonnet, of which he well knew the meaning, his heart was not so strong as it had been. He knew that his opponent must be a very brave man to wear those things.

And he knew that Sitting Bull meant fight, for he was singing a Strong Heart song:

> *Comrades, whoever runs away,*
> *He is a woman, they say;*
> *Therefore, through many trials,*
> *My life is short!*

Sitting Bull ran forward, faster than he ever ran again. He had only one shot in his muzzle-loader, and he intended to make it count. Very few of the Hunkpapa had guns in those days, mostly old flintlocks, and Sitting Bull was not yet the crack shot he afterward became. He ran right up to the Crow.

When the Crow saw his enemy so near, he threw up his gun to shoot. Sitting Bull instantly dropped upon one knee, threw his shield before him, and took aim at the Crow. The Crow fired first. Sitting Bull felt his shield jump as the ball pierced it, felt the jolt and the pang of the wound it made in the sole of his left foot. The Crow was blotted from sight by the white smoke, but not before Sitting Bull had taken aim and pulled the trigger. He saw his enemy leap into the air and fall mortally wounded, shot through the body. Sitting Bull jerked his long knife from its scabbard, and, limping forward, plunged it into the heart of the Crow chief.

The fall of their leader struck terror to the Crows, who retreated. Immediately, some of the Hunkpapa charged. Long Horn counted the second *coup* on the man Sitting Bull had killed, Many Sacks the third. The men who counted *coup* on the Crow whose war bonnet was torn were Loud Bear, Spotted Weasel, Thrown-on-Ground, and Red Fox (sometimes called Rattles). Scatters-Them, Running Hawk, and Wooden Gun struck the third Crow.

Having fulfilled his vow by killing an enemy, Sitting Bull turned back, caught his horse, and rode off with the others. The bullet of the Crow chief had struck his left foot just beneath the toes and plowed its way straight back through the sole to the heel. It is known that this wound was treated with a medicine obtained from the Rees. Possibly Jumping Bull treated his son, as he was a good doctor and had formerly had a Ree wife, mother of Sitting Bull's half-brother, Fool Dog. Whoever treated the wound made a botch of it, for when it healed, the sole of the foot contracted, and from that day Sitting Bull walked with a perceptible limp. The Hunkpapa never forgot his brave deed. Every time he took a step, his limp reminded them of the courage he had displayed in defending his comrades.

When the war party got back to camp, they mourned for Paints Brown four days, and then asked permission from his relatives to hold a victory dance. This was granted, and there was a great celebration. Sitting Bull gave away the horses he had taken, but was unable to dance because of his wound.

The Strong Hearts proposed to do great honor to their champion. Among them was a smaller club or society of picked young men known as the Midnight Strong Hearts. Whether they were so called because they met at night, or because they did their fighting then, is not known. But they were the cream of the Strong Hearts, and they made Sitting Bull their leader.

There is one strange thing about this single combat with the Crow chief which no one can explain.

The Hunkpapa made their shields round. They say that the sun is round, the moon is round, the earth is round, the sky is round like a bowl. So is the stem of everything that grows from the ground, and the body of everything that breathes. In fact, everything in the world is round—except the Rock. There is no straight line in Nature. Therefore it is clear that Wakan' Tanka, the Great Mysterious, likes round things: the circle is sacred. And so they make their tipis round, and pitch them in a circle. For the same reason they made their shields round. Round shields protected them better, they say. Now there is no doubt that round shields did protect them better than those of other shapes, for the simple reason that a round object attracts the eye, and, when a man is shooting, is likely to attract his aim also. It was a great advantage to have a shield which attracted enemy arrows—arrows which could not pierce it.

But when firearms came into use—what a change! The shield attracted bullets also, just as it had arrows, and the shield could not stop the bullets! After the Indians had the thing all worked out, along came the white men and broke their medicine. Firearms put a terrific strain upon the science—or art—of the Sioux shaman.

Now, as a rule, when a man's shield, or other war-charm (*wo-ta'we*) failed to protect him, he simply threw it away and got another, either in a dream or by purchase. The Sioux warrior wanted results. If his shield failed him, he threw it away. But Sitting Bull, although his shield had been pierced by a bullet, had allowed him to be wounded, crippled in fact, kept it—kept it until long after his surrender, when wars were at an end. This is something strange and unaccountable, which no one can explain. . . .

The importance of this single combat was very great in Sitting Bull's life. When the Sioux wish to say a thing is excellent of its kind, they say it is *sha*, red. The killing of the Crow chief—that was *sha-sha*, very red! A hundred Hunkpapa were witnesses to Sitting Bull's single-handed courage, to his success; and among Indians, nothing succeeds like success.

The chieftaincy of the Strong Hearts made Sitting Bull responsible for the tribal hunting. And owing to the steady decrease of buffalo, he was forced into wars of conquest, in order to win hunting grounds wide enough to maintain his hungry people. These hunting grounds had belonged for generations to the Crows, Rees, Mandans, Hidatsa,

31

Hohe, and Shoshoni. And for all that time the Sioux had been skirmishing with them, mostly for fun, without much change of base. But after Sitting Bull took command of the Strong Hearts, there was a sudden shifting of all these tribes. The Shoshoni fell back to Wind River and the mountains; the Hohe scuttled off to the country north of the Missouri River; the Crows (having lost one-third their number and all their horses) in 1864 cowered away yonder on Milk River and the Musselshell, enduring with what patience they could the persecutions of Piegans and Gros Ventres of the Prairie. The Mandans, Rees, and Hidatsa had long claimed all that great region between the Missouri River and the Little Missouri, clear down to the Big Cheyenne, and in 1851 the Sioux had admitted this claim at Fort Laramie. But by 1864, these nations were begging the Grandfather at Washington to buy their lands, on the novel plea that they themselves could not use them, as they dared not leave their fortified town to hunt, because of the Sioux! Not one of their delegation to the treaty of 1851 remained alive in 1864. The Sioux had killed them all!

Peaceful penetration was impossible among nations of such long-standing enmity. The Sioux needed their hunting grounds. War was the only solution, and one very congenial to the fighting spirit of the Hunkpapa. Sitting Bull and his fighters swept all those people out of the way. Having got the raw materials of his industry by war, he had only to steal good horses, buy guns and ammunition, properly organize his hunts, and see that successful hunters shared their kill with the poor and helpless. He did this by means of his Strong Hearts. As the old men say, "He fed the whole nation."

Sitting Bull himself was a master hunter. He knew how to make good bows, good arrows, and more than once shot an arrow clear through a buffalo cow into the snow beyond. It has been estimated that the total ration of his camp amounted to about thirty-six hundred tons of meat every year—some thirty thousand buffalo. He was a crack shot, and took great care of his buffalo ponies, which he trained to come at his call. Indeed, his success as a hunter, like his success in war, was firmly founded upon his fast horses.

Yet there was more than skill and good equipment in his success.

His attitude was correct. He thought of the animals he hunted as fellow creatures, many of them with keener senses and greater strength than his own. He was no game hog, no butcher. He thought it cruel to kill more than was necessary. The animals were his friends: wolves led him to game, knowing he would share with them; birds gave warning when foes were about. To have slaughtered these friends recklessly would have been black ingratitude, and he let them know how he felt about it.

When he was stalking an elk, or when (his head wrapped in a gray kerchief, so as not to be seen on the skyline) he took aim at a fat antelope, he always had the correct formula on his lips. Before his finger pressed the trigger, before his hand released the arrow, he would whisper, "Grandfather, my children are hungry. You were created for that. So I must kill you." And when he butchered, a part was offered to Wakan' Tanka, who had given it.

Even long after his kill, he remembered the respect due these animal friends. For when he rode across the prairie with his young men and came upon the bleaching skeletons of bison, where the Sioux had made a surround, he would dismount and turn the skulls to face the sun. "Friends," he would say, "we must honor these bones. These are the bones of those who gave their flesh to keep us alive last winter."

5. Big Brother

There can be no truer friend or braver man than the American Indian of the better type. —COMMISSIONER OF INDIAN AFFAIRS, 1878

WHEN THE FALL hunt was over and supplies laid in for that winter of 1857, the young men began to grow restless, and Stands-at-the-Mouth-of-the-River proposed a raid on the Hohe, or Assiniboin Indians. The Hohe lived north of the Missouri River, in what is now Montana. The tribe had once been part of the Sioux nation, and spoke a dialect which Sitting Bull's people could readily understand. But for a long time now they had been bitter enemies. Sitting Bull's rapid progress to honor in the Strong Heart Society had not cooled his martial ambition. When Stands-at-the-Mouth-of-the-River offered the war pipe to him, he smoked it. Among others who volunteered were Swift Cloud, High Bear, and one Bear Ribs (not the chief).

They slipped away from camp and pushed north toward the mouth of the Yellowstone. The weather was cold, and Sitting Bull wore his white blanket coat with the hood or capote. He rode a bay horse and carried his lance. But he also took along his precious gun—the smoothbore with which he had shot the Crow chief. And he carried the horned bonnet with ermine streamers, to wear when they attacked the enemy.

Soon after the party left camp, it turned bitterly cold, and when they reached the Missouri River, they found it frozen hard, with a light fall of snow on the ice. They struck it below Poplar River, not far from where Fort Buford was afterward built.

34

Right there they found a single tipi—one family—of Hohe, and immediately crossed on the ice to rub them out. The Sioux say that was just the luck of the Hohe: they were always getting killed and captured, they never seemed to know how to take care of themselves.

When the poor Hohe saw the Sioux coming, they tried to run away. The mother caught up her baby and ran, dragging her small son by the hand. The father of the luckless family tried to stand off the Sioux with his bow, and beside him stood a tall, weedy lad about eleven years old, ready to do his best in defense of his family.

In those days the Sioux had no more compunction about killing women and children of enemy nations in battle than an army aviator has when dropping bombs on a city. To kill a woman in the presence of her man was rated a brave deed. Every man of the Sioux had lost relatives to enemy arrows. Their wars were personal, like a Kentucky feud; and they never ended. Because of the frequent truces for trading, it was easy to talk over old battles, and very often the warriors knew their opponents by name. Under such conditions there could be no lofty, impersonal chivalry in those wars. And so the Sioux war party struck out after the Hohe.

In running across the ice, the Sioux had got strung out. The first ones to arrive shot down the Hohe man and his woman, destroyed the baby, and put an arrow through the little boy, as he ran screaming away. In less time than it takes to tell it, the four of them lay on the bloody snow, their bodies full of feathered shafts.

But the tall, weedy boy, aged eleven, though he saw his parents and brothers slain before his eyes, did not lose heart. He faced his enemies with his little bow and arrows, and shot at them until he had only one arrow left. Then the Sioux charged on him, counting the *coup*: first, Swift Cloud; second, Bear Ribs; third, High Bear; and last of all, Sitting Bull, who had arrived too late to have a hand in killing the family.

The Hohe boy was surrounded by his enemies. His time had come. *But he did not cry.* As he looked around at the hard, fierce faces of the Sioux, hot and excited by the run across the ice, by their recent kill, he had small hopes of survival. Only one face there showed any gentleness—Sitting Bull's. The boy turned to him, called out, begging for mercy, "Big brother!"

Sitting Bull had no full brother. That cry, and the lad's bravery, made instant appeal. Perhaps the gap left in his life by the recent loss of his first wife, Scarlet Woman, and their little son also counted at that moment. Sitting Bull took pity on the helpless, courageous Hohe boy, flung his arms about him, shielded him from the weapons of the Sioux.

"Don't shoot him!" he cried. "Don't shoot! This boy is too brave to die. I have no brother. I take this one for my brother. Let him live."

But the warriors did not want to spare the boy. They were hot with battle, still panting from their pursuit of those hated enemies. They would not shoot while Sitting Bull held the lad in his arms, but some of them were determined to kill him. He was a warrior, had tried to shoot them; why should they spare him?

However, some of Sitting Bull's friends intervened and kept on talking until the excited killers had time to cool off—which did not take long in that weather. At last all agreed to Sitting Bull's request for the time being, and the matter was deferred until they should reach home. Sitting Bull mounted his horse, took the captive boy up behind him, and rode back with the others, southward.

Because the Sioux believe that the south wind brings sickness, they think of the south as the land of death, and when a man is killed, they say he has "gone south." No doubt the Hohe lad was well pleased to be going south horseback, and not as his father and brothers had just done!

When the war party reached home, it received the usual ovation.

Of course, the faction led by No Neck opposed the adoption of the captive, as it opposed all that Sitting Bull wished. But Circling Hawk and others stood together, and the adoption went through. Sitting Bull gave the boy some nice new clothes, painted his face appropriately, and seated him in his own tipi. Then he stepped out into the frosty air and invited all the important men in camp to a feast. When they had assembled, he announced that he was going to adopt this captive as his brother, because he was so brave, and because he had called Sitting

Bull "brother." Sitting Bull then gave away horses in honor of this new member of his family.

One of the old men present then delivered a speech on the obligations and duties of brother-friends: The wish of one must be the law of the other: they must be one in thought and action. From that day, each must give preference to his brother before all mankind. Each must be willing to give anything to, or do anything for, the other. They must both pray and try to please the gods. Then the gods would give them success in forays against the enemy, and they would be enabled to steal horses and women from their foes. When they succeeded, the women would sing praise-songs in their honor, and when they made offerings to the Rock (the patron god of war), it would please the Earth and the Buffalo, and these two gods would give them industrious women to bear them many children. . . . "The Great Spirit will harden your shields and direct your arrows, and put breath into your war-horses when they get old. The Buffalo will provide you with plenty of robes and moccasins, you will have places of honor in the tents of your people, and when you die and 'go south,' your spirits will not be found unworthy and compelled to wander homeless over the world. . . ."

The lodge was crowded, and all around it stood a dense throng, trying to see what was going on inside. Those who could see beheld a boy, tall and weedy for his years, a boy about eleven years old, with a light complexion, who sat there silent in his new clothes and face-paint. Sitting Bull served the feast and all ate together with the newly adopted member of the tribe.

Some shook their heads over the matter, but their fears were groundless. For the captive boy grew into a strong, brave, all-round man, a chunky warrior of medium height, laconic always, but good-humored, who in time was to become a chief of the Strong Hearts. During his lifetime he performed many brave deeds, was wounded in the hip in battle, and had horses shot under him. He remained loyal to the Sioux and to Sitting Bull until he died with him at last.

The Hohe captive was so well treated that he had no wish to return to the Hohe camp, though his many relatives there tried to secure his release. He was well content to remain with his good brother, Sitting Bull. For this reason, Sitting Bull called him Stays-Back. Afterward, he was given the name of Sitting Bull's father, Jumping Bull. On the agency rolls his name appears as Little Assiniboin. But he was also known as Ota Ktepi, Plenty Kill or Kills-Often, for he was always striking the enemy.

Sitting Bull's adoption of this boy had several important results. In the first place, it brought a brave and honorable warrior into the Hunkpapa camp. Because of the fine character and success of the captive, Sitting Bull was encouraged to spare others, and not a few persons owed their lives to this event. Moreover, this adoption led, in later years, to a truce with the Hohe, which saved Sitting Bull's life in perhaps the tightest corner he ever occupied in 1875. Had Sitting Bull died then, he could never have assembled his warriors to fight Custer, and Custer might have lived to be president of the United States. Few events in the life of Sitting Bull had such far-reaching effects as his protection of the Hohe lad that wintry day on the frozen Missouri, and because of this the year 1857 is known in the Hunkpapa Picture Calendar as the Winter-when-Kills-Often-was-Brought-Home. This deed was one of the most celebrated Sitting Bull ever performed. It appears in sketch number 5 of his autobiography, and—after a recital of how Sitting Bull was wounded in battle—it is the first story about him the old men will tell you. They say it showed the heart of a great chief to spare that helpless enemy.

6. The One-Man Women

ABOUT THIS TIME, Sitting Bull made a double venture in matrimony. He brought home a young woman named Light Hair. They were very happy—until he added a second wife to his household. Then things began to happen. The new wife's name was Snow-on-Her, and there was nothing cold about her but her name. She quarreled with Light Hair from the first night. If Sitting Bull had been wiser, he would have married sisters, like most men, for sisters were used to each other, and the younger sister usually accepted with resignation her position of handmaiden to the first wife and concubine to her husband. But Sitting Bull was new to polygamous marriage, and made a mistake. Snow-on-Her would not act in a sisterly manner. She would not take orders from Light Hair, nor meekly go to bed by herself while her husband snuggled under the buffalo robes with Light Hair across the lodge.

Snow-on-Her insisted on sharing their couch. They slept three in a bed.

A Sioux warrior always stripped to the breech-cloth before retiring, so that, if an enemy attacked in the night, he would be ready for the fight. And every time Sitting Bull turned in, he found himself lying flat on his back, with Snow-on-Her clinging fast to his arm and leg on one side, and Light Hair—not to be outdone—clinging to his arm and leg on the other. Neither one would yield her place or permit him to face the other woman. Sitting Bull complained that he never got a good night's sleep after Snow-on-Her came to his tipi. He had to lie on his back all night, and in the morning his muscles would be so

39

cramped and sore that he could hardly walk. Sometimes he would wait until both the women were asleep, and then try to free himself and stealthily turn over. But when he did so, one of the women would be sure to waken, and begin to tug, and then the other would be aroused and pull him the other way, and there he was—flat on his back again.

This was hard to bear. Sitting Bull liked peace and quiet. He always insisted upon the decencies and proprieties of domestic life. He did not readily lose his temper, and was apt to be sympathetic with human frailty. When Snow-on-Her began to nag and quarrel and make trouble, he remonstrated with her. He told her it was the custom of her people that the first wife should rule. It had always been so. She came to his lodge as the second wife knowingly, and now she ought to be content with her position. The first wife was the chief of the lodge, would always be so. But Snow-on-Her would not listen: she had no ears. She cared nothing for the customs of her people: she made trouble from morning till night. And hell hath no fury like a jealous Indian woman.

Sitting Bull was very much annoyed by the turn things were taking: they were going from bad to worse. When he was away from home, he worried for fear Snow-on-Her might whip out her knife and stab Light Hair. And when he came in, tired from the day's hunt, he found his lodge boiling over with quarrels, scoldings, tears, and tantrums. And even darkness brought no relief: he could not sleep of nights.

Snow-on-Her was determined to get rid of Light Hair. She began to slander her behind her back, and accused her of being intimate with other men. Snow-on-Her stopped at nothing. The camp was soon humming with her slanders, and at last some kind friends of Light Hair brought her the story.

Light Hair was outraged. Everyone was saying she was a bad woman, an adulteress. And the punishment for unfaithful wives was severe. Something had to be done about it. She waited until Sitting Bull went off for the day. Then she called in an old woman who had lived with one man all her life. She explained the case, gave the old woman a present to get her help, and the two of them carried several kettles of food out into the middle of the camp circle. There they dug a shallow hole in the ground, and in it laid a gun, a knife, and an arrow. Light Hair intended to vindicate her honor then and there.

When all was ready, the old woman stood up, and facing the east, the south, the west, and the north in turn, shouted her announcement to the whole camp: "Light Hair's body has been enjoyed by one man only. Let all women who can say as much come here and eat."

Soon all the one-man women in camp had gathered about the weapons in the hole, and among them, of course, Snow-on-Her. She could not be absent: it was an anxious time for her. And surrounding the circle of women, shoulder to shoulder, a dense throng of males—all the men in camp, in fact—stood packed and staring.

Then the old woman got up and said: "If any man present has known any of these women, let him come forward and point her out. Let him take up the arrow, the knife, and the gun, and take his oath on them. If he swears falsely such a weapon will kill him."

Nobody came forward. Light Hair's honor was not impeached. She turned fiercely upon the woman who had tried to ruin her, this rebellious concubine who had slandered her behind her back. "You have thrown lies against me," she said. "If you spoke truth, where is the man who was intimate with me? Who is he? Produce him, and let him swear to your story."

The ring of packed, staring faces never stirred. The silence was tense, electric. Light Hair stood there, facing her rival, waiting. Snow-on-Her had nothing to say. Drawing her robe over her head, she pushed through the jeering crowd, and fled. With cries of contempt, the one-man women ran after her, pelting her with buffalo chips until she was outside the circle of tents. Then they returned triumphant and dined with great content.

This scandal annoyed Sitting Bull, but he was glad that his wife's honor had been publicly vindicated. Yet one thing was certain: there could be no peace in his lodge after that if Snow-on-Her remained there. When she came sneaking back to the tent, he told her to go home to her parents.

A person who had not the sense to recognize his lawful superiors was to him simply ridiculous, like that jealous woman. Sitting Bull's wife must be above ridicule.

That night he slept soundly.

7. Jumping Bull Has the Toothache

IT WAS JUNE, and Sitting Bull's band was in camp on the headwaters of the Cannonball River. Their tipis—rakishly tilted cones, with smoke-browned tops and gaudy, painted flanks—stood in a circle on the grassy flat beside the stream. Alongside each tipi stood its stacked travois, its rack for drying meat, its outdoor kitchen of willow boughs. There the children romped, the women worked and gossiped, and the young men gambled, or—grave as statues—muffled in their blankets to their steady eyes, shyly stared at the girls. All about, on the prairie, grazed the Hunkpapa ponies, the wealth of the nation.

One day someone saw two Crow Indians skulking about in the neighborhood, but before the alarm could be given and the fighters called out, these Crows had vanished. Perhaps they were scouts sent out in advance of some larger party. Such things happened often, and but few of the Hunkpapa paid any heed. Least of all did Jumping Bull, Sitting Bull's father, care what the Crows were doing. Day and night he sat in his tipi, rocking with agony. He had a raging toothache, and none of the many remedies known to the Sioux could stop the pain. He sat there, holding his jaw, wishing his time had come. He was getting old now, and his teeth had begun to trouble him.

Two days later, the pain was worse than ever. But the Hunkpapa were breaking camp to start off to the northwest and Jumping Bull had to go along. They were headed along the eastern flank of Rainy Butte, that great landmark near the eastern boundary of Slope County, North Dakota. Rainy Butte is almost a mountain, so long, in fact, that now there is a town at each end of it. It was named Rainy Butte because it rained almost every time the Hunkpapa camped there.

43

It was fine, sunny weather that morning, good for traveling, but so warm that it made people lazy. The Hunkpapa were slow in getting started. The women furled the white tents, lowered the lodgepoles, threw their dubbers and bags and parfleches, their children and puppies, into the family travois behind the old sore-backed nag, and moved out on the trail to the northwest. They formed a long straggling line as they strung out across the prairie, the horses of each family running in a bunch together, the women and children riding the plodding pack horses, or afoot. On the flanks and in rear, groups of men jogged along, joking and laughing. Two boys were in the lead.

Suddenly, without warning, over the nearest swell of the green prairie fifty Crows came pelting at the gallop, fast as their war horses could run. The ground thumped like a drum to the beat of two hundred hooves, the sunlight flashed from steel lance heads, bright and keen, from the garish war paint on those naked bodies, from the flaring splotches of color on the spotted ponies. The long tail of the Crow leader's war bonnet trailed behind him like some strange feather mane. On they came, cutting across the head of the Sioux column.

At the same moment the war whoop, like the quick rattle of a machine gun, pulsated upon the startled ears of the dawdling Hunkpapa, raising prickles along their spines.

Instantly all was confusion. Pack horses balked and reared as the women grabbed at their lariats. Dogs got in everybody's way. Women were wailing and crying, or singing Brave Heart songs for their men. Children squalled. Above all this din could be heard the high voices of the old men, telling the women not to run, to get together on the ridge and hold the horses there. The young men were gathering to resist the attack.

But before they could do anything, the Crows had cut off the two boys in the lead, had struck one of them down in plain sight of the Hunkpapa. The Crow attack was swift and sudden, they outnumbered the Sioux, and they had the enormous advantage of complete surprise.

Probably these Crows had come to steal horses, but, finding their enemies on the move, had recklessly charged them, trusting to superior numbers. Now it is one thing to steal horses from a sleeping camp, and quite another to charge upon the same camp in daylight when all the young men are awake and armed and in the saddle. This fact the Crows were soon to have rammed home to them. But at first the Hunkpapa attack, made by two separate groups of men, was not effective. The Crows gave ground slowly, retreating toward Cedar Creek.

One of these Crows, finding himself hard pressed, turned back to stand them off. But Swift Hawk swooped upon him, and, reining up his pony, knocked him out of the saddle and killed him. At his heels rode Little Elk, Chief Running Antelope, and Chasing Crow, counting their *coups* in turn. The Sioux warriors rode down the field like a polo team, one behind another, club or lance in hand. This Crow, the first to fall, had a lump on his neck, probably a goitre.

After he fell, the other Crows began to run. Their leaders, Bird-Claw-Necklace and Bird-in-the-Ground, could not hold them. Bird-Claw-Necklace himself turned to fly, bringing up the rear. But as he plunged on toward the creek, his horse stepped in a gopher hole, stumbled, and threw him. Regaining his feet, he could see the Sioux close upon him.

Bow in hand, he reached quickly for his arrows. But the quiver was empty. In the excitement of the battle he had used them all, or perhaps they had fallen out while he was racing away. There he was, unhorsed, unarmed, and the yelling Hunkpapa were almost on top of him. He knew he had seen his last sunrise. Tears rolled down his cheeks, and he wailed and cried like a woman.

The Hunkpapa sometimes spared a brave man, but they had no heart at all for a coward. Like an avalanche they were all over Bird-Claw-Necklace and cut him down. Sitting Crow hit him first, then Knocks-Them-Down, Knife Chief, and Two Eagles.

In this running fight, however, one brave Crow faced the Hunkpapa and stood them off. He rode back and forth on his war horse, with rifle ready, and nobody dared go near him. Just then Jumping Bull, Sitting Bull's father, came riding along. He was now getting on, a pretty old man. His hair was streaked with gray, and his legs and arms were a little shrunken. He was too old to be fighting hand-to-hand with a young man. But when he saw those Hunkpapa hanging back, afraid to jump that lone Crow, he showed a last flash of the fighting spirit which has made his family world-famous. He spoke to the timid Hunkpapa.

"Leave that Crow to me," he cried. "Last night I had a terrible toothache, and I wished I was dead. Now my chance has come. I have longed for such a day."

At once the old man started for the Crow. When the Crow saw him coming, he jumped off his horse and stood waiting. Jumping Bull, now also afoot, ran forward, an arrow on his bow-string. But before he could loose it, the Crow shot him in the shoulder. The old man had to drop his bow.

For all that, Jumping Bull did not stop. He was no woman. The wound did not delay him a moment. He ran to close quarters.

The Crow's gun was empty. He whipped out his butcher knife.

Seeing this, Jumping Bull reached for his own knife. But the knife sheath had slipped around behind him, it lay flat on his back. His fumbling old fingers could not find it, and before he could shift his belt and grab the hilt, the Crow was on him, stabbed the old man above the collarbone.

After that, Jumping Bull had no chance to recover his knife. The Crow grabbed him by his gray hair, stabbed him again and again in the breast and side. Still Jumping Bull struggled with bare hands against his strong young adversary, while the spiritless Hunkpapa stood still and looked on.

Many Horses, coming up just then, rushed forward to rescue the old man. But it was too late. Before he could get there, Jumping Bull sank to his knees. The Crow plunged his knife into the top of the old man's head, and he toppled over, snapping the knife blade as he fell. The Crow pushed him aside, mounted his horse, and was gone.

Someone told Sitting Bull that his father was being killed over yonder, and he came racing on his swift war horse. Too late. There lay his father, his withered limbs all awry, the broken knife blade sticking out of his skull, his gray hair dabbled with blood. And the Hunkpapa had let the man who had done this get clean away!

But Sitting Bull saw him going, raced after him, overtook him, lanced him, killed him. Then, jumping from his horse, he whipped out his knife and cut the body of his enemy to pieces. His heart was hot that day.

After that, the Hunkpapa, angry and ashamed, charged the Crows, yelling like devils, and chased them thirty miles. Now at last their blood was up; they cared nothing for the odds against them. The sun shone hot on their bare, sweating bodies, their horses were all in a lather. As the day advanced, it grew hotter and hotter: six good horses died that morning from overheating. But ten Crows fell on the prairie, while the great ridge of Rainy Butte, with its abrupt end, cut the sky with a long, slanting stroke, like a broken knife blade.

Pretty Weasel killed the next Crow to fall. Thunder Hawk and White-Bordered-Tail counted their *coups* on him. The next Crow fell by the hand of Shoots-Walking, who also claimed the second *coup* before anybody else could get there. Gives-Goose and Little Tusk struck this enemy after. Red Feather counted two *coups* in this fight, and others were garnered by No Neck, Chief Loud-Voiced-Hawk, Grindstone, and Running Against. Crawler, Gall, Two Bears, Red Fox, Brown Thunder, and Lame Deer were also active in this battle.

Sitting Bull, thirsting for the blood of those who had killed his father, pursued them so closely and fought so recklessly that at last his friends compelled him to turn back, saying that the danger was too great. Two Hunkpapa had already been killed: Makes-the-Enemy (father of Francis Fast Horse), and Running-Close, who was dying of his wounds. At the end of thirty miles, the Sioux turned back, worn out, riding their heaving, lathered ponies.

When the Crow warriors fled, they left behind them three women and a baby boy. The boy rode in his cradle, slung from the tall horn of his mother's rawhide saddle. When the women saw that they were cut off from their husbands, they made for the creek and tried to get away.

Feather Mane was the first of the Sioux to see them. He let out a yell and raced to count the *coup*. White Blackbird and Chief White Buffalo were right on his heels, Cloud Shield was fourth. All these struck the first woman they came to. The second woman, running away as fast as she could, was struck by Magpie Eagle, Bear Tooth (sometimes called Dry Bones), Feather Mane, and White Blackbird. Four others claimed these women as captives. The first woman was claimed by Water Carrier, the second by Looking Elk (Moses Old Bull's granduncle), and the third by Long Horns. Old Crow took the baby boy, cradle and all.

The men who owned the captives were very bitter about the killing of Sitting Bull's father. They determined to kill the captive women and the child.

Pretty soon, here came Sitting Bull through the camps, wailing and crying for his father. Tears streamed down his face, his hair was loose in mourning, and he had thrown away his comfortable clothing and was wearing old rags, barefoot. The Hunkpapa stood watching him, indignant and full of sympathy, almost ready to cry themselves. Sitting Bull was their friend, everybody liked him, and it cut them to the heart to see his distress. They were more determined than ever to destroy those captives.

Sitting Bull came and stood before his people. He had heard about these captives, and suspected what they were thinking.

"If you have hidden these captives for my sake, it is not right," he said. "Treat them well, and let them live. My father was a man, and death is his."

Sitting Bull knew that these women had lost husbands and brothers in this fight, that they were lonesome and grief-stricken. He felt the same, just as they did: he knew exactly how they felt. And so he took pity on them, since they were women.

Jumping Bull was buried with the other dead Sioux on the north bank of Cedar Creek, where the ridge and the butte made a valley, no very great way from the town of Lemmon, South Dakota. Sitting Bull became head of his family.

When four days of mourning had elapsed, he gave permission to hold a victory dance over the Crows they had killed. A special song was composed for this dance of triumph, and because the Crow leader, Bird-Claw-Necklace, had wept and wailed like a woman, the blackface warriors and their women stamped and sidled all night long to the taunting chorus: *"Crows cried! Crows cried!"*

At the end of summer, Swift Bull, Carries-the-Prairie-Chicken, and Wide Skirt brought horses and took the Crow captives home again. The Sioux gave these women a number of good horses, in fulfillment of Sitting Bull's wish, when they went away. No doubt these Crow women had many romantic tales to tell when they returned from their pleasant captivity in the Hunkpapa camp.

8. Killdeer Mountain

WHEN THE Civil War broke out, the fur traders (most of whom were Southern sympathizers) tried to get the Teton Sioux to make war upon the Union. They said that the Grandfather at Washington was weak, and helpless, and about to be destroyed; and the fact that his promises and threats made at Fort Laramie in 1851 and at Fort Pierre in 1856 had never been fulfilled lent color to their story. The Western (Teton) Sioux, however, though they had many grievances, refused to be stampeded into war; all they asked was to be let alone. Nevertheless, there was much jealousy in their hearts against the chiefs arbitrarily appointed by General "White Beard" Harney in 1856, and as these paper chiefs had never received the backing of white troops, they could no longer control their discontented people. For eleven years they had kept the peace and made their pledges good.

But now they found themselves in a hopeless minority, and could do so no longer. Accordingly, in 1862, when their agent came upriver, they met him at Fort Pierre, and with many expressions of regret formally repudiated their part of the broken treaties, renounced their agreements, and refused to accept the annuities he had brought for them. The agent kept at them, however, and at last Bear Ribs or Side-of-Bear (the head chief named by Harney) gave in and took the payments due his own small band. Bear Ribs did this under protest, declaring that his action endangered his own life and the lives of all his followers. He was right; within a few days some Sans Arc Sioux, who had vowed to have the blood of this "traitor" to the nation, came to

Fort Pierre and shot the chief's saddle mule. When he came out to see what was done, One-that-Limps shot him from the shelter of a tipi. The Peace Party died with Bear Ribs; henceforth what we may call the National Party led by Four Horns and Sitting Bull was dominant among the Teton Sioux and, within ninety days, the sorely tried Eastern (Santee) Sioux perpetrated the Minnesota Massacre, and thus involved the whole Sioux Nation in hostilities.

Sitting Bull, far to the west, had no hand in the troubles in Minnesota. But in June, 1863, when General H. H. Sibley attacked his hunting party of Western Sioux, who had been driven by the drought to hunt east of the Missouri River, he retaliated by skirmishing with Sibley's wagon train near Apple Creek, and ran off a mule under fire. (See sketch No. 14 of his Picture Autobiography.) Nevertheless, he did not consider himself at war with the whites; he went westward and continued his hunting peaceably.

In midsummer, 1864, Sitting Bull's people were camped above the mouth of the Little Missouri, not far from The-Hunting-Ground-Where-They-Killed-the-Deer, now known as the Killdeer Mountains. Pretty soon other bands of Sioux joined the camp, until there were hundreds of lodges and nearly every tribe of Tetons was represented. One of the Oglala, a man named Brings-Plenty, had a captive white woman with him. It was reported that the soldiers were coming up the Missouri—thousands of them—and that on the Little Cheyenne three Cut-Head Sioux had killed one of the soldiers who wandered away from the main body. Afterward, the soldiers had caught and killed these young men, and had cut off their heads and stuck them up on poles! It looked as if the soldiers meant to kill *all* the Sioux.

While the Tetons were discussing these things, here came a bunch of Eastern Sioux (Yanktonais and Santees), and pitched their lodges near Sitting Bull's camp. Sitting Bull's nephew, Bull-Standing-with-Cow, was then a lad of fourteen winters, and had heard that the soldiers were chasing the Santees and Yanktonais. He thought these people might be the ones they were after, but was not sure. It was the first time any Yanktonais or Santees had come to his uncle's camp, and the boy was timid about going among them, because they were perfect strangers.

A day or two after these strangers arrived in camp, some young men returned from a hunt and said that soldiers were coming. The chiefs sent out scouts, and the whole camp moved back into the hills. The women pitched the tipis on a flat part way up the mountain, where a big spring came out and made a fine pond of good water. This flat was at the mouth of a canyon, and all around were wooded ravines and breaks. The people hoped they would be safe there. Sitting Bull's own people had no desire for war with the soldiers. They were almost without ammunition, even for the few old flintlocks they had. Sitting Bull considered himself at peace with the white soldiers: he had no quarrel with them.

When the scouts came back, the herald announced: "Soldiers are coming close, and will be here tomorrow."

Next morning, the lad Bull-Standing-with-Cow went out to water and herd the family horses. While the horses were drinking, he heard a disturbance at the camp. So he drove the ponies back to camp, and sure enough he heard them saying, "The soldiers are here now."

Four Horns and Sitting Bull caught up their war horses, and the boy (who had never seen a battle) mounted his pony also. Sitting Bull selected a fine sorrel, a fast horse recently purchased from some Canadian Indians, whom he had met out hunting. He had paid many robes for this animal, which was very fast. He had his gun and a quiver full of arrows. The boy had only a bow. The three of them rode out with other Sioux to the top of a hill. The soldiers were coming from the southeast.

Then they could see a whole army of soldiers coming: a long line a mile wide of men on foot, bunches of horsemen following them, and behind these a string of wagons—or cannon. The Sioux waited, and as the soldiers came near, a man named Long Dog yelled out: "Let me go close to them. If they shoot at me, we will then all shoot at the soldiers." Long Dog had a charm, he was with a ghost, and nobody could kill him. He wanted to find out whether the soldiers were coming to fight, or not.

Long Dog charged toward the line of advancing soldiers, and when he got close, he turned and raced along across their front. He gave them a chance to shoot first, and they did: they began the war. They all shot at him, but he was invulnerable, bulletproof, and was not hit. When the other Sioux saw the soldiers shooting at Long Dog, they began to shoot back. Long Dog returned to his own line on the hilltop.

After a few minutes, Long Dog prepared to show off his power a second time. Bull-Standing-with-Cow was burning up with ambition to qualify as a warrior. And when Long Dog started to repeat his ride along the front of the enemy, the boy followed on his fleet pony. The soldiers all took a shot at the two of them, but neither was hit, and they rode back to their comrades on the hill, unscathed. Sitting Bull was proud of his nephew's bravery. He was glad the boy had taken this chance to show his courage.

While the Tetons were displaying their courage on horseback, the Yanktonais and Santees took cover in a ravine, naturally following the tactics of that forest warfare to which they had been bred. When soldiers came near, these men would shoot, and hit one or two. This ambush was on the left (east) end of the Sioux line. But as soon as the white men saw what was going on there, some cavalry charged these snipers, and killed about thirty of them. Forest tactics were no good in Plains country.

These thirty Yanktonais and Santees were about all the Indians killed that day, though the military estimate was much larger. General Sully was much criticized for having attacked Indians who had had no hand in the Minnesota Massacre. But as a matter of fact, it so happened that he caused most loss among the very ones he was after.

As the troops advanced, the Sioux fell back toward their camp. Shell-fire and good rifles were too much for men armed only with bows, lances, clubs, and old muskets. Sitting Bull had never seen troops fight before, and he had never heard such a lot of guns at one time. The cannon, which shot so far—and "shot twice"!—was a strange puzzle to the Indians. Yet the Tetons stood up to the troops in a way that made General Sully overestimate their numbers by 50 per cent.

On one flank there was a skirmish. Some Sioux swept down on the soldiers and Brackett's cavalry charged to turn them back. The Sioux, following their usual hit-and-run tactics, like so many buffalo wolves sped back again, and the soldiers chased them a long way. Another bunch of Sioux waiting behind a hill saw them coming, got ready, and when they approached, whipped up their ponies and charged. The cavalry wheeled and retreated at a run, but the Sioux ponies were fast and fresh, the Sioux overtook the troopers, and pulled several from their saddles. This action nearly ended in disaster for the soldiers. Though unable to face the cannon, the Sioux were first-class fighters in a melee. When the soldiers had gone, the Sioux went back to their hilltop again.

Meanwhile, the women in the camp were preparing to pull out. In that camp was a man called The-Man-Who-Never-Walked, a cripple from birth. His twisted, shrunken limbs had never been any good; he could not go on the warpath like other young men. But his heart was that of a bear, full of strong courage. And now, when he saw the soldiers coming right to camp, and the shells dropping among the tipis, he knew his chance had come. He told them to put him into the basket of a travois, or drag, and carry him out to the battlefield. He wished to play the part of a man, like other men, before he died.

The Sioux about Sitting Bull were sitting on their horses on the hilltop, watching the battle, when there came a man from the camp, singing, and leading a cream-colored horse with a drag tied to its saddle. In the basket of the drag was the cripple with the heart of a bear. When the man reached the Sioux line, he stopped his song and called out: "This man has been a cripple all his life; he has never gone to war. Now he asks to be put into this fight and killed. He prefers to die by a bullet, since he cannot be of any use."

The Sioux warriors looked at the shrunken, twisted limbs huddled in the basket, and Sitting Bull spoke up: "That is perfectly all right. Let him die in battle, if he wants to."

Sitting Bull's heart was full that day. He was proud of his nation. Even the helpless were eager to do battle in defense of their people.

So they whipped up the cream-colored horse, and the cripple in the basket of the drag sped away, trying to guide the animal with long reins made of lariats. He could use his arms a little, but he had no weapons. Away went the horse, dragging that strange chariot, galloping straight toward the line of soldiers. The Sioux on the hilltop were watching.

All at once, down went the horse, shot dead. The-Man-Who-Never-Walked was thrown from the drag, and sat facing the soldiers, singing his death song. That song soon ended, for he could not dodge the bullets. The soldiers killed him. Later, as they advanced and came upon his body, they were astonished to find that this man who had charged them alone so bravely was only a helpless cripple. So died The-Man-Who-Never-Walked, known also as Bear's Heart, because of his dauntless courage.

By this time the soldiers were getting close to the camp, and the Sioux made a determined stand to cover the retreat of their women and children. Sitting Bull and the Tetons had relied upon the advice of Inkpaduta and his Santees in selecting the campground in the hills, for the Tetons had had no experience in fighting soldiers, and Inkpaduta was the hero of half a dozen battles. Cavalry, it was true, could not get at the camp: but here came all the cavalrymen on foot, with rifles. And so the word was passed to the women to save what they could and get out up the canyon. Horses and dogs were being packed up and some of the tents were down, when the batteries opened upon the camp with all their power. Then all was confusion, and the terrified women scuttled away with what they could gather up, while the boys herded the horses before them and old men harangued amid the bursting shells. Children cried, the dogs were under everybody's feet, mules balked, and pack horses took fright at the shellfire or snorted at the drifting smoke of battle behind them. The captive white woman, Fanny Kelly, was hustled along with the others through the parching heat and dust, and has left a vivid account of the flight of the women into the hills.

Meanwhile, the soldiers charged upon the Sioux around Sitting Bull. The Sioux fell back, and as they retreated, Jumping Bull's horse was hit. At almost the same instant, Sitting Bull's uncle, Four Horns, called out, "I am shot!" but managed to stay on his horse.

Sitting Bull took his uncle's horse by the bridle and led him out of the field of fire. Then he examined the wound. The ball had hit Four

Horns in the ribs behind and was still in his body. Four Horns said he could feel the lead in his body, it hurt him so. Sitting Bull could not locate it, and had to let it be. He generally carried some of his father's remedies with him on the warpath, and now he applied first aid to his uncle's wound. Then he bandaged it, and gave Four Horns something to drink. Afterward, he and his nephew led Four Horns back to camp. Four Horns was able to ride.

It was near the middle of the day when the three of them left the fight, and as they went back, they found that the camp had gone. Many of the tipis were still standing, still full of everything the Indians owned—buffalo robes, tanned hides of elk and antelope, tons of dried meat and dried fruits prepared against the coming winter. The travois were still stacked together in rigid pyramids, the saddles still hung on the racks. Here and there a pony remained restlessly pacing about the picket to which it was tied, and puppies whined from their minia-ture tipis. Hundreds of lost dogs skulked about through the deserted village.

Indian women and children were likely to fall into panic when the soldiers came: the soldiers were apt to do crazy things, it was said. Yet, although the women had fled in panic, the men covered their flight in good order, and gave way deliberately, contesting every foot of the way from ravines and hilltops, saving all their wounded. When the troops tried to follow them into the hills, they were soon taught the folly of the attempt, and fell back to the captured village.

The Sioux did not have to retreat far. It was only ten miles to the place where Sitting Bull, when he got in, about sunset, found his people encamped. Even the women had suffered no harm from the troops. The only casualty during their flight was an old woman killed by a bear, which rushed upon her from some bushes along the trail.

That night, the Sioux attacked the troops and killed two soldiers. Next day, while the soldiers were burning the abandoned camp, some of the Tetons tried to make peace, showing a white flag. But Colonel R. N. McLaren, who was in command of the work of destruction, "didn't know what it meant," and paid it no heed. Having destroyed everything in the camp, including hundreds of dogs, he set fire to the surrounding forests.

After this battle of Killdeer Mountain, July 28, 1864, the Sioux scattered. Inkpaduta took his unpopular gang, which had caused all this trouble, and went off eastward toward Dog's Den, where General Sully tried, and failed, to catch him. The Hunkpapa went off by themselves, while the Minniconjou and Sans Arcs camped on Thick Timber River (the Little Missouri), not far from the site of the present town of Medora.

9. The Battle of the Badlands

ONE NIGHT soon after, runners came to Sitting Bull from the Sans Arc camp, and asked the Hunkpapa to come and help them fight the soldiers again. They said that the afternoon before, the soldiers had made camp on the flat by the river, and when the Sans Arcs were looking at them from the top of the bluff, the soldiers had shot at them with their big guns. It looked as if the soldiers were trying to follow the Sioux wherever they went. Would Sitting Bull come and help fight them?

Sitting Bull went out into the camp circle of tents, each glowing like a big taper lantern in the summer night. "Saddle up; saddle up! We are going to fight the soldiers again."

Then the Hunkpapa rode off to the Sans Arc camp, and next day there was quite a battle at the crossing of the Little Missouri. From the crossing on, the Sioux kept after the soldiers all the way to the Yellowstone, where the steamboats were waiting with supplies. The soldiers were in desperate haste to reach the Yellowstone. They were on quarter rations; drought and grasshoppers had consumed the forage all along the route. The wagons could hardly be dragged through the terrible badlands they had to cross, and there was no water but alkali, and little of that. Two thousand men were strung out over three or four miles of twisted trail. Hundreds of horses and mules starved and died in the Flat-Top Butte country. Sitting Bull's warriors no longer dreaded the troops, if—indeed—they *ever* had. It was sure now that in rough country everything was in the Indians' favor. The Sioux retreat from Killdeer Mountain was a holiday jaunt compared to Sully's "advance" on the Yellowstone.

58

In one of these fights, Sitting Bull's warriors drove the soldiers up a dry canyon. The fight began in the late afternoon, and the Sioux kept on fighting all night. While the Sioux were shooting across at the soldiers, someone among the soldiers called out to them, speaking in their own language: "We want to know what Indians you are?"

Sitting Bull's powerful voice replied, "We are Hunkpapa, Sans Arcs, Minniconjou, Yanktonais, and others. . . . Who are you?"

Back came that voice: "We are some Indians with the soldiers. One of us is badly hurt—shot through the arm. An Indian named Stuck-in-the-Mud is the one shot in the arm. Most of these white boys are starving and thirsting to death. Just stay around, and they will all be dead."

Sitting Bull smiled to his comrades, as they listened. It was clear that the Yankton Sioux scouts with the troops had despaired of their lives, and wished to make friends with the other Sioux. But he yelled back: "Why have you come with these soldiers? We have to kill you, too, and let you thirst to death. You have no business with the soldiers. The Indians here want no fights with white men. *Why is it the whites come to fight with us, anyhow?*"

There was no answer.

All that night the Sioux lay around, shooting at the soldiers as opportunity offered. In the morning, most of the Indians had used up all their ammunition, they had had nothing to eat for twenty-four hours and very little water. Soon after sunup, one of Sitting Bull's relatives was hit. He was a son of one of Jumping Bull's half-brothers, but his name has been forgotten. Sitting Bull had to take his cousin home. He said, "Let the soldiers go. Let's go home."

Probably Sitting Bull's motives were mixed on this occasion. No doubt he was hungry, thirsty, and tired. But these considerations would never have drawn him from a fight where he was needed. No, he was fighting a defensive battle, and as soon as he had put his enemy on the defensive, his task was finished.

Moreover, firing at long range was tedious business to men whose sole aim in battle was to strike the enemy with the hand or with something held in the hand. As the old men say now, "White man's war is just shooting." After World War I, some of the Sioux veterans (members of the American Legion) sought admission to the old tribal warrior orders. But the old men resisted their claims: they considered that killing men with rifle-fire was no qualification for standing as warriors. Such warfare is "just shooting."

Shooting might, of course, be necessary, but it was no fun. It could add nothing to a man's war record, his string of *coups*. It cannot be too often repeated that—except when defending his camp—the Indian was totally indifferent to the general result of a fight: all he cared about was his own *coups*. Time and again old men have said to me, in discussing a given battle, "Nothing happened that day," meaning simply that the speaker had been unable to count a *coup*.

Also, shooting used up very expensive ammunition, which might be more usefully expended in hunting. As game became wilder and scarcer, ammunition was more and more in demand. It is noteworthy that whenever Indians (of any tribe—peaceful or warlike) demanded ammunition, it was on the plea that they needed it for hunting. This was no subterfuge, as a rule. They meant it. Ammunition was not useful to them in battle; it counted no *coups*.

Probably Sitting Bull, on this occasion, would have remained longer had not his cousin been hit. But when that happened, his first thought was for his wounded relative. A war leader was held responsible for the casualties of his command. Sitting Bull had to face that unpleasant issue. And so, when his cousin was hit, he was bound to take him home. There was no Medical Service. When a man was wounded, his friends and relatives looked after him.

Indian wars were fought for defense, for glory, for loot, or for revenge. And revenge comes too high if it has to be paid for in the lives of one's friends. Victory is too dear at that rate. Those who have read *Revolt in the Desert* will recall how often T. E. Lawrence went into action with the distinct understanding that there were to be "no casualties." They will recall how often he postponed an attack rather than risk the lives of his Arab friends. To date, I believe no one has been stupid enough to suggest that Lawrence was a coward. Neither was Sitting Bull, who fought in the same spirit. He was brave, but he was not callous enough to send friends to their deaths for the sake of a "victory."

And so, that morning, he said to his fellows, "Let them go; let's go home."

Placing the wounded lad on his horse, they tied him to the saddle and set out. Sitting Bull led the horse. With him went his nephew, Bull-Standing-with-Cow, a man named Little, and another who belonged to the Icira band. A considerable number of others went after them.

In spite of Sitting Bull's suggestion, many of the young men remained behind to shoot at the soldiers. There were some two hundred warriors there, and of several bands. They were under no discipline, nor could Sitting Bull force them to do his will. Sitting Bull rode home astride the fast sorrel. In the late afternoon the others followed. The soldiers escaped with their lives.

Sitting Bull did not think much of the soldiers. Said he: "The white soldiers do not know how to fight. They are not lively enough. They stand still and run straight; it is easy to shoot them. They do not try to save themselves. Also, they seem to have no hearts. When an Indian gets killed, the other Indians feel sorry and cry, and sometimes stop fighting. But when a white soldier gets killed, nobody cries, nobody cares; they go right on shooting and let him lie there. Sometimes they even go off and leave their wounded behind them."

10. The Captive White Woman

GENERAL SULLY returned to Fort Rice via the Yellowstone and the Missouri. When he arrived at the fort, he learned that Captain J. L. Fisk, U.S.A., was piloting a party of three hundred emigrants (one hundred wagons) across Dakota to the west and had run into hostile Indians. Fisk was besieged in his fort—Fort Dilts —an improvised structure of sod with walls six feet high, having loopholes. This fortification was near White Butte, a few miles east of the Little Missouri, not far east of the site of the present town of Marmarth, North Dakota. General Sully immediately ordered out a detachment of six hundred men to the rescue of the embattled farmers.

One day the Sioux were moving camp, when word came that the soldiers had come again. About one hundred of the warriors rode out to meet them, to see whether they wanted to fight or not. When they came in sight of them, they saw that all the whites were on horseback. The whites began to shoot right away: they began the war. Bull-Standing-with-Cow and Circling Hawk were in this party.

Circling Hawk was on a good, fast horse. Among others, he charged the soldiers. The soldiers turned and retreated, and Circling Hawk knocked one or two out of their saddles. His horse became scared and ran away, right through the soldiers. Then he turned back, and the Indians caught up with the troops. The soldiers halted, and one of them turned and came back alone to meet the Sioux. The Indians thought he must be the soldier chief.

There was a man named White-Buffalo-Chief, who had no mount. He borrowed a pony, charged on this soldier, and pulled the white

62

man off his horse. Both fell to the ground and wrestled together. Fool Buffalo rode out to take a hand in the fight and tried to shoot the white soldier. But he dared not shoot for fear of killing his friend, White-Buffalo-Chief. The soldier soon got on top of White-Buffalo-Chief, and Fool Buffalo was afraid his friend would be killed. So he began to beat the soldier on the back.

Then the soldier turned on Fool Buffalo and took his gun away from him, and began to beat the Indian underneath and broke his collarbone with the gun.

Shoots-the-Bear, a third Sioux, dashed up. But when he saw the soldier get the best of the other two, he turned back to his own lines. The soldier had got the best of three of them, and now he was standing up, holding his horse. He was a brave soldier, and hard to kill. Now he was victor.

Just then Sitting Bull raced forward on his fast sorrel. He rode hanging on the left side of his horse. He was first to reach the soldier and grabbed the soldier's bridle rein. But the soldier had his pistol, and he fired at Sitting Bull and hit him. Then the soldier mounted and returned to his own lines.

The moment Sitting Bull was hit, he veered away from his enemy, clinging to his mount. As soon as he got back to his own lines, Jumping Bull took care of him and bandaged his wound to stop the bleeding. He had been hit at close range in the left hip, and out through the small of the back, a nasty flesh wound. Sitting Bull, however, did not faint or say anything. Jumping Bull and a friend took charge of him, and Bull-Standing-with-Cow went along. They took him home to camp. He was wounded about noon.

The casualties of the Sitting Bull family were heavy that summer. First, Four Horns, on Killdeer Mountain; then Sitting Bull's cousin, at Rose Butte; and now Sitting Bull himself. For a while thereafter he rode in a drag. But he was sound and brave and healthy: he was soon up and around.

This affair is represented in sketch No. 18 of Sitting Bull's Picture Autobiography.

About this time Four Horns felt better. He said the bullet in his body had dropped into his stomach, and troubled him no more.

During the time Sitting Bull was getting well from his wound, he had time to observe the captive white woman, Fanny Kelly. Brings-Plenty was using her as his wife and the frightened woman was doing her best not to incense her fierce captors. Sitting Bull watched her working with the other women, tending the wounded, enduring the hardships of the winter without complaint. Her submissive behavior contrasted markedly with that of the Sioux matrons, who (though white persons have always talked of them as slaves) were quite as independent and proud and touchy as their husbands. Brings-Plenty was delighted with his new wife and dubbed her Real Woman—a title of honor reserved for women of the most unquestioned character. She quickly won the respect and liking of the Sioux. In fact, she was so popular that several men tried to get her away from Brings-Plenty.

Sitting Bull also observed that this thin, pale woman in the outlandish dress and curious shoes was continually being demanded by delegations of Indians from the agencies, who came bearing gifts (supplied by the frantic Mr. Kelly in the settlements). Whenever this happened, Brings-Plenty refused to give her up, and a dangerous crisis followed, when somebody was likely to get hurt. The Hunkpapa became annoyed at this constant succession of visitors, trying to take away the woman of Brings-Plenty.

But Sitting Bull saw what must be done: he made up his mind.

He said: "Why don't you feed her up? Why don't you take better care of her? Traders will be coming. We must take this woman back and make a good showing."

One morning, early in December, 1864, a large company of Blackfeet Sioux rode into the valley of Grand River and halted opposite Laughing Wood, where the Hunkpapa were in camp. Laughing Wood is not far from the present town of Bullhead, near the mouth of Rock Creek. The leader of these men was Sitting Bull's close friend, the giant Crawler, that terrible warrior with the Mongol face and the interminable string of *coups*. Crawler said that they had come to try to buy the white woman from Brings-Plenty.

The Blackfeet Sioux knew that it was a dangerous errand—their coming to demand the woman from the Hunkpapa. Without Sitting Bull's consent, it would be impossible.

Sitting Bull said, "We will take her back." And he sent for Brings-Plenty, who flatly refused to accept the horses they offered him. He pretended that he wanted to trade the woman for food to the traders at Long Lake, because the soldiers had destroyed the Sioux food supplies at Killdeer Mountain. But he had no mind to give up Real Woman at any price. He went back to his tipi, took her inside, and sat down opposite the door. He had his knife ready.

The Blackfeet Sioux gathered about the tipi of Brings-Plenty and the Hunkpapa were all around them. It was a tense moment, for the Hunkpapa did not like to see these Blackfeet Sioux come into their camp and carry off a person in this highhanded manner. It was a breach of decorum, a violation of intertribal law. The Hunkpapa were always ready for a quarrel or a fight, and it looked as if there would be a big one if the Blackfeet tried to hurt Brings-Plenty.

But Sitting Bull said: "Friends, this woman is out of our path. Her path is different. You can see in her face that she is homesick and unhappy here. So I am going to send her back."

To Crawler, Sitting Bull said, "Go in and get her. And tell him I said so."

Crawler went in. He found a fire burning in the center of the room and Brings-Plenty sat near it on the farther side, and at Crawler's right Mrs. Kelly sat beside Brings-Plenty, at his left. Crawler told him firmly that he had come to take the captive and would forfeit his life if necessary in her behalf. The day was intensely cold, and he sat down to warm himself by the fire. As he huddled over the fire, rubbing his chilled hands, he said to Brings-Plenty, "I have come for this woman."

"My friend," Brings-Plenty replied, "I have no use for your horses. I will keep the captive."

Crawler drew himself a bit closer to the fire, still industriously rubbing his hands.

"My friend," he said, "I would advise you to exchange the captive for the horses."

Brings-Plenty answered, "My friend, I have no desire to part with the captive."

Crawler, still moving farther over the fire, again tendered the horses for the captive, and a third time was refused. He saw that Brings-Plenty had drawn his knife from his belt and laid it by his side. Still drawing closer to the fire, Crawler suddenly drew his revolver from his belt, flashed it in Brings-Plenty's face, and at the same instant, catching the woman by the shoulder, he threw her around the fire back of himself. Still covering Brings-Plenty with the revolver, he quickly backed out of the tipi, where his friends at the door hastily took possession of her and mounted her on one of the ponies.

By this time the camp was astir, and apparently divided about equally between the friends of Brings-Plenty and those who desired to let the captive go in exchange for the horses.[1]

But Sitting Bull and his Strong Hearts prevailed over the excited Hunkpapa, and, after a time of jockeying and bluffing, carried Real Woman away to their council tipi. There they selected certain men to accompany her as representatives of the Hunkpapa. At this meeting, Sitting Bull said: "Care for her well. Choose good men to see that no harm comes to her. We can trade on the same trip."

Among those chosen were Big Head, Kills-Enemy, Crawler, Pretends-Eagle, Wet Hand. Loud-Voiced-Hawk, the chief, was one of the group who supported Sitting Bull.

Real Woman was well treated by these Hunkpapa and Blackfeet Sioux. She herself says: "These savages proved very kind to me. Though their nation is regarded by the whites as very vindictive and hostile, they showed me nothing but civility and respect." She was housed with Crawler's family, and Mary Crawler adopted the white woman as her sister. The party went on to Little Oak Creek, to the home of Hollow Horn, and Hollow Horn's wife gave Real Woman a complete new outfit of clothing, for the weather was terribly cold. And when the Yanktons came trying to buy her, giving her a fine horse and saddle, the Hunkpapa sent the Yanktons away and presented Real Woman with four good horses and eight fine robes of

[1] *South Dakota Historical Collections*, IV, 114 ff.

their own. On Moreau (Owl) River, Sun-Flower-Face awaited her in the lodge of her husband, the Two-Kettle Sioux chief, Long Soldier. Then they rode down the west bank of the Missouri to Fort Sully.

Mrs. Kelly, not understanding the Sioux tongue very well and being fearful at all times, sent in a letter to the commandant of the fort by a young Indian named Jumping Bear, or Charging Bear, who was later to be known as Chief John Grass. This letter warned the soldiers that the Indians intended to overpower the garrison and take the fort. As a matter of fact, the great number of Indians who followed her along were simply hungry, and went down in the hope of sharing in the feast and the reward which they expected to receive for turning the woman over to the soldiers.

Eight Indians rode with the captive to the fort, one leading her horse. But no sooner had they entered than the gates were shut and the other Indians left outside. These, however, went peacefully into camp near by. After a few days spent in trading, the Indians prepared to go home again. They were a little hurt because their friend Real Woman had refused to come out and dine with them when they invited her. Sitting Bull was one of those who had been locked out of the fort.

Throughout her misadventure, Mrs. Kelly was always so upset that she took the wrong step whenever an opportunity was offered for escape. She scared Captain Fisk off, when he was all ready to rescue her, by a letter of warning, and did the same thing again when Sully's troops came to relieve Fisk. And now she had given the men in Fort Sully the wrong idea entirely. Sitting Bull and the Sioux acted in good faith. But Mrs. Kelly laid the blame on her Indian friends, and their effort at peace and good will was wasted.

Mrs. Kelly afterward wrote, or published, an account of her sojourn among the Sioux, a highly colored, incoherent story, in which geography and Indian names are terribly mangled. The book is not a success: it is an attempt at romance, and the Sioux were not romantic, but epic. Although the Moon is one of their greatest gods, they are not her minions. Long ago they discovered that she pays no heed to human supplications, and so they build no altars to Diana. One cannot help wishing that, if the author was determined to play the romantic heroine, she had had some other name. Hers somehow fails to suggest a romantic girl beloved in his youth by the great John Grass.

But it was not the fault of Sitting Bull that Brings-Plenty only brought one. He made the best of a bad business and restored her to her people as soon as possible. Her narrative has concealed him under some indecipherable spelling of an Indian name. Long after, a young pretender came up the Missouri River who claimed to be the son of Sitting Bull and Fanny Kelly. But none of the Hunkpapa took any stock in his story. Sitting Bull was not interested in Real Woman; he was compassionate, as always, when he saw someone unhappy and homesick. And he wished to make peace with the whites.

This deed of his is one of those which showed the generous heart of a great chief. It is well remembered among the Hunkpapa—so well, in fact, that the winter of 1864–65 is known in their calendar as The-Winter-When-the-White-Woman-was-Rescued.

Somewhat later, a delegation of Oglala chiefs signed an affidavit acknowledging the justness of Mrs. Kelly's claim for reparations from the Sioux. The money was to come from the monies appropriated for the agency Sioux. But when the talk was held, one of the chiefs, placing his finger on the breast of the Secretary, said: "Pay her out of our money. Do not give the money into any but her own hands. Then the right one will get it."

The speaker was a canny old man: he had been watching the officials of the Indian Bureau for some time.

It hardly mattered that Real Woman misinterpreted the motives of the Sioux who rescued her. For on November 29, 1864, things happened which were to make peace between Sitting Bull and the soldiers impossible. On that fatal day a thousand Colorado soldiers, mostly volunteers, led by a former parson, Colonel J. M. Chivington, attacked the friendly Cheyennes under Black Kettle and White Antelope near Fort Lyon, on Sand Creek, and destroyed almost a hundred families, mostly women and children, with a ferocity, cruelty, and brutality hardly to be matched in modern history.[2]

Spring brought the Cheyennes from the south. They carried a war-pipe, and told the dreadful tale of massacre to Sitting Bull. They offered the pipe to him. Would he smoke with them? Would he join his old boyhood friends, the ancient allies of his people? Said they: "We were told that white men would not kill women and children, but now we have lost all faith in white men. We took pity on them in the past, but we shall never do so again. We plan to strike the whites all along the Platte, and after that the settlements to the west. Are you with us?"

Sitting Bull took the pipe, put it to his lips, smoked it. It was lucky for Fanny Kelly that he rescued her before the news of Sand Creek reached Grand River!

Another captive white woman, Mrs. Eubanks, was brought in to Fort Laramie and turned over to the troops about the same time. Her escort, two Sioux chiefs, had bought her from her captors at great trouble and expense, and brought her a long way. But the officer in command of the post, instead of rewarding these chiefs, ordered them hanged in chains! For months afterward, their blackened bodies swung in the wind beside the trail.

Nearly everyone on the frontier wanted to kill Indians in those days. And it was *so* convenient to kill friendlies!

[2] See *Condition of the Indian Tribes, Report of the Joint Special Committee under Joint Resolution of March 3, 1865*, 26–98.

II. Sitting Bull and Sully

G ENERAL SULLY made no attempt to invade Sioux country in the summer of 1865. He soon discovered that the last campaign had produced no effect whatever, that the Sioux were perfectly willing to fight him again, and continually came right to Fort Rice or Berthold to do it. Says he, "I feel sure I could defend myself, but that is about all I could do." He adds, dryly, that if the soldiers under Connor, Walker, and Cole, then pushing into Sioux country from the southwest, really wished to find Indians, they could find plenty only fifty miles from his own base. But he himself made no effort to find them; he had tasted Sitting Bull's valor already.

All that summer the Government (though at the same time sending four columns against the Sioux) was trying to make a treaty with them, in order to get the Indians off the roads to the gold fields. Sully thought that to offer the Indians presents to make peace was to invite another war, in order that they might get new presents at another treaty. The officials of the Indian Bureau, he said, were always ready to make a new treaty, "for reasons best known to themselves." Said he, "After a peace has been made next spring, I would offer a reward for every hostile Indian captured, or for his scalp." This, he believed, would be an economy: at the time, the Government was paying around a million dollars a head for dead Indians. Probably Sully thought this rather dear. But he neglected to name the persons who were to harvest the hair. The cat remained unbelled.

Meanwhile, Governor Newton D. Edmunds was freely going among the Sioux, unarmed and fearless, and soon became aware of the power of Sitting Bull. He reported one reason why treaties in the past had failed: "There is in each tribe a band of soldiers—the Strong Heart band—who have in tribal affairs the control of the whole tribe. The chiefs should have an opportunity to act with the advice and consent of that band." Edmunds pointed out, somewhat caustically, that the Sioux war had already cost some forty million dollars, and that it might be cheaper to pay Indians to keep the peace, and stop their annuities when they misbehaved.

The only flaw in his theory was that Sitting Bull refused to accept annuities, and was perfectly self-supporting and able to defend himself.

This wrangling between officials of the Indian Bureau and the War Department went on for years with increasing bitterness. The Army men regarded the Bureau men as either "milk and rose-water philanthropists" and dreamers, or grafters steeped in corruption, and blamed both parties for causing Indian wars which the Army had to fight. The Bureau officials, on the other hand, professed to think the Army a lot of bloodthirsty butchers, sots, and lechers, whose presence near an agency would endanger the health and soul of the Noble Red Man, and accused the Army of fomenting Indian wars in order to keep up the military establishment and finance corrupt war contractors. Both departments kept up a constant barrage of accusations, insinuations, and charges. But as neither side was ever allowed to put its theories into practice without interference, it is impossible to say which was right.

One thing, however, is certain: so long as the Bureau kept on making friendlies out of hostiles, and the Army persisted in making hostiles out of friendlies, neither department could possibly lack employment. Sitting Bull summed up the matter in a nutshell: "The white men have too many chiefs."

Yet one thing all white men agreed upon: the roads to the goldfields in the West must be kept open. The country was bankrupt after the Civil War, and the precious metals were "our sole reliance to liquidate the accruing interest of the national debt." In those days we actually tried to pay off our national debt.

Sully set about making peace by his own methods. His position at

Fort Rice was unfortunate: it had a bad name with the Sioux, and they were reluctant to come, fearing a trap. The Fort Rice garrison were all greenhorns, men who had never seen an Indian before, and officers who (as Sully reports) "knew nothing of Indian character or manners, except what they may have learned from reading novels." Sully had to remove Lieutenant Colonel Dimon; he was making such a mess of things there. Says Sully: "Friendly Indians have sometimes gone to visit the post, and while they are there some hostile ones follow them up and make attacks on sentinels or steal horses. . . . Officers and soldiers, *who cannot tell one Indian from another*, retaliate by shooting the first Indian they see or by placing some friendly Indian in the guardhouse." Officers were shifted so often that the Sioux could never count upon finding a friend at the post when they came in, and "every officer had notions peculiar to himself for managing Indians."

When Sully's runners came to the hostile camp on the Little Missouri, offering peace, there was long debate among chiefs. Sitting Bull, whose whole importance was that of war chief of the Strong Hearts, led the opposition; he said the whites were not to be trusted. He himself, like other wild Indians, had seen almost nothing of white men (except traders) since the council at Laramie in 1851; he was dependent on hearsay. And he heard so little good, and so much bad, of white men, that he was suspicious of their every move. Like other wild Indians he relied much upon the mixed-bloods, because he supposed these "children of the white men" understood the whites and their strange customs.

Sitting Bull talked against the truce, dwelt on the troubles at Fort Rice, recalled how often the troops had attacked friendly Indians. Said he: "Right now the Cheyennes and Sioux are fighting white men on the Platte; this very day the soldiers are marching from the south into our hunting grounds on the Powder. Sully simply wants to get us all together at Rice, and then rub us out. Wait! Don't be in a hurry; take your time." As for signing away lands, "No!" As for allowing white men to make roads and forts in Sioux country, "No!" He stuck to his original policy: "Let us alone. The Black Hills belong to me."

But for all his talk, the big camp—three miles of tipis, circle on circle—was slowly turning away from him. The majority favored a truce with Sully; most men were not so keen on fighting as the war chief of the Strong Hearts. Sitting Bull was at his wits' end.

For Sitting Bull was not motivated merely by personal ambition, martial spirit, or distrust of white men. Years before, at Sylvan Lake in the Black Hills, he had seen what looked like a man perched upon the curiously rounded rocks which tower above that pretty water, and had heard singing. He climbed the rocks to find the singer. But as he got near, the person turned its head to look back at him, and Sitting Bull saw that it was an eagle. It flew away, but he remembered the song. Thereafter Sitting Bull believed himself "god-chosen," divinely appointed to lead and protect his people. This sober conviction was the driving, guiding force which sparked his whole career—a heavy responsibility which he fully accepted and carried conscientiously to his dying day. . . . And now his people were drifting away from his leadership.

Then, one day, his big chance came. He was returning from a hunt, his pony loaded with antelope meat. On the trail he was overtaken by a Sioux on a lathered, heaving horse, a Sioux who gasped out the dire news that General Sully had massacred all those who had gathered at Fort Rice to smoke with him. No, the man had not seen the massacre; but that was the story, he had come headlong from Rice to tell it.

Sitting Bull did not wait to verify that story; he rode like mad for camp. As soon as he arrived, he began to wail and mourn for the dead. Sully reports that "Sitting Bull, a chief who wishes to lead the War Party, rode through the different villages, cutting himself with a knife." As he rode, he sang the eagle's song, rousing his paralyzed people to action:

> *My Father has given me this nation;*
> *In protecting them I have a hard time.*

The Peace Party was thunderstruck. And before they could rally their wits, Sitting Bull forestalled all argument by shouting between his songs and his wailing, "Catch your war horses! Saddle up! Saddle

73

up! We'll go and see if this is true or not!" Thus he compelled his opponents to follow him; they could not refuse to investigate. He had the whole camp behind him. Then there was mounting and riding in haste. Five hundred warriors sped away to Rice.

There, they found the camp gone, sure enough. They learned that Sully's steamboat had slipped across the Missouri from the Indian camp to the soldier camp, to bring over the soldiers and rub out the Sioux. But a watchful mixed-blood had seen what was going to happen, and, riding through the camp, had loudly warned the Indians of the coming massacre. Thanks to the warning of the friendly mixed-blood, the Indians had time to strike their tents, hit the trail to the buffalo range, and so escape destruction. Nobody had been killed, not a shot fired.

Sully angrily declared that the whole story was a lie got up by the mixed-blood traders, who wished a monopoly of Indian trade, and had deliberately frightened the Sioux away from the white man's fort. But Sitting Bull refused to be convinced; who could be sure that Sully was telling the truth? Only last summer he had attacked the Sioux on Killdeer Mountain, for no reason at all. Why not again?

One thing was certain: the friendly Sioux had fled, and it was impossible to be sure that they might not have been massacred if they had remained. Sitting Bull felt, and made others feel, that a second Sand Creek had been narrowly averted. The Peace Party melted away, Sully's treaty fell through, Sitting Bull's faction triumphed. The war went on.

This report of Sully's is the earliest official mention of Sitting Bull in the records of the United States. After that date there were many, and always he is described as the "chief," the "leader," the "generalissimo," of the hostiles. Later, when he became an agency Indian, the word was spread that he was "only a medicine-man," but this false propaganda was never dreamed of in the days of his power.

Sully and those who followed him knew well enough who was chief in those days. For Sitting Bull knew how to seize an opportunity, turn it to advantage, and swing his people into line; his political sagacity was as remarkable among the Sioux as his dash and courage on the field of battle. And he was perhaps the only man among them who could see through the curious wiles of white men, who were as strange and incomprehensible to Indians as if they had been men from Mars.

12. War on Powder River

WHILE SULLY, on the Missouri, was making peace with the Sioux, out in the Powder River country his colleagues—Connor, Cole, and Walker—were busy making war. The Sioux were sadly puzzled at this state of affairs: they were never sure whether a bunch of soldiers was friendly or hostile.

In August, General Connor was busy building Camp Connor (afterward called Fort Reno) on Powder River, a few miles above the Crazy Woman Fork. Meanwhile, Cole and Walker had arrived on the Powder by separate routes, and their combined commands were having a bad time, what with drought, dying horses, no guides, and Cheyenne war parties. They were afraid to turn their animals out to graze, for fear the Indians would get them, and many of the poor creatures starved on the picket line. Early in September, they had turned back, and were moving slowly and painfully upriver toward the new fort. The Cheyennes under Roman Nose attacked them in force, but having so few guns could not break the soldier lines, and after a lively skirmish set off to the Black Hills for the autumn hunt. On September 8, the soldiers reached the mouth of the Little Powder, and there Sitting Bull ran afoul of them.

He was out with a big war party—fully four hundred Sioux—looking for enemies, not for horses. The party was well mounted: every warrior had two horses, one to ride while traveling and a war horse for fighting. Sitting Bull, armed with a gun, shield, and quiver, with rainbow-painted face, and two eagle feathers in his hair, jogged along leading the fast sorrel. With him were many of his relatives: Jumping

Bull, his adopted brother, now nineteen; Bull-Standing-with-Cow, his nephew, going on sixteen; Long Ghost, the brother of his brother-in-law Makes Room, husband of Good Feather Woman. It was quite a family party. Other well-known warriors there were Black Moon, Swift Bear, Brave Buffalo, and Red Leaf.

They had come west from Ptenatapi, sometimes called Stampede Prairie, or Running Buffalo, where the camp was. It is near Slim Buttes.

Sitting Bull had been going on the warpath constantly for some years past. He was always singing war songs he had composed for himself, and one of his favorites had these words:

> *No chance for me to live;*
> *Mother, you might as well mourn.*

The song well expressed his recklessness and daring.

His mother (in those days named Mixed Day, and later called Her-Holy-Door) was a witty, sensible woman, with many cares. Sitting Bull now had two wives and three children to provide for. He was thirty-four years old and had won honors in plenty. Already he had been lamed for life by an enemy bullet, and here last summer he was shot again. Four Horns, too, and that young cousin, had been hit. And once before Four Horns had driven her distracted by getting left for dead on the battlefield. She had not yet recovered from the grief and shock of seeing her husband, Jumping Bull, throw his life away. She was tired of all these casualties. That song of her son's got on her nerves!

And so, when she saw him getting ready to go off with this big war party, the old lady gave him a piece of her mind. Said she: "Look here, Son. You be more careful in the next fight, and hang back a little. Take pity on me. If you happen to be killed, it will be a heavy burden for me and my children. Try and use a little judgment. Be careful."

Sitting Bull had always listened to his mother. This time he said nothing. But it rather took the joy out of the expedition to have her talk like that.

As the Sioux approached Powder River, some of the young men, far ahead, found the soldier camp, and, relying upon Sully's peace talk, rode down to see if the white men would give them a little tobacco or something to eat. But the soldiers fired at them and killed several. Then the young men ran off a few horses and rode back to the main body. Sitting Bull and the others were angry: the soldiers had fired the first shot. He rode around calling out, "Brace up! Brace up! We'll get them yet!"

That day, however, he did not sing the song urging his mother to mourn. He had another song, more appropriate to his present mood and less offensive to the family circle. It ended in two "soldier yells," and acted as a spur to his emulous comrades. As the Sioux rode down into the valley of the Powder and sighted the soldiers just breaking camp—at noon—his resonant chant was heard:

> *Friends, I am a soldier,*
> *And have many people*
> *Jealous of me!*

When the four hundred Indians appeared—"three thousand Sioux," says the official record—the troops took a position in the timber of the river bottom, near a small hill. Bull-Standing-with-Cow said there were about one thousand soldiers, which is pretty close to the actual number. Some were afoot, some on horseback. They began to shoot right away, and the Sioux were all around them, shooting back. They were all well mounted and kept circling around and trying to advance toward the troops.

Suddenly the horseback soldiers charged out at the Sioux to the northeast, along the stream, the left bank. The Sioux easily ran out of the way, and on their fast horses kept ahead of the half-starved cavalry mounts. But when the troops turned back again, the Sioux swept down after them like hornets. There was one very brave man, Stands-Looking-Back, on a sorrel horse and armed only with a sabre. He charged far ahead of the other Sioux, rode right in among the soldiers, and knocked one of the troopers out of his saddle. After this skirmish was over, he rode across the river and joined the bunch around Sitting Bull, who was on the east side of the soldiers.

Sitting Bull and his comrades were shooting at the soldiers. And the soldiers saw that they could never get out of the bottom and go their way unless they could drive these Sioux away, for they were on all sides of them. This time the cavalry came straight for Sitting Bull. There they came, riding right across the river, all blue coats and splashing water, for the river was very low that droughty season. The bugle was sounding. When they got across the river, they charged.

The Sioux repeated their tactics, keeping out of the way, leading the soldiers on to a fruitless chase, and then—when they turned— charging back at them. Sitting Bull rode with the others, astride his fiery sorrel, loosing an arrow when he had a chance, his gun being only a single-shot muzzle-loader. But far ahead of the ruck of rushing ponies rode the brave Stands-Looking-Back, sabre in hand, and after him Bull Eagle. Together they raced in among the soldiers, and with sabre dangling from his wrist, his painted face distorted with anger and triumph, the leader seized a soldier with his hands and hurled him down from his horse. Bull Eagle also knocked a man off his horse and counted the *coup*. Sitting Bull did not much enjoy his new rôle of "hanging back," that day.

Away went the soldiers with a thunderous thudding of hooves, back across the bottom, back across the river, back to their comrades in the timber. After them went the Sioux pell-mell.

As they came on, they saw the foot soldiers turn to face the south, a long line of them, already shooting, half-hidden by bursts of white smoke which bloomed along their front and veiled them as it drifted off. Straight for this line went the Sioux, and far in the lead Brave Buffalo, emulous of the courage of his two friends, dashed toward the waiting soldiers. But when he was within twenty paces of the troops, they fired, killing horse and man.

Brave Buffalo was not the only casualty. Long Ghost was shot through the leg, the ball also piercing his horse. And Red Leaf was hit in the right side of the body. They were badly wounded, but both survived. The Sioux turned back, mourning for Brave Buffalo, caring for their wounded. Not long after, they reached home. Sitting Bull's mother shook her head over Long Ghost's wound. One more casualty in the family!

General Connor had issued orders "not to receive overtures of peace or submission from Indians, but . . . kill every male Indian over twelve years of age," instructions which his superior, General Pope, described as "atrocious. . . . If carried out, they will be disgraceful to the Government." There was no cause for alarm, however. Though the Indians "did most of their fighting with arrows," they more than held their own. Connor afterward wrote of this campaign, "Harm rather than good was done, and our troops were . . . driven from their country by the Indians." Almost the only Sioux killed that summer were killed by the Pawnee Scouts.

The troops who fought Sitting Bull had been very unwilling to fight Indians. Some of them had mutinied at the start, and had had to be coerced by the threat of cannon, with gunners ready to fire. Their fears were justified. The night after the fight with Sitting Bull, a cold snap came, and the horses, half-starved, and exhausted by the charges of the day before, died on the picket line. Next day they had to burn or bury all their supplies, saddles, wagons, extra ammunition, and hike into Camp Connor hungry, ragged, and half of them barefoot, "as completely disgusted and discouraged an outfit of men as I ever saw." General Connor was relieved of his command because of the wretched failure of his campaign.

When the Sioux got back to camp, Sitting Bull had the unusual experience of sitting still and listening while other men recounted *coups*. He had counted none.

His only wound that year was the hole left by a bad tooth which had to come out. And even this, surprisingly, was soon filled by a new tooth!

Sitting Bull lived too far to the north to have a hand in the skirmishes of Red Cloud's War, and was not present when the Minniconjou, aided by the Oglala and Cheyennes, lured Colonel W. J. Fetterman's command into the ambush near Fort Phil Kearny, December 21, 1866, and destroyed the soldiers to the last man. Bull-Standing-with-Cow, a Minniconjou on his father's side, was present, and told me that no Hunkpapa took part in that battle. And certainly the young man could not have been ignorant of his uncle's presence had Sitting Bull been there.

Yet it must not be supposed that Sitting Bull knew no danger that year of 1866. He was attacked in his own camp, on the Yellowstone —and by one of his own people. Bull-Standing-with-Cow witnessed the affair.

Two Rees had come to visit Sitting Bull, and passed the night in his lodge. Next morning a Hunkpapa named Turns-Over found that someone had stolen two fine buckskin horses from him. He scouted round, and suspected from the sign that the animals had been taken by these Rees or by their skulking relatives. He was very angry and complained to Sitting Bull. Sitting Bull knew his two guests were blameless; they had been with him all night. Yet, seeing how angry Turns-Over was, he thought he had better walk with his guests when they left and see them safely out of the Sioux camp.

Meanwhile Turns-Over tied up his hair in a knot on his forehead— a warrior's coiffure—and with several friends waited near a cutbank on the edge of camp for the Rees to pass. It was a crime to shoot within the camp circle, more especially at a guest, and Turns-Over was not foolish enough for that. But once the Rees had left the camp, they were no longer guests; he could kill them. Before long he saw them coming, and with them Sitting Bull. As they passed by, one of the Rees was walking abreast of Sitting Bull, the other a little behind him.

When Turns-Over saw Sitting Bull escorting these Rees out of camp, he lost his temper. Already the three men were twenty-five steps away; soon they would be gone. Turns-Over said to his friends, "It seems like Sitting Bull has no ears. Get him! Hold him!" With that he jerked out his revolver, loaded with buckshot, and fired at Sitting Bull's back.

Many of the customs of the Sioux were borrowed from the Animal People. For example, when a man was about to attack another, he was likely to give one or two guttural "brave grunts," or growls, like a wounded bear about to charge. It would be hard to imagine a sound which conveys more ferocity or brute courage than those same brave grunts.

Turns-Over's shot hit the Ree behind Sitting Bull in the buttocks. The moment Sitting Bull heard the shot, he whirled around, uttering two brave grunts. Those with Turns-Over knew what that meant; they tumbled over the edge of the cutbank quick as scat. But Sitting Bull had already thrown up his rifle, and, without aiming, pulled the trigger just as Turns-Over went over the bank. Turns-Over went headfirst, backwards, over the cutbank; the bullet had struck the knot of hair on his forehead, knocking him flat. But he was unhurt.

Such crack shooting terrified Turns-Over. Bull-Standing-with-Cow said that Sitting Bull meant to kill Turns-Over. But Turns-Over thought Sitting Bull's marksmanship quite good enough as it was. He left camp that day and moved to the agency.

That was the only time Sitting Bull took a shot at another Sioux. Many chiefs did shoot members of their own tribe or band: Sitting Bull never. Those who saw him shoot that day did not need to be warned to leave him alone. His career as a warrior had raised him high in the estimation of his fellows.

13. The Testing of the Chiefs

THE FOUR CHIEFS created by the Hunkpapa in 1851 had not lived up to the expectations of the tribe. Hard times always bring criticism of government, and the Sioux had been having difficulty in feeding themselves. Cold weather, wars, and broken treaties may also have counted against the leaders. It was the general opinion that the experiment had not proved a great success. But worst of all, the chiefs themselves seemed not to have the dignity and forbearance demanded of men in their high office.

Running Antelope had run away to the Ree village with another man's wife; Red Horn had stolen *two* women from the same man, Bear-Skinned, one of his own warriors; Loud-Voiced Hawk became involved in a fatal stabbing affray. Even Four Horns, Sitting Bull's uncle, was being criticized. Some of the head men got together and decided that something must be done to test these chiefs and find out whether they were fit for office, or not.

A chief (I-tan'-chan) was supposed to be greathearted, magnanimous, generous, and above all personal spite or selfishness. For this reason, few men were willing to undertake the responsibility. It was asking too much to forgive everything, never to lose one's temper, and continually to give and share with those who could never by any chance repay benefits. Most men had not enough of the father in them to be father to a whole tribe. Famous warriors—like the Cheyenne Roman Nose—sometimes declined chieftaincy—not feeling themselves fit for it. Among the Sioux, men were sometimes made chiefs for their lovable, gentle qualities, even though they were hardly

83

warriors at all. Black Eagle, of the Sans Arc Sioux, is an example. Great warriors sometimes lacked the kindly qualities demanded of a civil chief.

When the Hunkpapa head men assembled, they devised a plan for testing the chiefs who had so grievously fallen from grace and displayed the weaknesses and passions of ordinary men. It was agreed that a sure way to test these chiefs would be to steal their wives and see how they took it. Therefore, certain men were secretly appointed for this job and sent to the scattered camps where the four chiefs were then living.

As had been expected, Running Antelope, Loud-Voiced-Hawk, and Red Horn all lost their tempers when they found men meddling with their wives, and one of them even went gunning for the disturber of his domestic peace. The head men nodded; it had turned out just as they expected. And now it was the turn of Four Horns.

One day the wife of Four Horns left his tipi without saying where she was going. All day she was missing, but Four Horns made no inquiries. It was not the part of a chief to disturb himself about a woman. Night fell, and she did not come back. He sat in the lodge alone, but made no effort to find out what had become of his woman.

Early in the morning, the wife of one of the Hunkpapa came into the tipi of the lonely chief. Said she, "I wish to marry you. I have long wished to do so, for you are a great chief, and have performed many brave deeds. Besides," she added, "my husband has stolen your wife; he has her now."

Four Horns sat still. He said nothing, nor did he betray any emotion whatever. She watched him, and after a few moments went to work preparing breakfast for the chief. When the meat was cooked, she cut it up, and, sitting before him, fed him with her own hands— four morsels. He ate the food she had prepared for him. The woman remained in his lodge that day.

A little before sunset, when the rays struck through the yellow lodge-skins and dimmed the small fire in the middle of the tipi, someone came to the door of the tipi and coughed, to let Four Horns know he was there. Four Horns asked him to enter. It was a messenger from the man who had stolen the chief's wife. He said, "My friend wants his wife back."

Then Four Horns got up and went out of the lodge and caught his best war horse and brought it to the tipi and put on its back his finest saddle. The saddles of that family were celebrated among the Hunkpapa, for Sitting Bull's uncle, Looks-for-Home, was an excellent saddler.

Over the saddle he threw a decorated buffalo robe, and put his best bridle on the horse's head. Then he called the woman out of the lodge and placed her in the saddle. "Certainly," said the chief, "if my cousin wants his wife again, he may have her. Let there be no hard feelings between us."

The woman went back to her husband, riding the fine gift horse. Four Horns went back into his lodge, and soon after his own wife returned to him. He said nothing to her about her desertion, but treated her just as if nothing had happened. His relations with the man who had stolen her remained friendly as before.

Then the head men of the Hunkpapa, who had planned the testing of the chiefs, rejoiced. Four Horns had justified his election. He alone, of the four, had shown the great heart of a real chief. Henceforth, though the others were chiefs in name, Four Horns was regarded by the people as supreme.

But Four Horns was not happy. He was terribly ashamed and humiliated, because his three colleagues had brought such disgrace upon their high office—which he shared. He thought long, and then decided that he would create a chief who should restore the honor of the chieftaincy and wipe away the tarnish from that office. He looked about for the right man, and he did not need to look long.

Four Horns had children of his own, sons who might have been chiefs after him. Also he had adopted two young men—Noisy-Walking-Elk and Red Arse. But he passed them all by. His choice fell upon the chief of the Midnight Strong Hearts, his nephew, Sitting Bull. His qualifications made him the only candidate.

Sitting Bull: there was a young man who was brave, who usually led the charges on his fast horses, and never reined them back in a battle. A man who had been severely wounded in battle twice, once so badly that he was a cripple. A man who was a peacemaker in the camps, and never quarreled. A generous man, who was always capturing horses from the enemy and giving them away, a man who constantly shared his kill with the poor and helpless when hunting, a man who could not bear to see one of the Hunkpapa unhappy. An affable, jocular, pleasant man, always making jokes and telling stories, keeping the people in a good humor, a sociable man who had tried to please everybody all his life, and was not in the least haughty or arrogant—in spite of his many honors. A family man, who stood well with matrons and old women whose domestic quarrels he had patched up, whose larders he had filled. A man who had the gift of prophecy, and could foretell the event of a battle, so that he was almost always victorious. A good singer, always in demand. A man who could speak, and think, and never was swindled by the whites. A man whose unshaken purpose was to maintain Hunkpapa laws and customs, and hold the Hunkpapa hunting grounds against all comers. A man who—and this weighed strongly with the conscientious Four Horns—was devoutly religious, whose prayers were strong, and who generally got what he prayed for. Finally, a man who—in five short years—had swept away the surrounding nations and occupied their hunting grounds.

Not least important in Four Horns' calculations was the fact that Sitting Bull had the unqualified support of the Midnight Strong Hearts, the most powerful warrior society in the tribe, without whose consent no chief could be named at all. Under Sitting Bull's leadership, this society had grown to have more than two hundred members. When they charged, they charged shouting, "We are Sitting Bull's boys!" A cry that struck terror to the enemy.

When Four Horns proposed Sitting Bull's name to the Midnight Strong Hearts as his nomination for a chieftaincy, he met with no opposition. The society was unanimous in supporting his nephew's candidacy. They all remembered that day when he was shot in the foot—that day when he killed the Crow chief. Many of them believed that the qualities of a man killed entered into the slayer: if Sitting

Bull had the qualities of a chief, it was no surprise to them. That exploit had much to do with the approval of the warriors.

The old councillors, however, were perhaps more impressed by the thoughtful and studious cast of Sitting Bull's mind. It was certain that he spared no pains in getting ready for his enterprises; his forethought, among the heedless Sioux, made him remarkable. The old men now recalled a portent at his birth, which had been hard to explain at the time. It happened that shortly before Sitting Bull was born, an epidemic struck the camp on Grand River, and in the general grief and alarm, the unborn child turned over in his mother's womb. This strange and unusual event had puzzled men at the time. Now its meaning was clear: even before he was born, Sitting Bull was *thinking* of the welfare of his people!

A meeting was held, and Sitting Bull was sent for to be installed as chief. Four Horns was master of ceremonies.

II. Chief

14. The Inauguration

The name of Sitting Bull was a "tipi word" for all that was generous and great. The bucks admired him, the squaws respected him highly, and the children loved him. He would have proved a mighty power among our politicians—a great vote-getter with the people. —FRANK GROUARD.

AT THE ELECTION of a head chief, it was necessary to assemble all the bands and tribes concerned. The nomination of the warrior society had to be confirmed by everyone. As it happened, the Northern Sioux, Cheyennes, and Arapahos were weary of the continual uncertainty of peace and war with the white men and with other tribes. A man never knew whether he could safely approach an army post or not, because individual chiefs waged war or made peace at discretion. No one knew when to expect trouble. When Four Horns and the Hunkpapa warrior societies proposed to create a high command, a single head chief, the tribes responded readily.

Five big camps were strung along the river: Hunkpapa, Minniconjou, Sans Arc, Crazy Horse's Oglala, and the Cheyennes. The Yanktonais, Two Kettles, and Blackfeet Sioux were also represented—but not in force. Some Arapahos camped with the Cheyennes. When this book was written, well over a hundred men were living who had witnessed this ceremony. Among them were Judge Gray Eagle, Circling Hawk, Chief One Bull, Old Bull (chief historian of the Hunkpapa), Crazy Bear, Red Bird, Bear Ghost, and Chief Joseph White Bull, then known as Big-in-the-Center.

Chiefs who took part in the ceremony were, in addition to the four

91

Hunkpapa head men already mentioned: of the Hunkpapa, Long Horn, Iron Dog, Black Moon, Crow King, and Gall. Gall was also known as Walks-in-Red-Clothing, or The-Man-Who-Goes-in-the-Middle; of the Sans Arc, Black Eagle, Blue Coat, Two Eagle, His-High-Horse, Brown Thunder, and Spotted Eagle; of the Minniconjou, chiefs Makes-Room, Black Shield, Flying-By, White-Hollow-Horn, Lame Deer, and yet another Black Moon; of the Oglala, Crazy Horse, Sweat; of the Cheyennes, Ice, also called White Bull. Chase-the-Tiger, also a Sioux chief, was present.

It was a great occasion, an earnest attempt to reunite the whole Teton Sioux nation against the encroachments of the white men and other enemies and to organize the hunting on a grand scale. After seventeen years, the plan proposed by the Commissioner at the Laramie Treaty in 1851—the plan of having *one* chief—had at last begun to take hold upon the imaginations of the Tetons. That day they tried to put it in force, choosing a man of their own, quite without interference by white men who did not understand the thoughts and standards of the Sioux.

Of course, such an attempt could not be a complete success. The Brûlé Sioux, far to the south, never admitted Sitting Bull's claim to be head chief of all the Tetons. Their leader, Spotted Tail, truckling to the whites, led them another way: he aspired to that position himself, but trusted to the power of the Grandfather for his election. As for the Southern Oglala, led by Red Cloud and his three hundred Bad Faces, their power was already spent. Red Cloud was even then preparing to sign a treaty of peace. They were remote from Sitting Bull's influence, and though many of them visited his camps and even fought with him as volunteers, they never—as a tribe—acknowledged his authority. But Crazy Horse, the fighter, would have no treaty for *his* band of Oglala: he brought his people north and threw in with Sitting Bull.

A special lodge was set up—a big lodge, open on one side, made of several ordinary tipi covers stretched on a framework of poles. There the chiefs assembled and preliminaries were completed. Then four chiefs—Four Horns, Red Horn, Loud-Voiced-Hawk, and Running

Antelope—took a buffalo robe and went to the lodge of Sitting Bull. They led him out of his tipi. Spreading the robe flat on the ground, they seated him upon it, and, taking hold of the four corners, carried him in state to the council lodge. There he was seated in a place of honor, and the ceremonies began with the smoking of the long pipe in communion. The day was fine and bright—a good omen.

When the pipe had been lighted, the mouthpiece was extended toward the earth, that it might hold them good and strong; then to the four winds in turn, that no harsh winds might blow upon them, bringing distress and ill luck; then to the sun, that they might see their way clearly, and so avoid danger and death. It was then passed from hand to hand, from right to left around the circle, as the sun moves, and every chief inhaled a puff or two of smoke, blowing it out from his lungs with a prayer which it would carry upward to Wakan' Tanka, who loved the sweet savor of the sacred weed.

This pipe was decorated with duck feathers and other symbolical adornments. It was presented to Sitting Bull as the badge of office. The duck feathers, impervious to water and wind, urged a like endurance and patience upon him. Men use a pipe to pray with, and it was his duty to pray for his people.

There he sat, that homely cripple, in his plain clothing, and with only two eagle feathers in his hair—one red, in remembrance of his wounds. He had never put on any airs, was never a snob, though pleasantly conscious of his own undoubted merits. Some of the chiefs, in whose family that rank was hereditary, became very arrogant after watching army officers lord it over the privates at the frontier posts. But Sitting Bull was arrogant only to the whites. He was a man of the people, and never pretended to be anything else.

There were many speeches, many songs, that day. Some spoke of his bravery, some of his generosity, and others of how, since he was a small boy, he had always been merciful and kind to all, both men and animals. They reminded the people that he had abolished slavery in his band, had told the people to adopt captives or set them free. They recalled his mercy to his "brother" Jumping Bull, to Real Woman, and referred gracefully to his many deeds in battle, when he had rescued a comrade.

93

Four Horns, master of ceremonies, declared: "Because of your bravery on the battlefield, and your reputation as the bravest warrior in all our bands, we have elected you head chief of the entire Sioux nation, head war chief. It is your duty to see that the nation is fed, that we have plenty. When you say 'fight,' we shall fight: when you say 'make peace,' we shall make peace."

Afterward, Crazy Horse, who brought such an accession of strength from the Oglala, was created second in command. Though a much younger man than Sitting Bull, he was justly famous for his valor. Unpretentious, laconic, scorning all possessions but his horse and weapons, he was an ideal man for the post. He and Sitting Bull had the decision in every crisis thereafter. They were always close friends.

Black Moon, upon whom the prophetic mantle of the shaman Sun Dreamer fell, urged Sitting Bull to remember the two halves of his duty: "First," he said, "you are to think always of God, of Wakan' Tanka. Second, you are to use all your powers to care for your people, and especially for the poor."

Sitting Bull was then presented with a bow and ten arrows, and a flintlock gun. He was reminded that he must be like the eagle, for the eagle is the chief of all birds, its feathers are the rewards of valor, it flies highest. A chief should study to resemble the eagle.

Then they brought out a magnificent war bonnet, with beaded brow-band, ermine pendants, and swagger crown of lustrous black-and-white eagle plumes. This splendid headgear had a trailing double tail of eagle tail-feathers cascading down the back to drag on the ground. Every feather in that bonnet represented some brave deed, some *coup* performed by the warrior who had contributed it. It was in fact the symbol of the combined valor of the Northern Teton Sioux. With it, Sitting Bull was publicly crowned.

Afterward they led him out of the lodge. There he found a fine white horse awaiting him, a gift horse. Gall and Running Antelope then lifted Sitting Bull into the saddle; the warrior societies (Strong Hearts, Crow Owners, Mandan, Badger, and Fox Soldiers), formed in column in all their might and panoply, rode behind their new chieftain and his staff. All were dressed in shirts of deerskin and mountain sheep profusely decorated with human hair, stained horsehair, red and yellow, and devices worked in porcupine quills and beads. Long fringes trailed from sleeve and leggin, and every face was painted as if for war. Shields were uncovered, displaying their sacred and heraldic devices to the sun, eagle feathers fluttered from the hair or stuck upright in the rider's scalplock. Tassels of scarlet horsehair or red flannel pennons waved from every lance, and some bronze-chests swelled beneath necklaces of bear claws. On they rode, chanting their virile chorus, their painted chargers prancing with the consciousness of pomp and warlike spirit. And at the head of that long column, the flower of the manhood of what to him was the greatest nation in the world, rode the lame man, brave, kindly, and gracious, who had risen from the common people to be head chief.

That was a proud moment for Sitting Bull, and an humble moment, too. As they passed slowly around the great camp circle, the city of his nation, his heart was full. Then the warrior-poet broke into song—a song composed by himself for that occasion:

> *Ye tribes, behold me.*
> *The chiefs of old are gone.*
> *Myself, I shall take courage.*

15. The Black Robe Makes Peace

I know of no Indian war that could not have been avoided by a little common humanity of frontiersmen, honesty of the Indian Ring in Washington, and common-sense by the commissions sent out.

—CHARLES ERSKINE SCOTT WOOD.

SOON AFTER SITTING BULL was made chief, some of the more thoughtful and public-spirited Strong Hearts formed a men's dinner club with a limited membership of twenty, for the sole purpose of discussing tribal affairs, with a view to helping the people. Because of the serious purpose of the club, it held no dances and seldom sang songs. Joking and storytelling were barred, and the meetings were usually secret. Because of the novel character of the club, it was known to the tribe as the Silent Eaters.

Though unofficial, the Silent Eaters soon dominated Hunkpapa affairs. The chiefs constantly consulted and deferred to them, and after Sitting Bull became a member (some two years later) the Silent Eaters became the cabinet through which he governed. The Midnight Strong Hearts had voted him into office: the Silent Eaters kept him there. For the members were men who shared and could appreciate his qualities. All of them were known as being in the thick of things in a fight, all of them were generous, all of them often brought home captured horses, and most of them had been wounded or had had horses shot under them. With their backing, Sitting Bull was able to feed his nation, so long as buffalo ran.

The immediate result of his inauguration was reflected in the *Re-*

96

port of the Secretary of War for 1867, which states that attacks by Indians were "less frequent than they ordinarily have been." And the Secretary blames the rumors of Indian outrages on white frontiersmen, saying that the rumors "originated in a natural rivalry for business on the three great roads across the Plains, the friends of each aiming to damage the business of the others by these exaggerations."

Sitting Bull had won distinction by battling with the Indian nations; he cared little about the whites, so long as they left his game alone. And the first thing he did as chief was to launch war parties at the Crows, Hohe, Rees, Hidatsa, Mandans, and Flatheads. Like other wild Sioux, he had no deep animosity toward white men, but for his ancestral Indian enemies he had a hatred deep and rankling, and a fixed determination to drive them out and destroy them root and branch. He never attacked the white settlements; he asked only to be let alone. And *all* his demands (which may be found repeatedly in official records) were simply for *rights guaranteed by the very treaties which the government had made.* They show how far he was from seeking war with white men, much less leaving Sioux country to make war. Those demands were, briefly: (1) Close the roads; (2) burn the forts; (3) stop the steamboats; (4) expel all whites except traders. If those demands could be granted, there would be peace. Otherwise, he was forced to fight, he could not allow stray white men to ruin his nation, destroy the buffalo industry, starve his family. That old pagan loved his native soil with a love almost carnal, a love wholly mystical. Up before dawn always, he liked to bathe his bare feet, walking about in the morning dew. "Healthy feet," he used to say, "can hear the very heart of Holy Earth."

And so now, uplifted upon a great wave of popular, wartime enthusiasm, out of a full heart he composed a song for his warriors, and sang it to strengthen their courage:

> *Young men, help me, do help me!*
> *I love my country so;*
> *That is why I am fighting.*

At the end of May, 1868, Father Pierre Jean De Smet, the Jesuit, arrived at Fort Rice, with authority of the Peace Commissioners and General Sherman to visit the camp of the "hostile" or hunting Sioux, in the interests of peace. For two years the good father had been trying to bring this mission about, and he was well content. There was good hope that he might succeed, though all feared for his life on the journey. Of all the heroic company of Jesuit missionaries to the Indians, none was more generally beloved by them than Father De Smet. He was a genial, cheerful, courageous man, honestly intent upon helping his Red friends, whom he sincerely loved. We have it from his own mouth that he was happier and more at home at a feast in a tipi than when dining with the dignitaries of the Church. He was affable, even-tempered, laughter-loving, and without any of that lust for unnecessary martyrdom which so often interfered with the success of Jesuit missionaries. For many years this saintly man had been longing to found a mission for the Sioux, and had visited them whenever he could. No man in North America had more influence with them than he.

Father De Smet was not merely saintly: he was practical. He had long before obtained the promise of Major Charles E. Galpin, the Indian trader, to accompany him. Galpin was well liked by the Hunkpapa, and his wife, a Yanktonais, was a woman of unusual character and intelligence, respected by everyone. She promised to act as interpreter with her husband.

When Father De Smet announced to the Indians at Fort Rice that he intended to visit the camp on Powder River, they were amazed at his courage. For years now, no white man in his senses had ventured a mile from a fort without an escort or a gun and a good horse. But when he told them that prayers were being offered for him daily by a thousand children before the altars of the Holy Virgin Mary, they cried out: "That is good. We will go with you. When shall we start?"

Next morning they started, De Smet in his carriage with a large black cross fastened to the dashboard over the horse's tail, and an escort of eighty friendly Sioux. The escort contained representatives of the Yanktonais, Yankton, Blackfeet Sioux, Hunkpapa, Minniconjou, Oglala, Sisseton, and Santee tribes. The leaders were such famous chiefs as Running Antelope, the Hunkapapa, Two Bears, the Yanktonais, Bear Ribs II, Log, All Over Black, one Red Cloud (*not* the Bad Faces' war chief then fighting the soldiers), Little Dog, and Sitting Crow. Blue Thunder, the celebrated Yanktonais scout, drove Father De Smet's carriage. Many of the escort were Strong Hearts.

Blue Thunder had served as scout against the hostile Sioux, and his presence was not auspicious. He was a well-known herald, with a voice that could be heard five miles away. In fact, when he was broadcasting, he had to cover his own ears with his hands, to keep from hurting them with the noise he made.

No sooner had the party started than runners sped far ahead on their fleet ponies to bring the word to Sitting Bull and the other chiefs at their camp near the mouth of Powder River. There was much talking, but in the end the matter of a treaty was referred to Sitting Bull, who controlled the flower of the warriors. Galpin and De Smet were both old friends, who had always dealt justly with the Sioux. Their tongues were straight. Sitting Bull said, "If they come, we will hear what they have to say."

He sent a delegation of eighteen men back with the runners to Father De Smet. "Tell the Black Robe," said Sitting Bull, "we shall meet him and his friends with arms stretched out, ready to embrace him. No man living can remember that I ever treated a peace commission with contempt, or gave them hard words, or did them any harm. Say to the Black Robe: 'We have made room for you in our hearts. You shall have food and water, and return with a glad heart. We wish to shake your hand, and to hear your good words. Fear nothing.'"

In anticipation of this visit, Sitting Bull moved his camp. The six hundred tipis were pitched in a grand circle on the right bank of the Yellowstone, four miles above the mouth of the Powder, in the forks between the rivers. Across the Yellowstone, some miles away, loomed blankly down the mountainous, sterile badlands, ash-color and rose, above the gray, rushing water, and the sound of the wild rapids at the mouth of Powder River rumbled steadily in the ears of all, both day and night. Around the camp circle thousands of ponies grazed, and the people kept a bright lookout for the runners, who were expected hourly.

On Thursday, June 18, some fifteen days after Father De Smet left Fort Rice, the runners returned to say that the Black Robe would reach the camp next morning. Immediately, all was preparation and bustle there. Hunkpapa and Sans Arc, Minniconjou and Blackfeet Sioux—all caught up their best horses, got out their finest war clothes, their paints and charms and weapons. When morning came, the standing scouts signaled with hand mirrors that the Black Robe was coming, and four hundred warriors, dressed in all their regalia, mounted and rode up Powder River singing. At their head rode Sitting Bull, Four Horns, Black Moon, White Gut, Gall, No Neck, and Bull Owl. It was a fine June day. The sun shone, the grass was green in the lovely valley of the Powder.

After a four-mile ride they made out the dark mass of the visitors coming down the right bank of the river. Sitting Bull, in the lead, saw that mass halt. Then suddenly, over it, a flag was unfurled. Sitting Bull reined in his black war horse. His heart beat fast. What flag was that? Was it the flag of the soldiers? Was a trap laid for his warriors? He and three others raced forward, galloped around the Black Robe and his escort, looking carefully, anxious to reassure themselves. Sitting Bull saw that on one side of the flag was some strange hierogylphic (the name of Jesus), and on the other the picture of the Holy Woman, surrounded by a circle of golden stars. Reassured, he rode straight up and shook hands with the Black Robe; it was the flag of peace, not of war. To Sitting Bull, brought up to reverence the White Buffalo Maiden, it seemed entirely natural that the white men should worship a virgin. Dashing back to the main body, the four chiefs led them forward in a long rank, singing and shouting their joy at the meeting. The whole line charged, then halted two hundred yards off. All was wild and joyous, but admirably ordered. The four chiefs rode forward, shook hands with De Smet, and soon after the whole body of warriors rode up and shook his hand also. Then, in the general rejoicing, the warriors of both parties embraced each other and exchanged horses and clothing in token of their friendly feeling.

But all was not friendly. The flag had aroused suspicions nothing could kill. White Gut said, "Here comes another white man to cheat us." He wished to kill the Black Robe, and even more he wished to kill Blue Thunder, who had fought as a scout against his own people for the soldiers. One of the Sioux said to Blue Thunder, "Last time I shot you in the leg: this time I'll kill you." It was a tense moment for the escort of the Black Robe.

But Sitting Bull interfered. He and Four Horns, Black Moon, and Gall rode close beside the Black Robe, and the other chiefs of his escort were right behind him. They protected him and saved his life. It was not only White Gut they feared: many men in that camp had cause to avenge the death of some relative, and had sworn to kill the first white man they met. Sitting Bull had given his friend the Black Robe safe-conduct: he was taking no chances of its being broken now. For some miles they rode so, approaching the camp. They kept careful watch over their beloved guest, the Black Robe, who was so affected by their welcome that he rode blinded by tears. No man ever loved the Sioux better.

And so, preceded by the banner of the Virgin and guarded by four chiefs, the peacemaker came to the great camp of the Sioux, which no white man had dared approach for four years past. Five thousand Indians swarmed about the compact cavalcade, which had formed in a square around the Black Robe after they forded the sandy bed of the shallow Powder. They cheered and sang in welcome. But Sitting Bull, fearing that some hothead might make trouble, ordered his Strong Hearts to disperse them. He led the Black Robe directly to his own lodge, a big one in the middle of the camp circle. He stowed the priest's baggage within it and posted a guard of twenty warriors around that tent. Sitting Bull gave orders to this body-guard: "See that the Black Robe has plenty of meat and drink. Do not allow the white men to stray far from their tent. And see that no one stabs or steals away their horses."

Galpin and De Smet remained in the lodge, and the Father, worn out by the fatigues of his long journey and the excitement of his reception, fell asleep. Mrs. Galpin passed the afternoon going from lodge to lodge and from feast to feast. She was a general favorite.

At sunset, Sitting Bull, "generalissimo of the warriors" (as De Smet calls him), came to change the guard. Black Moon, Four Horns, and No Neck came with him, and took seats within the lodge, waiting until the Black Robe awakened. Afterward, they talked.

Sitting Bull said: "Black Robe, I hardly sustain myself beneath the weight of white men's blood that I have shed. The whites provoked the war; their injustices, their indignities to our families, the cruel, unheard-of, and unprovoked massacre at Fort Lyon of hundreds of Cheyenne women, children, and old men, shook all the veins which bind and support me. I rose, tomahawk in hand, and I have done all the hurt to the whites that I could. Today you are here, and my arms hang to the ground as if dead. I will listen to your good words. And bad as I have been to the white men, just so good I am ready to become toward them."

Father De Smet then explained briefly the purposes of the Peace Commissioners at Fort Rice and sketched the outline of the treaty. Sitting Bull listened attentively. The Black Robe said: "Your Grandfather wishes you to live among your people on your own lands. You will never starve. You will always have plenty of rations. You will not be captives, but at liberty. You will receive warm clothing."

Sitting Bull answered, "It sounds good, but I am satisfied with the old treaty for the hunting tribes if the whites would keep it."

Afterward he added, "Listen, my friend. I have a message for the Grandfather. I do not want anyone to bother my people. I want them to live in peace. I myself have plans for my people, and if they follow my plans, they will never want. They will never hunger. I wish for traders only, and no soldiers on my reservation. God gave us this land, and we are at home here. I will not have my people robbed. We can live if we can keep our Black Hills. We do not want to eat from the hand of the Grandfather. We can feed ourselves."

All the time Sitting Bull was talking, the Black Robe held his pencil to show that he was taking Sitting Bull's words. But nowadays the old men ask, "Why have those words been forgotten?"

They talked long that night, and at length slept together in the lodge. And at last day broke—the day of the grand council.

The complete minutes of that council long remained unpublished.[1] Had they been published at once, much of the popular misunderstanding of Sitting Bull and the Sioux would have been impossible. For the speeches of the chiefs set forth clearly the causes of wars in the past and the situation out of which future wars arose. Carefully considered, this council exhibits almost every factor in the relations between Sioux and whites. It also has the interest of being the only great council between the "hostile" or hunting bands and the United States for which exact contemporary record exists. The chiefs spoke freely, man to man, and not as at the agencies. The interpreter, also, was excellent, and Major Galpin took down the speeches word for word on the spot. For us, this council has extraordinary interest, because it gives us the first important speech of Sitting Bull of which there was immediate record made in writing.

Early in the morning the women began to erect the amphitheater for the council. This was made by setting tall, slender tipi poles upright in the ground in a circle, and suspending from them great curtains made of the leather coverings of these tents. The amphitheater enclosed half an acre. In the center four buffalo robes were spread down for seats. At ten o'clock the chiefs escorted the Black Robe to his seat on one of these robes. Beside him was his interpreter. In front Four Horns and Black Moon sat, holding their pipes.

Opposite them, Sitting Bull, White Gut, Gane, and No Neck sat at the head of their five hundred warriors, and behind them every foot of space was filled by the throng of women, children, and old men who crowded in to listen to the good words of their old friend, the Black Robe. Five thousand people were present.

For perhaps an hour the warriors. dressed in all their finest war clothes, danced and sang. Then, when they had become pleasantly tired and were in a mood to listen, Four Horns lighted his peace pipe,

[1] Though a partial account is given in *The Life, Letters and Travels of Father Pierre–Jean De Smet*, by H. M. Chittenden and Alfred T. Richardson, on which I have drawn for certain details.

presented the stem to Wakan' Tanka, the four Cardinal Points, the Sun and the Earth, summoning them as witnesses to the proceedings of the council, imploring their favor. Afterward he walked round, offering the pipe to every man in due order of rank, beginning with Father De Smet. Each one took a few puffs. When all had smoked in communion, Black Moon stood up and said, "Speak, Black Robe, our ears are open to hear your words."

After a short prayer, Father De Smet addressed them.

"Friends, I have been trying to see you for the last two years; and this day, through the help of God, I now have that pleasure. I hope you will listen well to what you hear from my mouth, which speaks the sentiments of my head, which will be entirely upon the importance of your making peace with the whites. This cruel and unfortunate war must be stopped, not only on the account of your children, but for a thousand other reasons, which the great men, whom "the President of the whites" has chosen to meet you at Fort Rice will show you. I have come only as an adviser to aid you all, knowing that your Grandfather means you well and will help you. Indeed, in the name of the Great Spirit, and in the name of all good, in the presence of your chiefs and braves, and all assembled here, I most solemnly beseech you, one and all, to bury all your animosities against the whites, forget the past, and accept the offering of peace which is now just sent you. My mission to your village is now completed with one exception. I have brought you tobacco to smoke, which you will accept as an assurance of the truthfulness of my sentiments. I will now thank you for your kind reception of myself and party. And with all my heart I will ever pray for your future happiness."

Father De Smet then caused the banner of the Holy Virgin to be set up in the middle of the enclosure. Afterward he said: "The flag which now stands in the center of this circle is the holy emblem of peace. And I am most happy to have it said that is the only one that has ever been carried so far. But on this occasion I deemed it most necessary, and now will leave it in the hands of your chiefs that you may regard it as a token of my sincerity and good wishes for the welfare of the Sioux nation. I pray to God you will look upon it as a blessing to your tribe. It is to Him you must look for all blessings, and from Him all blessings flow. And while you live, let it not be said you had evil thoughts; for evil thoughts and doings bring troubles in your land. I will always do, as I have always done, continue to offer my feeble prayers for your good, but remember, peace must reign in your land. I will now listen to your words."

Father De Smet sat down. Black Moon rose from his seat to give the address of welcome and set forth the cause of past wars. Having offered his pipe to the Sun and the Earth, he pointed the stem to Father De Smet. "Touch it with your lips, and let your hand rest after doing so," he said.

Then, turning to the crowd, he said: "This man has come far to meet us. He looks tired and careworn. I am glad to see him, and welcome him with all my heart. His words are good and full of meaning and truth. He speaks well, and everything he says is my heart's desire. But there are many thorns in our hearts, many wounds to heal. Our country is desolate and impoverished by a cruel war, which was commenced by the Cheyennes and the Eastern Sioux. It was forced upon us.

"And now, when we travel over our country, we often see red spots. They are not the red spots of slaughtered buffalo, but of our own comrades, or of white men. Our country was full of game. But since the war the animals seem to detest their native haunts, and I believe it is by the smell of human blood that they are driven away. Again, the whites have been cutting our country up with roads, and building forts at various places. They often and unkindly put our people in prison for little or no cause. They cut our timber, ruin our country with impunity.

"I told them I did not want their annuities, nor could I sell my country. My father lived and died here; so would I. And if our white brothers would do right, we would never have had war. I always liked to have goods to trade for, but I cannot bear the idea of having the country filled up with white men. Some are good, but many are bad, and they often treat us badly. Our people are often shot down by travelers over the plains while they are seeking food for their families.

And for no cause we have been badly treated. But these things past I now hope will be forgotten from this day. I will say no more, but end my remarks by thanking you, in the name of all my people, for the welcome news you have so kindly brought. We will accept your tobacco and your kind advice. And extend our hands in the sight of the Great Spirit and all of you, as the hands of peace." Then, turning once more to his people, Black Moon said, "Let the past be forgotten," and returned to his seat.

Then Sitting Bull "came boldly forward," and after going through the usual ceremonies with great dignity and due respect, began to speak:

"Father, you pray to the Great Spirit for us. I thank you. I have often besought the kindness of the Great Spirit, but never have I done so more earnestly than today, that our words may be heard above and all over the earth. When I first saw you coming with that flag, my heart beat fast, and I had evil thoughts, caused by the remembrance of the past. I bade my heart be quiet: it was so! And when on the prairie I shook hands with you, and my cousin and sister, I felt changed and hardly knew what to say. But my heart was glad and quickly scouted deception. I am, and always have been, a fightin' fool;[2] my people caused me to be so. They have been troubled and confused by the past: they looked upon their troubles as caused by the whites, and became crazy, and pushed me forward. For the last four years I have led them in bad deeds; the fault is theirs, not mine. I will now say in their presence, 'Welcome, Father—the messenger of peace.' I hope quiet will again be restored to our country.

"As I am not full of words, I will thank you in the hearing of our chiefs and braves, in sign of peace, hoping you will always wish us well. I have now told you all. All that can be, has been said. My people will return to meet the chiefs of the Grandfather, who wants to make peace with us. I hope it will be done, and whatever is done by others, I will submit to, and for all time to come remain a friend of the whites."

Sitting Bull then shook hands with Father De Smet and Major

[2] Literally, "a fool and a warrior." Sioux idiom.

GENERAL GEORGE "THREE STARS" CROOK, 1875
(*National Archives*)

LIEUTENANT COLONEL GEORGE ARMSTRONG "LONG
HAIR" CUSTER, ABOUT 1867
(Custer Battlefield National Monument)

Galpin and returned to his place. There he turned to his people and asked if they heard his words.

"*Hau, hau, hau!*" was the thundering response. Sitting Bull knew how to reach the hearts of his people: the more one knows of the Sioux, the cleverer his remarks appear. How brief, how direct! And yet how adroitly he reminds them of his piety, dramatizes for them the first suspicion which he shared with them on the approach of the peace party, and the following revulsion on meeting the good father and their old friends. How courteously he remembers to include the Major and Mrs. Galpin in that reference. And then the reminder that he was war chief, that he had always been a "fightin' fool," and that his people shared the blame, that they had pushed him forward. That shows the true statesmanlike adeptness, to carry them with him, when they might have turned upon him as the scapegoat for their own deeds. And afterward, his greeting, with his promise to abide by the action of the representatives sent to make peace with the commissioners at Fort Rice. The insinuation that no more need be said is also entirely characteristic of the leader of that society of jealous, rival chiefs. And the confident appeal to his people, resulting in their assent, from which they could never retreat. It would be difficult to find a more skillful speech of like brevity, so consummately meeting the situation in all its phases. Yet, Sitting Bull declares himself the man of action, merely— "not full of words!"

And this was not all. Having got the crowd with him, he rose again to add the essential point to his speech, saying, "I have forgotten two things." This was a favorite trick of his, to make his speech appear wholly impromptu and informal, and hammer in the important words in the most memorable part of his speech—the end.

"Friends," he added, "I have forgotten two things. I wish all to know that I do not propose to sell any part of my country, nor will I have the whites cutting our timber along the rivers, more especially the oak. I am particularly fond of the little groves of oak trees. I love to look at them, and feel a reverence for them, because they endure the wintry storms and summer's heat, and—not unlike ourselves— seem to thrive and flourish by them. One thing more: those forts filled with white soldiers must be abandoned; there is no greater source of trouble and grievance to my people."

Sitting Bull once more shook hands with his guests, "and sat down, amid the cheers of young and old." Thus Sitting Bull laid down the terms of peace. He had met a most difficult situation with entire success, carried his people with him, and yet budged not one inch from his first policy. One wonders why this speech was not permitted to reach the press in Sitting Bull's lifetime. Or perhaps one need not wonder.

"After a few minutes, quiet was restored," says the record, and the Yanktonais chief Two Bears came forward. As leader of the peace party and head man of the Black Robe's escort, he must be heard from, trying to soothe the hunting bands, and also—in some measure—defending the stand of his own people, who were regarded with some suspicion and derision in those days.

Running Antelope then brought the council to a close. After he sat down, the chiefs escorted Father De Smet back to his guarded lodge, while the earth trembled and the valley of the Powder rang with the songs and shouting, as the warriors resumed their dancing. The peace party began to prepare their baggage for an early start: they planned to leave in the morning. They assured the Black Robe that his mission had been a complete success. The chiefs spent the night with him, making arrangements for the coming council. It was decided to send a delegation to Fort Rice with Father De Smet.

Sitting Bull refused to go. He said, "I will sit here on the prairie, and listen. Everybody knows my terms." He said, "Send Gall. He has lived over there; he knows those people." Gall was a good choice, the chiefs agreed, because Gall had been roughly handled by the whites, and would not be likely to forget it and yield to them too easily. Too well they knew how easy it was for white men to talk an Indian into something he afterward regretted. There was constant communication between the hunting bands and their people at the agencies. They knew how the agency Indians were swindled.

Sitting Bull gave Gall his instructions: "You go down there and see what they have to say. Take no presents: we don't want them. Tell them to move the soldiers out and stop the steamboats; then we can have peace."

The whole evening, however, was not spent in talk about the treaty. Father De Smet blessed many children and baptized some of the Indians in the camp who came to his tent. He told his hosts stories from the Bible: of Daniel in the den of lions, of Jonah and the whale, of the three men in the fiery furnace, of how Lazarus was raised from the dead. He told them how, when people got so bad that something had to be done about it, God sent His only Son among them, and how the white men killed him. The chiefs listened and said nothing: that was just what you might expect of white men. They readily accepted the miracles, and as for the fiery furnace, there was a society among themselves whose members could pick up hot coals or take meat from a kettle of boiling water without burning their hands.[3] With that tolerance characteristic of old-time Sioux, however, a number of men, including Lone Man, were baptized. It was difficult to refuse anything to the Black Robe. And they were ready to try anything once.

Some believe that Father De Smet also baptized Sitting Bull that night. Certain it is that he gave Sitting Bull a crucifix of brass and wood, which long remained a treasured possession in the family. (I own it now.) It may be seen on his breast in a well-known photograph of the chief by D. F. Barry—the one in which he wears a white buckskin shirt and a single feather in his hair. But Sitting Bull was not the man to be converted overnight, and it is inconceivable that Father De Smet would have failed to record such a conversion had it taken place.

Nowadays the old men say, rather sadly, "The Black Robes were Sitting Bull's best friends while he was out on the prairie, but when he came to the agency, they were the first to turn against him." This could not have happened had he been a convert.

Gall and Bull Owl went down to meet the Peace Commissioners, and on July 2, 1868, signed the "Treaty of Laramie" (as it was called)

[3] Said to have been done by smearing the hands with the juice of the narrow-leaved purple cone flower (*Echinacea angustifolia D. C.*) or comb plant, an Indian panacea. See Bureau of American Ethnology, *Thirty-third Annual Report*, 131.

at Fort Rice. This treaty established the Great Sioux Reservation (Dakota Territory west of the Missouri) and provided that the country "north of the North Platte River and east of the summits of the Big Horn Mountains shall be held and considered to be unceded Indian Territory," and that "no white person or persons shall be permitted to settle upon or occupy any portion of the same; or, without the consent of the Indians first had and obtained, to pass through the same." The military posts on the Montana Trail were abandoned, and the Trail itself closed. Article II provided that the Sioux had the right to "hunt on any lands north of the North Platte River . . . so long as buffalo may range thereon in such numbers as to justify the chase."

The treaty also provided that no future treaty would be valid unless signed by three-fourths of the adult males of the tribe. The Sioux, on their part, were to keep the peace. That was *all* that was demanded of them. It was a complete victory.

Naturally the army, loath to abandon their posts on Powder River, and still itching to avenge Colonel Fetterman, could not rest easy under such a treaty. Within three months after the proclamation of the treaty (February, 1869), the War Department issued an order which violated the clause providing for the right to hunt outside the limits of the Reservation. The order admitted that the Indian Bureau had jurisdiction over the Indians on their reservations, but declared that "Outside the well-defined limits of their reservations they are under the original and exclusive control of the military, and *as a rule will be considered hostile*"! Already, in November, 1868, General Custer had attacked the Southern Cheyennes on the Washita in what is now Oklahoma. But Sitting Bull was unaware of these orders. He went peacefully about his work of policing his hunting grounds.

It must not be forgotten that Sitting Bull had plenty of white men backing him up in his attempt to keep his country free from wandering whites. For thirty years the fur traders had been encouraging the Sioux to kill or drive out white strangers, because such men were generally a menace to the fur traders' monopoly. Missionaries constantly warned their converts against the danger of contamination by white frontiersmen. Indian agents deplored the evil influence of squaw-men and half-bloods, and urged their charges to drive them from the Indian lands. And military men were stationed at posts on the Missouri for the express purpose of keeping out white squatters and emigrants. General Harney, at his council at Fort Pierre in 1856, had asked the Sioux chiefs to arrest or kill deserters from the army found in their country, and had offered a reward for them dead or alive. All the white men for whom the Sioux had any respect had *always* encouraged them in this. And the Peace Commission had just pledged the government to that *identical law*. It is hardly surprising that Sitting Bull felt justified in dealing severely with any whites he found inside his hunting grounds.

Sometimes—as in the case of Tom Campbell the trader—he let them go with a warning. Sometimes the rash adventurer paid for his folly with his horses, gun, and clothes. Sometimes, resisting arrest, he was killed. But sometimes he was spared. On January 2, 1869, Sitting Bull captured a mail carrier on the trail between Fort Hall and Fort Peck. The Indians lay in wait for him in a ravine on the big flat between Fort Peck and the Bend of Milk River—a gulch about twenty feet deep, with steep sides and a little timber. They could see him coming a long way off across the snow.

Snow was falling, and the wind was in the white man's face, so that he kept his head down, riding along—a dark ball of grizzly bear fur —across the white prairie. They could see that he was leading another horse. On he came, keeping no lookout, and rode down into the gulch. They let him cross it and start up the other side: then they were all over him. One of them struck him across the back, others grabbed the horses, and a third pulled the rider to the ground. Before he knew what had happened, one of the Sioux had snatched his gun and was trying to shoot him.

Luckily for the white man, one of the Indians was trying to strip off his bearskin coat, and this made it difficult for the other to shoot. Naturally, the white man did his best to keep that Indian between himself and the one with the gun. It was a rough-and-tumble, everything happened very quickly.

Just then Sitting Bull rode up.

It happened that the mail carrier, Frank Grouard, was the son of a sailor and a woman of the Sandwich Islands, and his mother's blood had given him the coloration and something of the appearance of an Indian. Sitting Bull saw that Indian face, and called out to the man with the gun, "Let him go: let him go!"

But the man with the gun was too excited to heed his chief and kept trying to get a fair shot.

Immediately, Sitting Bull jumped from his pony, walked over to the struggling trio, raised his bow, struck the Indian with the gun a heavy blow on the head, and knocked him flat. The other Indian at once let go of Grouard and stepped back. Sitting Bull stood waiting, talking to his young men. The one he had knocked down got up and went off toward the river. When he was safely out of the way, Sitting Bull sat down, got out his pipe, and smoked with his prisoner. Then he put the white man on a horse and rode away with him toward camp. By means of the sign language, which Grouard could understand, he told the white man he was Sitting Bull.

On the third day they reached their camp on Bark Creek. Everybody turned out to see the prisoner Sitting Bull had brought home, crowding around his horse to have a look, "but they gave no sign of anger, and raised no shout of triumph." Of course not, the war was over. Grouard feared a dreadful fate, but Sitting Bull adopted him, made him a member of his family. Grouard remained in the chief's camp for three years, and was given the name Sitting-with-Upraised-Hands, or Hands-Up, a reference to a bear, because of his bearskin coat. He soon took to Sioux ways, learned the language, and became an excellent hunter and scout. Sitting Bull's nephews remembered him with affection, though regretting that he later turned his coat and served with the troops. It was impossible to make them believe that he was not an Indian.

16. Thirty Crows Are Killed

No man in the Sioux nation was braver than Sitting Bull.

—FRANK GROUARD.

WHITE MEN were not the only poachers who felt Sitting Bull's wrath. He was always jumping other tribes, who were rash enough to hunt in Sioux preserves, and often raided their horse herds successfully. Of all these tribes, the Crows gave him most trouble. Indeed, the winter of 1869 saw Sitting Bull's boys engaged with them in one of the hardest fights in all Hunkpapa history —so hard a fight, in fact, that it gave its name to that year in their calendar.

It was cold, with snow on the ground. The people were hunting along the Yellowstone, their camp being near the mouth of Powder River. One day two young men went out to kill buffalo for the family. In the late afternoon they started home. All at once the two boys saw enemies running after them across the snow. The boys threw down their meat and robes, and took to their heels. They knew they had no chance against thirty Crows.

On came the Crows, yelling and running hard as they could. But the Sioux boys were swift, they were running for their lives, and the Crows could not overtake them. One of the Crows had a horse. It was not in very good condition, as an Indian horse had only cottonwood boughs to eat in winter, and it had come a long way that day. Still, the horse could run as fast as the Sioux boys.

The Crow on the horse took another Crow up behind him, raced his horse until he was even with the Sioux boys, and then dropped his passenger, turning back to bring up another. In this way he brought one Crow after another forward into the running fight. That Crow must have been a great coward, or else he was so generous that he wished his comrades to count all the *coups!*

Before long the Crows had killed one of the Sioux boys, but they could not catch the other one, their horse was exhausted, and they had to give it up. Knowing that the alarm would be given, they turned back and hurried northwest toward Big Dry Creek. The Sioux boy ran home, panting and crying for his dead comrade, and gasped out his story.

Instantly Sitting Bull was out in the frosty evening air, shouting the news. *"Hopo! Hopo!* Let's go! Let's go! Take action!"

Within a few minutes a hundred Sioux were mounted and pushing hard on the trail, led by the boy. Within an hour they had found the body of his comrade, all cut to pieces, stripped, and scalped, lying in the dusk on the frozen snow, now dark with blood.

Away they went over the snow, keen to avenge their comrade, eager to wipe out the cowards who had butchered him. Thirty to one! At sunrise they came up with the Crows.

But the Crows were in a strong position. On the headwaters of Big Dry Creek, south bank, there is the Spoon Horn (Mountain Sheep) Butte. Between this butte and the creek, there is a knoll entirely surrounded by large rocks, now known as Crow Rock, Montana. Within this natural fort the Crows stood ready, gun and bow in hand.

But the Sioux were too eager to be careful that morning. They charged right up on their fast horses, hoping to jump off, scale the rocky walls, and kill the Crows in a minute. They met with a hot reception. Many were hit. Turning Hawk was shot in the buttocks, and fell from his horse. The Sioux turned back.

Sitting Bull, however, urged on his men—not that they needed much urging. Said he: "We must not let them escape! It would be childish. Everyone would laugh at us if we did. We are not women! I'll go first, you follow."

Jumping Bull said, "I will first empty their guns." He circled the fort at a gallop, only a few yards away from the rocks where the Crows were shooting. He was wearing the sash of a Strong Heart chief, and was not hit.

The Sioux were all around the fort, waiting. As soon as Jumping Bull had emptied the enemy guns, they all rushed up toward the rocks. As soon as they got near enough, they jumped from their horses and rushed the rocky walls, each one as he thought best, trying to reach across the rocks and strike or shoot the Crows. It was impossible to scale the rocks until they had killed most of the Crows. Many of the Sioux were hit and killed at the rocks. It was like fighting across a wall of stones. The Sioux were determined to destroy the Crows or die in their tracks.

Sitting Bull counted three *coups* in this fight. Pretty soon the Sioux had killed most of the Crows, and they began to leap over the barrier and fight hand to hand. One of the first to go in was Sitting Bull.

Once the Sioux got inside, it did not last long. The last of the Crows was killed within half an hour after the Sioux sighted their fort. Those who say that Plains Indians will not charge a position in the face of gunfire should hear eyewitnesses tell the story of that battle. That was a stand-up fight on both sides.

When the Crows were all killed, Sitting Bull took several scalps, stripped off the coat of one of his dead enemies, and gathered up some of their arrows to take home to his mother for trophies. She could dance over them when the period of mourning was over.

For there was plenty of crying among the Sioux tipis after that battle. The thirty Crows had sold their lives dearly. The Sioux counted fourteen dead that day, including the boy killed the night before: Strong-as-Buffalo, Bear Eagle, Hog Bear, Hog Bear [No. 2], Buck, Short Bull, Long Bull, No-Name, Longest One, Roan Bear, Long Balls, and Looks-for-Home. Looks-for-Home (Tiole aupi), sometimes called Bakiula or Stooping, was Sitting Bull's youngest uncle, and a chief. Once more the family had cause to mourn.

There were also the wounded—eighteen Sioux: Turning Hawk, Holy Soldier, Ready-to-Shoot, Lone Man, Little Eagle, Young Black Crow, Yellow Horse, Bad, Chief Bear, Little Wounded, After-the-

Bugs, Fool Dog, Bear Tooth, Young Eagle, Dog, White Thunder, White Whiskers, and Iron Ribs.

They laid the dead Sioux in a row. Looks-for-Home was shot with an arrow through the belly just below the breast, as he was scaling the rocky wall to jump in among his enemies. He died just as bravely as his brother Jumping Bull had done. Four Horns was in this battle also. That was a fighting family.

Three months later, when the weather had moderated and their relatives had all assembled, the Hunkpapa returned to the scene of the battle, camping about three miles away. They went to the place and recovered the bones of their dear ones. The relatives of Looks-for-Home carried him back to the camp, placed him upon a nice bed in a fine tipi, and when the camp moved, left him there in the burial lodge, lying in state.

Sitting Bull had always been very fond of his youngest uncle, Looks-for-Home, and proud of him too. When they had buried him, Sitting Bull threw away his leggins and went barefoot. He cut his hair and left off painting his face. Instead, he smeared his hair and face with mud, in token of grief. His nephew, Chief Joseph White Bull, was present at this burial, and long remembered Sitting Bull's crying.

One of Sitting Bull's *coups* in this battle with the Crows is shown in sketch No. 31 of his picture autobiography. He is shown striking a Crow with his bow, as the Crow fires at him with a gun, and misses.

This sketch, No. 31, is the last but one completed in the unfinished autobiography of Sitting Bull. He made a set, showing all his sixty-three *coups*[1] soon after this battle, and gave it to Jumping Bull, his "brother." Soon after, Four Horns began to make a copy of this set of pictures, adding to it a number of exploits performed by Jumping Bull. Four Horns had completed fifty-four drawings and had begun on the fifty-fifth (forty of them being Sitting Bull's deeds) when some other Indian got hold of the book and sold it to an Army officer, adding a meager interpretation. Thus the series came to an end in 1870.

[1] Frank Grouard bears witness to the number of Sitting Bull's *coups*, which he heard recounted at the Sun Dance camp of 1870.

Sitting Bull carried arms for eleven years after he finished the autobiography. Fortunately, plenty of eyewitnesses lived to tell of his
battles in this later period. It was considered miraculous that he was
not hit in that battle with the thirty Crows. Bullets flew all about him;
men fired in his face, yet he came out unscathed. And even when he
was hit, he pulled through. He seemed to bear a charmed life, to have
that divine protection to which every warrior aspired; it was not every
man who could survive gunshot wounds at close range. He had even
killed the Crow chief after he himself was wounded, a rare feat which
gave him the right to wear a red X painted on the right shoulder of
his war shirt.

There was a sacred horse belonging to the Hunkpapa, a dark sorrel,
which the warriors used when they wished to attack a strong position,
because it was bulletproof. It had been hit nine times, but never could
be killed. Because of the animal's wonderful power to survive dangerous wounds, they called it Sitting Bull, after their chief. This horse
was led at the head of all their parades around the camp circle.

Sitting Bull—*there* was a chief the young men were proud to follow.
For they were confident of success when they rode with him.

17. The Fight with the Flatheads

I am not ashamed to tell that I was a follower of Sitting Bull. I have no ears for hearing anybody say he was not a brave man. He had a big brain and a good one, a strong heart and a generous one. In the old times I never heard of any Indian having spoken otherwise of him. If any of them changed their talk in later days, the change must have been brought about by lies of the agents and soldier chiefs who schemed to make themselves appear as good men by making him appear as a bad man.—A Warrior Who Fought Custer, *Interpreted by Thomas B. Marquis.*[1]

THE HUNTING SIOUX were in camp on the Yellowstone at Big Bottom, below the mouth of the Rosebud. Hunkpapa, Oglala, Minniconjou, and Sans Arcs were there—a big camp, almost a thousand lodges. The summer hunt was over, the drying racks and parfleches were thick with meat. Young men began to say it was time to go on the warpath.

Beyond the mountains to the northwest, in Montana and Idaho, were the Flatheads, Pend d'Oreille, and Nez Percé. Ever since the white men had settled in their country looking for gold, these nations had been coming into Sioux country for buffalo, because their own game was killed off. Sitting Bull organized a war party to rub out these trespassers. It was a big war party—more than four hundred men. Sitting Bull and Flying-By were the principal chiefs. They set out in high spirits, horseback, leading their war horses, full of fight. They headed northwest toward the Musselshell.

[1] Page 383.

There were many young men in this party, and they were a jolly, cheeky bunch. One of the ringleaders was Sitting Bull's nephew, Big-in-the-Center, then just twenty-one, and now known as White Bull. When the party camped, they made shelters or war lodges in a circle: the seasoned warriors slept together and the younger men by themselves, every tribe separately. One day White Bull thought he would have some fun at the expense of these older honor men; they had been on the warpath for several days and had done nothing. So White Bull got on his horse and rode around the little camp circle, stopping before the shelters of famous warriors to sing a song he had composed:

> *My friends, when we go home to report,*
> *What have I to report to my father and mother?*

He would end the song with a sharp yell, then ride on to another group and sing again. It made the young men laugh: they praised White Bull for his song at the older men's expense. For as yet there was nothing to report.

When they had been out for some days, the chiefs sent scouts out to look for enemy camps. While they waited for the return of these scouts, some of the warriors became impatient, and went to Sitting Bull. They asked him to divine what was going to happen, to make a prophecy. He had often done this, and nearly always his prophecies came true.

Sitting Bull said, "I will try to find out something."

He walked away from the crowd some distance, and walked up and down, singing. They could hear him singing, but he was too far away for his words to be understood. After a while he came back. They had a pipe ready to light waiting for him.

Sitting Bull lighted the pipe and smoked. When he had finished, he said, "In the smoke I see a battle within two days. Many enemies and several Sioux will be killed." After a few moments, he added: "When I was out there singing, I saw a little ball of fire—a spark— coming toward me. But it disappeared when it reached me." The warriors all knew what that spark meant: it was a sign that Sitting Bull was going to be wounded.

Soon after, the scouts got back, and the war party struck out for the Flathead camp, reported to be on the Musselshell. They left their saddle horses hidden, and rode their war horses. All night they rode, and about dawn were close to the camp of their enemy. There they halted and Sitting Bull announced his plan for the attack. Said he: "Let's all act together; that's the best way. Let's pick a small party of young men with fast horses and send them against the enemy. The rest of us will stay behind, out of sight. When the Flatheads see how few they are, they will chase them. Then our young men can lead them straight into the trap we have prepared."

This arrangement was satisfactory to everyone. It allowed the young men to make the first attack—which they would probably do anyhow. And it gave the older men a chance to take part in the fight and distinguish themselves, since the young men would bring the enemy back to them. Old men and young men are jealous of each other. It is probable that strategy originated in a desire on the part of the old men to turn the young men's headlong courage to their own advantage.

The whole party was filled with martial ardor that morning. One of them, Badger, stood up, and, jerking off his breech-cloth, displayed the tokens of his virility, saying, "Look at me. I am brave. I want to distinguish myself. I can do anything. Go to war, kill the enemy. I am a *man!*"

Mole and Herald were chosen to lead the advance party. Other young men chosen to act as decoys were Bull Eagle, Hump, Owns-the-Warrior, Red Gun, Drops-Two, Red Circle, Looks-for-Enemies, Bear-Shoot-Him-as-He-Runs, Eagle Thunder, Red Thunder, Use-Him-as-Charger, Red Thunder (No. 2), Crane, Two Eagle, Red Tomahawk, White Shield, Turning Bear, Charging Bear, Long Ghost, and Running-Wild. Long Ghost was Sitting Bull's relative. White Bull, his nephew, went with this bunch on his own hook. Day was breaking as they started for the Flathead camp.

The reserves, under Sitting Bull and Flying-By, remained about two miles behind—to the west of the camp.

As the young men advanced, they could see the Flathead tipis, about one hundred of them, sharply outlined against the brightening east. They kept a sharp lookout, not making much noise. One of the Flatheads was driving his ponies out onto the prairie; he was heading south from the camp. As soon as the Sioux saw him, they rushed him. He was half a mile from his camp before he saw them coming. At once, he let his horses go and raced for his life, back to his friends among the tipis. The Sioux were after him, yelling and lashing their horses, but he had a start, he rode hard, and got back to the camp. The Flatheads swarmed out of the tents like hornets. The Sioux rounded up the lone Flathead's seven ponies, and started back, as if they had got what they wanted. Sitting Bull's plan worked perfectly.

Away went the young Sioux, running off with their capture, back toward the four hundred warriors in the ambush. And after them, pell-mell, came a hundred mounted enemies, riding like mad. The Flatheads were well armed with guns and pistols, and were shooting all the time.

It was two miles back to the ambush. The young Sioux raced for that place. But White Bull wished to distinguish himself and keep the enemy coming. He kept charging back at them, as if trying to hold them so that his comrades could get away. He rode last of all the Sioux young men. All at once he gave two yelps and turned his horse back, charging his enemies. All alone he charged them, chased them back alone. One of the Flatheads was in the rear, waiting for White Bull. White Bull struck at the Flathead with his spear three times. The Flathead fired his revolver at White Bull, but missed. White Bull then drew his own revolver, pumped three bullets into his enemy's horse. The man's horse dropped, and White Bull thought he had him. But the man afoot ran in among the tents, and White Bull couldn't touch him.

White Bull then turned to follow his comrades, and once more the Flatheads pursued. Again White Bull chased them back a way, but was unable to strike anyone. And as he fell back, the Flatheads came after him. It was back and forth that day.

The third time he chased them, they nearly caught him. But the other Sioux stopped and waited for him, and he reached them safely. The Flatheads dismounted, and they all had a good fight.

One of the Flatheads came right after White Bull, and jumped off his horse to shoot. White Bull turned and charged him, with lowered lance. The Flathead did not run, as White Bull expected, but stood his ground, with gun up, ready to shoot. White Bull, however, though all alone, wished to do as chiefs and chiefs' sons do; he was Sitting Bull's nephew. He had started after this Flathead, and, if he did not strike him, people would say he was a coward. So he went right ahead, lance against rifle. The Flathead shot at him, and the ball broke his lance-shaft. White Bull struck the Flathead. This deed is reckoned the bravest of all White Bull's thirty *coups*.

By this time the Sioux reserves had come piling out of their ambush, the fight became general, and a hot fight it was. The Flatheads were well armed, fought on foot, and hit a number of the Sioux, killing Standing Bull and Hunts-the-Enemy, and wounding Crow-Going-up-in-the-Air.

One of the Flatheads was very brave. The Sioux were all around him, and he had wounded three of them. White Bull saw his wounded comrades, and he got mad. He jumped off his horse and rushed this enemy. The Flathead had a bow, and just as White Bull came up, he loosed an arrow. *Tchk!* It went by—a miss. White Bull had thrown away his broken lance. He knocked the Flathead over with his pistol butt, jumped on him, and cut him about the face and throat. The Flathead was apparently dead. White Bull scalped him. While he was ripping off his hair, the man grunted, came to. He jumped up and ran around dizzily a few yards before he fell dead.

Seeing how many the Sioux were and how many of their comrades were killed, the Flatheads ran back to their camp. It was a regular stampede. The Sioux were eager to follow. White Bull and another young man raced to strike one of these men, who was afoot, with a revolver. But before they reached the Flathead, one of the Sioux behind them shot and killed him. They struck his dead body: White Bull counted the second *coup*.

MAJOR MARCUS A. RENO

CAPTAIN FREDERICK W. BENTEEN
(*Custer Battlefield National Monument*)

GALL, FIGHTING CHIEF OF
THE HUNKPAPAS

TWO MOON, WAR CHIEF OF
THE CHEYENNES
(Custer Battlefield National Monument)

Just then they could hear Chief-Flying-By shouting to the Sioux: "Stop! That will be all for this time! Some good men have been wounded already."

So they turned back, and let the Flatheads go. If Flying-By had not given that order, all the Flatheads would have been wiped out that day.

But Sitting Bull did not want to stop. He had not yet begun to fight. He paid no attention to the advice of Flying-By. Six young men felt just as he did. These were his "brother" Jumping Bull, His Cup, Bad Horse, Dresser, Top-of-Lodge, and one Crazy Horse (not the famous war chief). They all remained on the field. Pretty soon some of the Flatheads came back to see their dead, and these seven Sioux began to shoot at them. They chased these men back toward the Flathead camp.

Just before reaching the camp, the last Flathead got off his horse to fight. One of the Sioux captured his horse and ran it off. Sitting Bull, on horseback, charged the Flathead. He had no shield, only a gun, held in his right hand. The Flathead had a bow and arrows, and when he saw Sitting Bull coming, he jerked an arrow from his quiver, snapped it on the string, drew it back to the point, and waited. An instant later, Sitting Bull was right on top of him. The Flathead let fly. Sitting Bull tried to avoid that deadly shaft. He threw up his left arm to shield his face, and dodged to one side. But the Flathead did not miss, the arrow found its mark. It hit Sitting Bull, passed clear through, between the bones of his forearm.

Instantly, Sitting Bull flung himself to one side of his racing horse and sheered off before another arrow could reach him. He rode back to his friends, carrying the bloody shaft through his arm. When he was out of range, they cut off the head of the arrow, and drew out the shaft. The wound was painful, dangerous, they thought. He "died" for a while; that is, he fainted. Back at the camp of the reserves, Sitting Bull found a number of wounded. The two dead men were laid out in state, and their horses shot alongside. They carried their wounded and the horses they had taken back toward home. On the way home three wounded men died: Crow-Going-up-in-the-Air, Dog Eagle, and Bull Eagle.

They found the camp of their people on the Yellowstone below the mouth of the Rosebud. Before they reached the camp, the war party sent in a messenger to break the news of the casualties. Because they had lost some comrades, they felt bad, and they wished to make the people feel better, and cheer them up. Therefore the messenger was ordered to say that Sitting Bull had died also.

When this news arrived, the family began to cry and rend their garments. And then, just when everybody was feeling so bad, here came Sitting Bull, riding his own horse, still alive. Then the people laughed and almost forgot the losses they had suffered. Once more Sitting Bull had shown his courage and his strategy, and had survived a bad wound. Nearly everybody in camp came running out to embrace him and stroke him all over, they were so glad to see him again.

After they had mourned four days, a big victory dance was held, and the people danced over the scalps the men had taken. White Bull had a Flathead scalp with hair as long as his arm. He also brought home an enemy quiver and belt. These he gave away, according to custom. Sitting Bull was unable to dance at this celebration, because of his wound. But before long it had healed nicely, and he was all right again.

For all that, his mother shook her head. It looked as if that son of hers would never learn to stop playing with fire!

Sitting Bull, however, was content. The Flatheads never troubled the Sioux buffalo herds again.

18. The Bravest Deed of All

*He was by far the most influential man of his nation for many years—
neither Gall, Spotted Tail, nor Red Cloud . . . exerting the power that
he did.*   —MAJOR JAMES MCLAUGHLIN.

ALL THE SUMMER of 1872, Sitting Bull was busy fighting
the Crows. His peaceful intentions toward the whites are well
shown by the report of the Commission sent out that year to
arrange for the survey of the Northern Pacific Railroad along the
Yellowstone.[1] They traveled unmolested for more than six thousand
miles through the territory of so-called hostile Indians, without any
military escort whatever. At the agencies they did find disaffection, of
course, but not on the Plains. They wished Sitting Bull to visit Washington, but he was too busy. He sent in word by his brother-in-law,
His-Horse-Looking, that he would be ready to talk when snow flew,
provided he could find a white man who would tell the truth. At last
the grand peace council was held at Fort Peck, August 21. One week
before that date the soldiers had already opened fire upon Sitting
Bull's boys!

Colonel D. S. Stanley, commander of the escort detailed to accompany the surveying party of the Northern Pacific Railroad, reached
the Yellowstone about the middle of August, 1872, and had a number
of skirmishes with the Indians under Gall and other chiefs on that

---

[1] See *Annual Report of the Commissioner of Indian Affairs, 1872*, 456–60, which
gives much space to appraising Sitting Bull's character and influence.

river and its tributaries. The survey placed the railroad on the south bank of the river, in violation of the recent treaty.

Gall and his warriors returned from the east to Sitting Bull's big camp on the Powder, and reported that soldiers were coming up the Yellowstone. Sitting Bull said, "We'll go out and meet them, and warn them off. They have no business in our country." He had Oglala, Minniconjou, Hunkpapa, Sans Arc, and Blackfeet Sioux in his camp. All of them rode with him downriver, dressed in their war clothes, carrying arms. It was the custom to go to meet strangers so—whether they came in peace or war. It was just like going to meet Father De Smet. Sitting Bull rode his fleet bay and carried a quiver and his gun. Eight young men were ordered to ride with him, in advance of the main party. They were: Circling Hawk, Red Thunder, Long Dog, Hunts-for-the-Bear, Many Dogs, Wrinkled, Strikes-the-Kettle, and Old Bull.

They found the soldiers in the valley of the Yellowstone, below Arrow (Pryor) Creek. They reached the soldier camp about daybreak, and immediately all the soldiers came out to fight them. The soldiers fired the first shot. Sitting Bull had no chance to talk to the soldiers: they began the fight. They fought all the morning. The soldiers were behind a cutbank, and the Sioux were out on the prairie, both on the same side of the stream. For some time the young men dashed back and forth along the soldier lines on their swift ponies, while most of the Indians stood at a distance of a quarter of a mile and shot at the soldiers. Plenty Lice was killed, and a good many Indians were wounded.[2]

A medicine man named Long Holy had recently organized an order of seven young men and, following the instructions received in his vision, had made them, as he and they believed, bulletproof. Though he had wounded several of his young men during a test made in the Indian camp, *none* of the bullets had *gone through*. So now he saw that here was ideal ground for his display of power. Just after sunrise

[2] Four hundred soldiers (182 of them cavalry) under Major E. M. Baker, Second Cavalry, escort of a surveying party of the Northern Pacific Railroad Company. The engagement took place August 14, 1872.

he shouted, "Now I am going to make these men holy [bulletproof]. We are going to make four circles toward the white soldiers, and each time we shall ride a little nearer to the enemy. When we make the fourth circle, we are going to charge, and all of you must charge with us."

White Bull led off, then came Bear-Loves, With-Horn, Little Bull, Leading-Him, and Takes-the-Bread. Last of all rode Long Holy. The soldiers were all shooting at them all this time. As they dashed along, they were singing the song Long Holy had taught them:

> *There is nobody holy besides me.*
> *The Sun said so; the Rock said so;*
> *He gave me this medicine, and said so.*

White Bull was expecting to be hit, he was waiting for a bullet to strike him or his horse. Suddenly, as he rode ahead, he heard Long Holy, and then Leading-Him, call out, "I am hit!" He looked back, but they were still on their horses, galloping along, apparently unhurt. The second time they circled nearer the soldiers, within forty yards. White Bull could hear his comrades sing out, one after another, "I am hit!" or "I am shot!" He kept expecting to be hit himself. By the time they had finished the second round, four men had been hit. Leading-Him had been shot in the neck, below the chin; the bullet passed *clear through!* He bled freely.

As the young men were starting on their third circle, Sitting Bull galloped out upon the prairie between the lines. He was yelling at Long Holy and his young men: "Wait! Stop! Turn Back! Too many young men are being wounded! That's enough!" He kept ordering them to turn back, to give up their circling. The young men hardly knew what to do. Leading-Him had been shot through the neck, Takes-the-Bread was hit in the ribs, With-Horn had been hit twice in the back, Long Holy himself had been hit in the right breast.

But Long Holy did not wish to stop; nobody had been killed, only one of the bullets had gone through. He was indignant at Sitting Bull's interference. Said he, "I brought these men here to *fight.* But of course, if they *want* to quit, they can."

127

Sitting Bull paid no attention to Long Holy. He kept insisting, shouting to the young men to stop. And so, reluctantly, they did.

Then White Bull, stripped for action, was with his uncle, Sitting Bull, and close by them was Crazy Horse, chief of the Oglala detachment, and second in command (under Sitting Bull) of all the hunting Sioux.

As usual, Crazy Horse had his face painted all over with white spots, and wore his hair hanging loose. He wore a white buckskin shirt and leggins, but no feathers. That was the way he always dressed for battle, White Bull said; and White Bull was a close friend of Crazy Horse. That day Crazy Horse carried only a lance—nothing else. He was mounted, like all the Sioux. Slim, not very tall, with a light complexion, serious and laconic, he was a warrior through and through.

For a while then the fight was "just shooting." All that time Long Holy kept complaining because the chief had interfered with his demonstration; he kept saying that Sitting Bull was getting "mouthy."

Sitting Bull was never a braggart: all the old-timers agree on that point. But he *was* free with his advice, for he knew he was smarter and more experienced than most men. Meanwhile Crazy Horse kept dashing back and forth in front of the soldiers, and the Sioux and their Cheyenne allies were saying how brave and how lucky he was. It was about time the commander-in-chief did something to remind his people that he was the greatest man among them.

All at once the Indians saw Sitting Bull lay down his gun and quiver, and carrying only his long, narrow tobacco pouch, with the pipestem protruding from its mouth, walk coolly out in front of the Indian line, as if he were taking a stroll through the camp at evening. He walked right out toward the soldiers, and sat down on the grass a hundred yards in front of the Indian line, right on the open prairie, in plain sight of the firing soldiers. There he got out his flint and steel, struck fire, lighted his pipe, and began to puff away in his usual leisurely fashion. Turning his head toward his own astonished men, he yelled to them, "Any Indians who wish to smoke with me, come on!"

It was amazing. But his nephew, White Bull, was not the man to ignore a dare. He and another Sioux named Gets-the-Best-of-Them, went forward. With them went two Cheyennes. White Bull had his six-shooter and breech-loading rifle along. The other Sioux had a bow and arrows. They left their horses behind. When they reached Sitting Bull, they all sat down in a row.

Sitting Bull was calmly puffing away, and handed the pipe to his nephew, and so on down the line. They smoked, as usual, from right to left.

Said White Bull: "We others wasted no time. Our hearts beat rapidly, and we smoked as fast as we could. All around us the bullets were kicking up the dust, and we could hear bullets whining overhead. But Sitting Bull was not afraid. He just sat there quietly, looking around as if he were at home in his tent, and smoked peacefully."

While they sat there, Two Crow was making a circle between them and the soldiers at the gallop. Just as Two Crow passed between them and the troops, his horse was shot dead and fell headlong, kicking up the dust in their faces. White Bull, seeing the horse shot right in front of him, shut his eyes and dropped his head upon his knees in the face of all that shooting.

After the pipe was smoked out, Sitting Bull got out the little sharp stick he used for cleaning his pipe, cleared the bowl of ashes, and put the pipe and cleaner back into the pouch. Then he got up slowly and sauntered back to the Indian line. White Bull and the other three ran back. Gets-the-Best-of-Them was so excited that he forgot his arrows, and White Bull had to run back after them.

Such absolutely reckless, cool daring beat anything those Indians had ever seen. It was the bravest thing Sitting Bull had ever done. There was no necessity for that stunt, no excitement to spur him on. It was sheer nerve—a grandstand play to teach those saucy young men a lesson and put them in their place again. It worked to perfection. None of them had ever seen anything like that. It was not a *coup*, of course, but it was braver than any *coup!*

When Sitting Bull had got back to his own line, he took up his weapons, mounted, and called out, "That's enough! We must stop! That's enough!"

It was then about noon.

But Crazy Horse was unwilling to stop fighting. All the morning he had been the star performer of the Indian team, and he could hardly reconcile himself to being second—and a bad second—all at once. He had been too brilliantly outdone. He turned to White Bull and said, "Let's make one more circle toward the soldier line." That was all Crazy Horse could think up.

White Bull was not the man to ignore the challenge. When Crazy Horse charged away on his fast war horse, White Bull rode right at his heels. The soldiers shot at them as they passed and turned back toward their own line. They all fired, and dropped the pony of Crazy Horse, stone dead. But Crazy Horse was near the Indian line: he got up and ran in afoot. White Bull and his horse were untouched.

Crazy Horse was brave as a lion, but he lacked the intelligence, the imagination, and the originality displayed by his chief. His charge could not compare with Sitting Bull's brilliant feat. And so, finding himself afoot, he rode double with some other man, and went back to camp with the others. For Sitting Bull, having demonstrated his unexampled courage, promptly led his men back home. There his novel deed was the one topic of conversation. Everyone swarmed round him, everyone came to see him and congratulate him. Everyone wished to be friends with this man who was so brave, and so marvelously lucky.

When they had all gone, he could sit there on that summer's evening in his tent, humming to himself the air of that favorite song: "*Friends, I am a soldier, And have many people Jealous of me!*"

That was a happy evening. Yet the sword Jealousy, though it may give the accolade, may be used to slash and stab. And in that prestige-mad society, even the most gracious and kindly of men must some day feel its edge. There is a jealousy which has nothing to do with sex—the envious rivalry of warriors. And it, too, is cruel as the grave.

This fight, like others that season, was hardly more than a show of force. Sitting Bull did not consider himself at war with the whites. And he had long ago given up hope that the white men would ever make up their minds whether they were at war or not. They never seemed to know their own minds. What should he do?

This knotty problem was finally solved by Sitting Bull and Crazy

Horse in conference. Crazy Horse said to his chief: "My friend, if any soldiers or white men come in here and do not shoot first, we'll not bother them. But if they come shooting, we'll go after them."

Sitting Bull was in full accord, but more determined to resist. Said he: "Friend, you are right. I hear there is a government of white men somewhere east, and it is sending many soldiers to fight us. That is no way for them to act; it is not right. But if they come, we'll fight them and kill them. Some Indians will be killed, too, until we reach a settlement."

This was the policy to which Sitting Bull and his friend Crazy Horse adhered until the end. "If they come shooting, shoot back."

It seemed as if there might be considerable shooting in the near future. Congress directed the issue of one thousand needle guns with ammunition to settlers of eastern Montana for protection against Indian raids. The Governor distributed these arms in September, 1872. That same autumn there were a number of attacks upon Fort McKeen (later called Fort Abraham Lincoln) on the Missouri, and a few white men were killed when away from their posts and commands. Gall, seeking revenge for the loss of friends killed by Stanley's troops on the Yellowstone, succeeded in shooting Lieutenant Eben Crosby. Crosby was a one-armed veteran of the Civil War. It is said that Gall collected his remaining arm and took it home as a trophy.

19. Indian Peace

Only by kind treatment and faithfully keeping every promise ever made them can any permanent influence be secured or retained over the Sioux.

—JOHN W. DOUGLAS.

THE NORTHERN PLAINS were quiet during 1873 and 1874. Sitting Bull was busy with his hunting. Even at the agencies there was peace. At Standing Rock Agency, where the Hunkpapa contingent had always been troublesome, they had become so orderly that troops were withdrawn from the post there. Red Cloud's people took no action, even when asked to yield their right to hunt south of the Platte. And at Fort Peck, that hotbed of dissatisfaction, the agent reports the Sioux "docile," and begs for ammunition or extra rations, so that they can be somehow fed.

But General Sheridan was set upon establishing a post in the Black Hills, and hit upon the plan of sending Colonel George Armstrong Custer from Fort Abraham Lincoln on the Missouri to reconnoitre the sacred mountains of the Sioux, on the plea that a post there would enable the military to "threaten the Indian villages and stock if the latter raided the settlements." As the only "settlements" raided by the Sioux for some years past had been Fort Abraham Lincoln itself, this was a rather startling proposition. *It violated flatly every treaty made with the Sioux.* But army men had never been able to forget the loss of their forts on the Powder. The plan was carried out.

Custer marched through the Hills without opposition from Indians, and on returning gave to the press a glowing account of the country—

132

a perfect gem of Ballyhoo—ending with the announcement that he had found gold in the grass roots! It is pleasant to be the bearer of good news—especially if one has one's eye on public office.

There was a rush for the Black Hills, a rush which the army was perhaps unable—and certainly unwilling—to stop. The miners moved in, the army made a pretense of driving them out, and the fat was in the fire.

All the work of the Indian Bureau for thirty years past was undone by Custer's march. Even the dullest Sioux could see now that the Grandfather was not to be trusted. It was bad enough that he had not enforced the treaties, worse that he violated them himself. But worst of all, the miners were not kept out of the Hills. The army had no heart for the job of disciplining its best friends—the frontiersmen— for the benefit of Sitting Bull. Sheridan appealed, asking that something be done to relieve the soldiers of a "most embarrassing duty"!

Having occupied the Hills, the miners compelled the government to send a Commission out to buy them, or at least secure mining concessions. But the agency Sioux now demanded cash—and a fair price!

As for Sitting Bull, he had no land to sell. "We have plenty of game," he said. "We want no white men here. The Black Hills belong to me. If the whites try to take them, I will fight." The chief was not inclined to compromise with white men just then, for his "brother" Frank Grouard had betrayed him, fled, and joined the troops as a scout. The fact that Grouard was the man sent to invite Sitting Bull to council with the commission did nothing to mollify the chief. And so the commission went back to Washington, unsuccessful.

However, the miners in the Hills remained. They said the Hills were "too rich for Indian blood." The deer and the eagle gave way to the sweet society of Deadwood.

Yet, even then, the Sioux were slow to attack these invaders. Sitting Bull was far to the north, and Spotted Tail and Red Cloud looked to the Grandfather for an adjustment. Later, when hostilities between miners and Sioux became frequent, Sitting Bull took no part in them; White Bull, who was in three of these scraps, was certain that his uncle took no part. And even in those trying times, Sitting Bull's habit of sparing enemies still held.

One day he and his young men came upon a starving white man, lost on the prairie. The poor wretch had been eating rosebuds and the bark of trees. The young men proposed to kill him. But Sitting Bull said: "No. That man is wearing a blue coat, he is a deserter from the army. Besides, he has nothing worth killing him for—no horse, no gun. He is leaving our country, let him go." He fed the deserter, sent him on his way. All Sitting Bull asked was to be let alone.

Indeed, the chief was so quiet that the Commissioner of Indian Affairs that year reported (confusing him with an Oglala of the same name) that he was a peaceful agency Indian, and captain of the Indian Police!

Soon after, White Dog, the Hohe chief, came to make peace with the Sioux, who were then at the mouth of Powder River. Ever since Sitting Bull had captured his Hohe "brother" Jumping Bull, he had always been ready for peace with the Hohe. He gladly smoked with White Dog, and made him many presents. The treaty held until 1879, when Silas Adam and other Hohe served as scouts with General Nelson A. Miles against Sitting Bull.

After the truce with the Hohe had been arranged, Sitting Bull thought he would take advantage of it and pass through the country of his new allies on a horse-stealing expedition. It seemed a good time to take horses from the Slota, Metis, or Canadian mixed bloods, who always had plenty of good stock. This expedition had far-reaching effects upon the fate of Sitting Bull and his people, and also put him into one of the tightest corners he ever occupied.

Because the warpath lay through friendly territory, Sitting Bull wanted only a small party. He asked his nephew, One Bull, to go along, and gave him his own repeating rifle—a gift to Sitting Bull from Bad Soup, that lean and hungry-looking man, one of Gall's warriors. With these two went Iron Claw (Horseshoe) and One Bull's wife, White Buffalo Woman. The four of them left the Sioux camp at the Shallow Crossing of the Yellowstone below the mouth of the Powder, and struck out horseback for the Canadian boundary. It was early autumn. Sitting Bull was then a chief of the Fox Soldier Society, and wore the bonnet and sash which indicated his rank.

After several nights' riding, they reached the Missouri River below Fort Peck, crossed it, and pushed up Little River (as they called the stream in those days) to a point north of the present Hohe (Assiniboin) Reservation. There they found a big camp of strangers, whom they thought must be Slota. It was right across the stream, and they could just make out the white blur of the massed tents in the darkness, and the dim forms of horses grazing about. Sitting Bull told Iron Claw and the woman to remain concealed in the timber while he and his nephew went after the animals.

Sitting Bull stood on the bank of the little stream, looking at that big camp full of sleeping enemies. He was afoot—and lame. If they were roused, it would be hard to get away. There must be lots of dogs there, too, ready to give the alarm. And the Slota were always well supplied with guns and ammunition. He had seldom attempted a more delicate or daring raid. Of course, he was an old hand at stealing horses, knew all the tricks. But there is more in success than a capacity for taking pains. Sitting Bull knew that there was also luck, and he turned to the Source of luck before he went to work.

Standing there on the riverbank, he raised his open palms to the dark sky and vowed to make a Sun Dance if he should be successful. "Wakan'Tanka, take pity on me, blameless as I am. Give me some horses to take home with me, and I will give You a scarlet blanket and a filled pipe next summer."

By a "scarlet blanket" Sitting Bull meant his own blood.

Afterward, uncle and nephew crept forward, waded the little stream, and came out upon the flat, open prairie of the bottom, taking care to make no noise. The smell of the horses came to their nostrils, borne on the faint night breeze, for of course Sitting Bull was going against the wind, so as not to arouse the dogs of that big camp. Slowly they went on, until they found themselves among the hobbled ponies snuffling over the dusty grass, their lips clap-clapping as they tried to snap off a mouthful of sun-dried herbage.

At intervals, Sitting Bull could hear the clink-clink of the lead mare's bell, and he silently drifted in that direction. Soon he saw her white form looming through the dark. Stepping gently up to the staring animal, he passed his soothing hand over her withers, and soon had hold of the bell-strap about her neck. While she stood there, uneasily regarding him, blowing softly through wide nostrils, he slipped his lariat around her neck, tied it, and quickly cut the strap from which the clinking bell depended. Then, stooping, he cut her hobbles. It was the work of a moment to loop the lariat about her nose, making a rope bridle. In another moment, Sitting Bull had slid upon the mare's back. As he had expected, the lead mare was a gentle animal.

All this time One Bull had been busy with his knife, cutting the hobbles of the other horses—the best he could select in the darkness. And when the lead mare started off, of course these others followed, as they always followed her everywhere. It was all done as quickly as one can read about it. Within a few minutes, Sitting Bull and his nephew were back at the rendezvous in the timber, with ten good horses. Iron Claw and the woman grinned happily in the shadow of the cottonwoods. They started home, traveling as rapidly as they could with ten head of horses to herd before them.

Next day, while passing through the Hohe country, Sitting Bull had a most unpleasant surprise. A party of twenty Indians jumped him, and, to his intense disgust, he saw that they were Hohe! They came running forward, afoot, and nearly all of them had guns. Sitting Bull threw his herd toward the shelter of the timber, called out to Iron Claw and the woman to watch the horses, and, as the last of them disappeared into the brush, he and his nephew flung themselves down in the grass of the open prairie to stand off their pursuers.

Here they came, yelping the war whoop, jumping from side to side to avoid being hit. As soon as they got within range, they began to shoot. The traitors! Sitting Bull was quite sure they could see he was Sioux. But there was no time for parley. Uncle and nephew lay there side by side, firing away, and it looked as if they would certainly be rubbed out. That day Sitting Bull might well have remembered his death song—*Mother, you might as well mourn!* No chance for him to live.

Time wore on. Hungry, dry, anxious, their shoulders sore from the kick of their guns, the pair lay low and saved their few remaining cartridges, trying to make them last as long as possible. Their throats were parched with the heat, the fever of excitement, the reek of the rifles. They had no water. And Sitting Bull was burning up with indignation at those treacherous Hohe out there trying to kill him just after he had made peace with them—a peace they themselves had sought!

And then, looking across the prairie, he saw another bunch of Hohe coming, horseback. There they came, and, when they had come near enough, one of them shouted, "Who are you, anyway?"

Sitting Bull stood up so that they could see him clearly. His voice, hoarse with anger, bellowed back at them, "I am Sitting Bull!"

Immediately, it was clear that his words had caused a sensation. The leader of the mounted Hohe rode out before his men and shouted, "I am Chief Red Stone, just arrived. The Hohe will fight no more." All the nations knew Sitting Bull.

That was good news. Sitting Bull answered, "I am kin to the Hohe and speak the same language, yet they have played a dirty trick on me." He was furious to think that those people would treat him like that.

Red Stone rode back and forth, driving his young men away, threatening them with his quirt. Reluctantly, they withdrew. Red Stone rode with Sitting Bull for some distance to make sure that none of his warriors returned to renew the attack on the Sioux.

Afterward, Sitting Bull's little party pushed hard for home. They found the Sioux camp on Beaver Creek, a branch of the Little Missouri. It was beginning to snow when they got home. One Bull said they thought they were stealing horses from the Slota. But my friend Big Darkness, a Hohe on the Assiniboin Reserve in Canada, who remembers this fight, says that Sitting Bull raided a camp of Crees that time.

Maybe so. All the same, they were good horses!

20. White Man's War

ON NOVEMBER 9, 1875, a United States Indian Inspector, one E. C. Watkins, having just arrived in Washington from a tour of the agencies, reported to the Commissioner of Indian Affairs on the "attitude and condition" of "Sitting Bull's band, and other bands of the Sioux nation under chiefs of less note, but no less untamable and hostile." He complained of their attacks on friendly tribes, lauded their country as "the best hunting grounds in the United States," and expressed resentment of their "lofty and independent attitude and language to government officials." Watkins went on to say that these Indians numbered but "a few hundred warriors and these never all together," and urged that a thousand soldiers, striking the Indian camps in winter, would be amply sufficient for their capture or punishment. He also blamed Sitting Bull for the failure of the Indian Bureau to civilize the friendly tribes, when—as a matter of fact —Sitting Bull had done more to tame them than the Indian Bureau ever dreamed of doing. Sitting Bull had forced them to abandon their hunting grounds in the buffalo country, had taken away their arms and their horses, had done to them, in truth, exactly what the War Department would have liked to do to him.

Watkins's plea for war on the Sioux was based, oddly enough, on the duty of the government to fulfill its treaty stipulations (!) and he ends this curious document with a glowing tribute to the frontier settlers, civilization, and humanity.

A small spark was enough. On receipt of this report, a conference was held. There were present the President of the United States; the

Secretary of the Interior, the Honorable Z. Chandler; the Assistant
Secretary; the Commissioner of Indian Affairs, the Honorable E. P.
Smith; the Secretary of War, the Honorable William W. Belknap,
soon to be impeached for graft; and an army contractor who later
spent some years in the penitentiary. It was voted that the Sioux Indians must go upon their reservation, or be whipped.

Accordingly, on December 3, 1875, the Secretary of the Interior
wrote to the Commissioner of Indian Affairs: "Referring to our communication of the 27th ultimo, relative to the status of certain Sioux
Indians residing without the bounds of their reservation and their
continued hostile attitude towards the whites, I have to request that
you direct the Indian agents at all Sioux agencies in Dakota and at
Fort Peck, Montana, to notify said Indians that unless they shall remove within the bounds of their reservation (and remain there),
before the 31st of January next, they shall be deemed hostile and
treated accordingly by the military force."

This message reached Standing Rock December 22. It would appear that the gentlemen who framed it were either unaware of the
rigorous climate of that region, or wished to make it impossible for
the Indians to meet the conditions laid down. That winter of 1875 was
even worse than usual: as early as November, General Sheridan reported that because of the terrible severity of the weather, the army
in Dakota had been compelled to suspend operations.

Sitting Bull was then in camp at the mouth of Powder River, some
240 miles as the crow flies from Standing Rock Agency. Other hunting bands were farther up the Powder and over on the Box Elder. The
runners sent out with the message had a hard time winning through
the drifts and blizzards on those bare and bitter plains, and not one of
them succeeded in getting back within the time allowed by the order
for the bands to come in. It was a sheer impossibility to transport
women and children through that frozen waste on half-starved ponies
within the time allowed.

Said White Bull, "Maybe, if we had had automobiles, we could
have made it."

But the runners knew, and Sitting Bull knew, that—if they went in—*there was nothing to eat at the agency*. His camp was full of agency Indians who had come out to hunt with him for that very reason. If he had gone in, many of his people would have starved.

Not all the camps were located by the runners. Those which could be found sent back word that it was impossible to travel with their families in such weather, that they were then busy hunting, and that they would come in early in the spring. There is some doubt whether Sitting Bull received this summons. Sooner or later, of course, he must have heard of it. But it is unlikely that he would have come in, and it is certain that he did not.

And so, on February 7, the War Department was informed that Sitting Bull was "hostile," and directed to deal with him accordingly.

No sooner had war been declared upon Sitting Bull for not bringing his women and children through the snow from Powder River to the Missouri than it was discovered that the winter was too severe to permit a military expedition to march from the Missouri to Powder River! "It was thought advisable to postpone the expedition" from that side, "the snow being so deep and the number of men badly frozen so great." Therefore General George Crook, or "Three Stars" (as the Sioux called him from his insignia of rank), was ordered to attack the hunting bands from the south. He made elaborate preparations for a winter campaign.

On March 1, 1876, Crook set out from Fort Fetterman, Wyoming, heading for Powder River. With him went one of the strongest single outfits ever seen in Sioux country. Crook was looking for Crazy Horse and his Oglala, said to be a few miles above the mouth of the Little Powder, in Montana. It was reported to contain 120 lodges. Actually this was the camp of Two Moon's Cheyennes which Crazy Horse's Sioux friend He Dog had joined in order to go into the agency. The scout Grouard, recognizing He Dog's horses, led the troops in attack; this brought the Cheyennes into the war. Colonel J. J. Reynolds captured the camp early on the morning of March 17, and burned the lodges, but was driven back, losing the captured ponies. He went home to be court-martialed for his failure.

Meanwhile, the freezing Oglala and Cheyennes set out to find succor in that bitter weather. And at last, cold and hungry, in the Blue Mountains on Beaver Creek, some sixty miles down the Powder, they found the camp of Sitting Bull.

Sitting Bull heard their story, took them in, fed them, gave them horses and saddles, robes, and powder and ball, and told his people to double up and let the refugees have some of their tents. He made them welcome.

When Sitting Bull first heard of that attack, he made up his mind. Ever since the Black Robe came to smoke with him eight years behind, he had put up with everything and kept that peace. He was a patient, gentle, long-suffering man, as many great fighters have been. Probably he would not have resented an affront to himself; it was the business of a chief to bear and forbear. But now his people had been wantonly attacked. He had come to the end of his patience. He was angry, and when he was angry, he was a different man. At the council on Tongue River, he said: "We are an island of Indians in a lake of whites. We must stand together, or they will rub us out separately. These soldiers have come shooting; they want war. All right, we'll give it to them!"

Many a white man lost his horses and his scalp that season. Sitting Bull had accepted the challenge.

Runners sped away in all directions, to every camp of the hunting bands, to every Sioux, Cheyenne, and Arapaho agency west of the Missouri—all the agencies. They rode hard, and when they arrived, slipped from their fagged ponies, dived into the tipi of the chief, and spoke the words of Sitting Bull: "It is war. Come to my camp at the Big Bend of the Rosebud. Let's all get together and have one big fight with the soldiers!"

That word swept the camps, the agencies, like a prairie fire. All the restless young men, patriotic and adventurous, weary of lazy starvation at the agency, opened their ears. They began to trade for guns, for powder and ball, for horses, and as soon as the grass was high enough to feed their ponies, their women struck the tipis and they hit the trail to the Rosebud. Red Cloud, who had been in Washington, seen countless white men, and measured their big guns with his fan, despaired of victory: he advised his people to cover their ears and sit still. But his own son, Jack Red Cloud, rode away with the rest; he would not listen to the old man. For this was the day of young men, and Sitting Bull's medicine was good; it was what the young men wanted.

Of course, not all the people who went to join Sitting Bull went to fight soldiers. Some of them went to hunt, as they had done every summer for years. Some went because their children were hungry. Some went because they expected their relatives out there to give them presents. Some young men had girls in mind. And even the warlike ones thought more of the chance of killing the Crow and Shoshoni scouts known to be with the troops than of scalping white men.

Then, too, there were many who—though entirely peaceable—feared to remain at the agency, now that the war was on. Said they: "You know how it was at Sand Creek and Ash Hollow. You know what happened to the Santees when Inkpaduta ran amuck. Look at those poor people at Crow Creek: they are still being punished for the sins of others. The Grandfather will surely take it out on us too, after Sitting Bull begins to fight. We shall be a heap safer with Sitting Bull than we are here at the agency. Let's go." That was what they said, and they were right: within six months the Grandfather had taken away all the horses and guns from the Indians at the agencies, just as if they had been hostiles. He treated them all alike.

And so the trails were filled with people, all heading for Sitting Bull's big camp. There the people would see them coming: first, young men racking in, singing a riding song. Then, a few hours after, the older men and the pack train, women and children, travois and loose horses, dogs and colts. The tired mules would halt, the women would run about like ants, and in half an hour the smoking tipis would be crowded together on the flat, circle on circle, while grazing ponies covered the hills around.

It was a jolly, sociable camp. Drums were beating, and every night there was dancing, the chink and clash of sleigh bells as the warriors stamped and postured, the high-pitched yelps, the male voices chanting. Every day there were feasts, and family parties, courting and gossip, and almost every hour the fresh excitement of new arrivals and reunions.

Here they came, Oglala under Crazy Horse, Low Dog, Big Road, and "Sweat"; Minniconjou under Makes Room, Hump, Lame Deer, Flying-By, Black Shield, and Black Moon; Sans Arc following Spotted Eagle, Two Eagles, His-High-Horse, Black Eagle, and Blue Coat; Hunkpapa led by Four Horns, Black Moon, Long Horn, No Neck, Red Horn. Cheyennes with Ice and Little Horse. And not a few Arapahos, Brûlés from Spotted Tail's camp, Southern Cheyennes. Not to mention some Yanktonais, Two-Kettle, and Blackfeet Sioux, who—with Inkpaduta's Santees—camped with Sitting Bull and the Hunkpapa: three hundred lodges in one circle.

When all had come together, Sitting Bull called the chiefs to council. The first thing was to choose leaders for the coming campaign. As the Cheyennes were guests, the Sioux courteously suggested that they name their own leader first. Perhaps because his people had been the first to resist the soldiers, the Cheyennes named Two Moon. He was to command the Cheyennes in the war.

It was then the turn of the Sioux. There was only one nomination. Two Moon rose and said: "I can see that it will not take you long to choose your leader for this war. You already have the right man— Sitting Bull. He has called us all together. He is your war chief, and you always listen to him. I can see no reason for another choice."

"Hau! Hau! Hau!" was the hearty response. Sitting Bull was elected by acclamation, without one dissenting voice.

When the warriors heard who had been named, they were satisfied. Said they: "He knows how to lead us: he can always bluff us into charging: we always feel like fighting when he is urging us on. He is lucky, too, and brave. He never sends another man where he will not go himself." That was what those who knew him said to the strangers from the far-off agencies. It was good news.

No sooner had Sitting Bull been given high command of the campaign than he went to work. He began to prepare. He sent his young men out in all directions, to rustle horses for the war. He said: "Go in small parties—two or three or four in a bunch. Then the soldiers cannot catch you, they will not chase you." And he added: "Listen, young men. Spare nobody. If you meet anyone, kill him, and take his horse. Let no one live. Save *nothing!*"

Now that he had made up his mind to fight, Sitting Bull was a changed man. His heart was hard; he had no heart at all for the white men. He was so ruthless, so callous, that some of the Sioux were afraid of him and wanted to go back to the agency. Kill Eagle and some of his Blackfeet Sioux got cold feet and wished to leave camp. But the Warrior Societies which policed the camp would not permit it. Said they, "If soldiers come, you won't be the only ones killed!"

To hearten such timid souls, Sitting Bull rode through the camps singing a new song he had made:

> *You tribes, what are you saying?*
> *I have been a war chief.*
> *All the same, I'm still living.*

He knew how to put fight into his people, how to make their hearts strong.

Those were thrilling days for Sitting Bull. He was in supreme command of one of the largest camps of Plains Indians ever brought together for war. There were two hundred lodges of Cheyennes alone, and six camps of Sioux, each one as large or larger than that. Besides, there were many men without women who camped in bowers or wickiups, or slept in tipis as guests of some family. Sitting Bull had never seen so many people together: to him those crowding tents, those hundreds of warriors, were the greatest city, the greatest nation, the greatest military force in the world. It is no small thing to be leader of the greatest nation in the world. It makes the heart big; it goes to the head. Sitting Bull was a proud man in those days. And nobody who knows the old-time Sioux, and can realize the competition he had, can blame him. For they were then, as General Frederick W. Benteen said, "good shots, good riders, and the best fighters the sun ever shone on."

Few people realized the strength of Sitting Bull's small army at the time. But military men, though ignorant of the number of his warriors, were fully aware of their splendid efficiency. Read Custer's high praise of their tactics, their "individual daring," their horsemanship (in his opinion the best in the world, surpassing even that of the Cossacks). Read the statement of one of Crook's staff officers, "the finest light cavalry in the world." Read the words of General Charles King, "foemen far more to be dreaded than any European cavalry." Read Colonel Ford's official report, calling the Plains Indians "the finest skirmishers" he ever saw. Read the words of General Anson Mills: "They were then the best cavalry in the world; their like will never be seen again." Finally, cap all this by the statement of Mr. P. E. Byrne, who has made a special study of this phase of history, "the greatest mounted fighters of all time."[1]

Where is the man who could rise from the ranks to supreme command in such an army and not be proud? He was full of fight in those days.

It was not only those tame Blackfeet Sioux who feared him. Even some of Two Moon's Cheyennes—that hardy race—were a little timid about serving with such a merciless chief. Said young Two Moon, nephew of Chief Two Moon: "Sitting Bull was a goodhearted man to his own people. But he was a mean warrior; he loved to kill. I have seen our own chief, Little Wolf, kill a man and laugh to see him die. That summer of 1876 we thought Sitting Bull was like that. In those days only one thing smelled good to him—gunpowder."

The Cheyennes, however, had no cause to worry. Sitting Bull was extremely courteous to them. When the camps moved, he told Two Moon to go first, that the Sioux would follow their guests, the Cheyennes. The head and tail of the column were the dangerous posts of honor. Sitting Bull's Hunkpapa marched last of all. He, himself, of course, rode with other chiefs at the head of the whole outfit.

And so Sitting Bull's young men sped away in small parties, scouring the country for horses, and there was a lively time on the frontier that spring and summer. The Black Hills then contained more than

[1] See P. E. Byrne, *Soldiers of the Plains.*

twenty-five thousand whites, and whenever there was the least chance, the young Sioux attacked them and took their stock. Then they rode home, bringing hair and horses, bringing a few captured guns, sometimes mourning, but generally singing songs of triumph, all set to dance the victory dance. Horses were easy to get.

Guns were not—nor ammunition. The Indians could not manufacture these, and the cost of a gun was exorbitant—beyond the means of most Indians. Two pounds of powder cost a well-tanned head-and-tail robe, and few women could tan more than twenty robes in a season. Any kind of gun cost from five to eight robes and upward. In the seventies a good repeating rifle cost around twenty-five dollars in the East. On the frontier it would cost ten or fifteen dollars more—to white men. Indians had to pay even more, and the top price for buffalo robes was never more than six dollars in *Eastern* markets. Only rich Indians could afford repeaters or buy fixed ammunition, and rich Indians were no more numerous per capita than rich white men are. There was no Ordnance Department to supply warriors with arms or replace a lost or broken weapon. Every Indian had to arm himself at his own expense. Most of them could not afford guns of any kind, and the sorriest old weapons were treasured as family heirlooms.

After the greatest effort, only half of Sitting Bull's warriors were able to obtain firearms, and of these the majority had old flintlocks, condemned muskets, muzzle-loaders, smoothbores. There was plenty of propaganda claiming that the Indians were even better armed than the troops—a fantastic yarn: read the reports of the guns turned in when Indians surrendered. Granted that they may have hidden some, would men who were well armed with repeating rifles have retained the wretched old-fashioned guns that they did turn in? Those weapons were mostly so old-fashioned that they belonged in the museum; the best of them were Spencer carbines, old-fashioned Henry rifles, and old Sharps military rifles. The gun which Sitting Bull presented to his "brother" Frank Grouard was a Hawkens rifle—forty years out of date!

Two guns, said to have been turned in by Sitting Bull himself at his surrender in 1881, are now in the National Museum, Washington,

D.C. One is a Model '66 Winchester with brass frame; the other a "sawed off" smoothbore flintlock, with the lockplate imprint "Barnett, London, 1876." Perhaps these two guns tell the story of Sioux armament better than guesswork statistics.

Fixed ammunition was so hard to get that the Indians all learned to save, reload, and recap empty cartridge shells. No doubt the Indians were better armed in 1876 than in 1866: so were the whites. Other tribes were just as eager for guns as the Sioux, yet the government had to arm the Crows and Rees for military service. They had the same chance to get arms as the Sioux, and needed arms far more desperately. Yet they had to be supplied by the Grandfather.

21. The Vision of Victory

There was nothing of the traitor about the man . . . he did not hide his enmity. —FRANK GROUARD.

SITTING BULL did not spend all his time at councils of war. Horses and guns were needed, of course. But he soon went about something far more vital to his success. One day he loosened the braids of his long hair, removed the feathers from his head, washed off the red paint he habitually wore on his face, and filled his long pipe with tobacco. Then he bound silver sprays of wild aromatic sage—a sacred plant—about the pipestem. When he was all ready to start, he called his nephew White Bull, his adopted brother Jumping Bull, and the son of his close friend and fellow chief Black Moon. He asked them to go with him to the top of a butte some distance south of the old camp site, downriver. The four reached the hilltop about noon.

There Sitting Bull renewed his vow before witnesses. He stood facing the Sun, holding the pipestem upward and wailing for mercy. When he had wailed for a while, he made his prayer: "My God, save me and give me all my wild game animals. Bring them near me, so that my people may have plenty to eat this winter. Let good men on earth have more power, so that all the nations may be strong and successful. Let them be of good heart, so that all Sioux people may get along well and be happy. If you do this for me, I will perform the sun-gazing dance two days, two nights, and give you a whole buffalo."

Then all four smoked the pipe in communion, and after Sitting Bull had wiped his face with the sage, set out for camp.

Sitting Bull immediately went hunting. He shot three buffalo. Of these he chose the fattest. Then, with the help of his nephew, he rolled the cow upon her belly, and together they stretched out the legs in four directions to prop it so. The head was stretched out also. Then Sitting Bull stood with raised hands and wailed for pity. Afterward, he prayed: "Wakan' Tanka, this is the one I offered you awhile back. Here it is." In this manner he offered the buffalo to God, and made his vow good.

Within a few days, the Sun Dance was begun. Black Moon conducted it, holding the office of Intercessor. Sitting Bull, having vowed the dance, was Chief of the Dancers.

That was a big Sun Dance, well remembered by the Sioux and Cheyennes, scores of whom now living were present. Because of the wonderful prophecy that Sitting Bull made there, and because he vowed the ceremony, it has ever since been known as "Sitting Bull's Sun Dance."

All the people—both Sioux and Cheyennes—went into camp in one big circle for the ceremony. The camp was on the bank of the Rosebud, not far from the carved rocks, where the prehistoric pictures are. There the ceremony began. The virgin cut the sacred tree, the chiefs carried it into the camp circle on poles, as if it had been the body of an enemy. It was dedicated and decorated with its symbols and its offerings. A square "bed" of ground was smoothed for the altar, a buffalo skull placed thereon, and a pipe set up against the little scaffold before the skull. All the elaborate ritual of the Sun Dance was gone through with. It was all familiar to Sitting Bull: he had danced the Sun Dance many times, and his breast and back bore the scars of the torture. At last it came time for him to fulfill his vow made last autumn—to give his flesh to Wakan' Tanka. Naked to the waist, he went forward to the sacred pole.

This time he had decided to give one hundred pieces of flesh—that is to say, skin—from his arms. Jumping Bull had agreed to do the cutting.

Jumping Bull came forward, bringing a sharp steel awl, and a knife ground down to a thin, narrow blade, very sharp. He knelt beside Sitting Bull, who sat leaning back against the sacred pole, his legs straight out on the ground in front of him, and his relaxed arms resting on his thighs. Jumping Bull began at the bottom—near the wrist—of the right arm and worked upwards. He stuck the awl into the skin of the arm, lifted the skin clear of the flesh, and then used the knife. Each time he would cut out a small bit of skin, about the size of the head of a match. Then he would let the skin fall again, withdraw the awl, and begin again just above. Sitting Bull's arm was soon covered with blood.

All the time Jumping Bull was slowly and carefully cutting away on him, Sitting Bull remained perfectly still. He was wailing all the time—not because of the pain—but for mercy to Wakan' Tanka, the Great Mysterious. When Jumping Bull had worked up to the top of the right arm and cut out fifty pieces of skin, he then got up and went over to the left side. There he cut in the same manner, beginning at the wrist and working toward the shoulder, Sitting Bull sat there, wailing, never wincing, while that endless piercing, endless cutting went on, cruel and sharp, over and over. Jumping Bull was careful, his hand was sure, he worked as rapidly as he could. But it was a painful ordeal for the half-hour it lasted. White Bull stood looking on. One Bull was dancing. Sitting White Buffalo was pierced at this dance, also. Everybody in camp was looking on.

Having paid his ounce of flesh, it now remained for Sitting Bull to dance the sun-gazing dance. He took his place, and, facing the Sun while the blood ran down his fingers and slowly congealed and closed his wounds, began to bob up and down, staring up toward the Sun. All that day he danced, and that night, and the next day about noon, the crowd noticed that he appeared faint and hardly able to stand.

Black Moon and others took Sitting Bull and laid him down. He was almost unconscious. They threw cold water on him to revive him. His eyes cleared, and he spoke in a low voice to Black Moon. He had had a vision: his offering had been accepted, his prayers were heard.

Black Moon walked out into the middle of the Sun Dance enclosure and called out in a loud voice: "Sitting Bull wishes to announce that he just heard a voice from above saying, *'I give you these because they have no ears.'* He looked up and saw soldiers and some Indians on horseback coming down like grasshoppers, with their heads down and their hats falling off. They were falling right into our camp."

Then the people rejoiced. They knew what that meant. Those white men, who would not listen, who made war without just cause, were coming to their camp. Since they were coming upside down, the Indians knew the soldiers would be killed there. The people had what they wanted: Wakan' Tanka would care for His own. The Sun Dance was swiftly brought to an end. It was June 14, 1876.

Afterward, Sitting Bull warned the people: "These dead soldiers who are coming are the gifts of God. Kill them, but do not take their guns or horses. Do not touch the spoils. If you set your hearts upon the goods of the white man, it will prove a curse to this nation." Twelve lesser chiefs heard this warning, but said nothing. All the people heard of this, but some of them had no ears.

The prophecy, so soon to be fulfilled, fired the Sioux and Cheyennes with martial spirit. Ice and Two Moon, Crazy Horse and Gall, all of them had faith in Sitting Bull, believed in him. They had heard him prophesy before, and nearly always his prophecies came true. Others also divined the future at this camp, and when Custer's troops reached it, ten days later, his Ree scouts found traces of ceremonies that made them tell him, "The Sioux are sure of winning."

So long as old-time Indians retain their memories, Sitting Bull's Sun Dance on the Rosebud will never be forgotten. For many years the Sacred Pole where he shed his blood and had his vision of Custer's doom stood on the flat no great distance from the Northern Cheyenne Agency at Lame Deer. Even after the pole fell, the stump remained, for no Indian would go near the site of a medicine lodge—that was holy ground. But at last some white men removed it. And now in the midst of the subdued grandeur of that lovely valley, which Sitting Bull worked so hard to hold his own, the site of that pole is lost beneath the modern motor road.

22. The Battle of the Rosebud

He was no coward, and I do not agree with Major McLaughlin in his esti-
mate of Sitting Bull's character. He was no medicine-man, but a statesman,
one of the most far-sighted we have had. —C. A. EASTMAN.

ALL THIS TIME, both before and after the Sun Dance, Sitting
Bull kept sending out scouts to look for soldiers. Sometimes he
sent ten scouts, as when Bob-Tail-Bull went; sometimes he
would send sixty, as when Yellow Nose (a Ute captive among the
Cheyenne) was leader; sometimes only six, as when Little Hawk,
Paunch, and Goes-and-Gets-the-Meat were chosen. Always they returned, sending flashes of sunlight from their hand mirrors at long
intervals to indicate that they could discover nothing. But at last, after
the game and the grazing on the Rosebud had been exhausted, and
the camps had moved over to Reno Creek (Ash Creek) between the
Rosebud and the Little Big Horn, something definite was reported.
One evening, June 16, hunters returned to say that the valley of the
Rosebud was black with soldiers.

A great war party—almost one thousand men—were organized. Of
these about one hundred were Cheyennes, the rest Sioux. Crazy Horse
led the Oglala; Sitting Bull, the Hunkpapa. There were also Sans
Arc, Brûlé, Minniconjou, and small parties of other Teton Sioux
tribes. Half these Indians had guns. It took some time for all these
men to paint, arm, and mount themselves. After they had paraded
around camp in their regalia, they headed off in the darkness up the

south fork of Reno Creek and down Corral Creek, and reached the battleground shortly after daybreak.

"Three Stars" Crook had more than 1,000 soldiers and 260 Indian scouts—Crows, Shoshoni, Rees. Altogether, his force was more than 1,300 men. The Sioux and Cheyennes who attacked him were less than 1,000 in number; half of them had guns.

The story of the battle of the Rosebud has been told too often to be repeated here.[1] It lasted all day, and when it was over, "Three Stars" Crook was glad to take his men back where they came from and spend the rest of the summer hunting and fishing. Sitting Bull put him out of the campaign. "Three Stars" knew where Sitting Bull could be found, but he made no further effort to find him.

Sitting Bull carried his repeating rifle that day, and wore two feathers in his hair. But the Sun Dance had used him up. Crazy Horse therefore directed operations, and because of this some have supposed that Sitting Bull was not in the fight, and even that the two chiefs had separate camps! Sitting Bull did not count a *coup*, it is true. But his voice was loud in urging on his warriors: "Steady men! Remember how to hold a gun! Brace up, now! Brace up!"

One Bull, White Bull, and Old Bull were close beside Sitting Bull in the fight. Gray Eagle and Bear-Comes-Out, Owns-a-Horn and Bear-with-White-Paw, Bob-Tail-Bull and Swift Bear were all taking a lively part. So were Appearing-Bear, Gray Bull, Elk Nation, Chasing Eagle, Red Bird, White Swan, Red Fox, Bear Soldier, Black Bear, Flying-By, Hail Bear, Pretends-Eagle, Bear Shield, Little Moon; all were Hunkpapa.

That night the Cheyennes and Sioux, well pleased with their success, rode home again, leaving scouts behind to watch the retreat of "Three Stars." They were short of ammunition after that all-day fight, but otherwise quite content. It had been a good fight, a victory. It was all very well.

[1] See my *Warpath*, Chapter XIX, also *Warpath and Council Fire*, Chapter XX. See also Brig. Gen. Anson Mills, *My Story*; also George Bird Grinnell, *The Fighting Cheyennes*, and J. W. Vaughn, *With Crook at the Rosebud*. General Crook's autobiography significantly ends just short of this battle.

Yet they were still waiting for the fulfillment of Sitting Bull's prophecy. His vision had promised soldiers falling right into their camp, and Crook had not come within twenty miles of their camp.

As for Sitting Bull, it needed all his tact and skill to keep that huge camp together. Game always deserted the country overrun by so many people and horses. He had to keep them moving to find meat. Before the Battle of the Rosebud he had been hunting on the Little Big Horn (the Greasy Grass). And now he decided to return there and try to find buffalo.

That great moving camp was worth seeing, old men say. The crawling ruck of travois and pack animals, the bunches of loose horses, people mounted and on foot, the dogs—it was like a lot of ants running over the prairie. That straggling column was half a mile wide (each band and family traveling by itself), and it was so long that the Cheyennes in the lead would have their tents pitched and supper over before the Hunkpapa in the rear had even reached the campground. Sitting Bull managed things well. The chiefs led, the young men rode flank and rear as a guard. After the Cheyennes trailed the Oglala, four hundred lodges and more; then the Sans Arc and Minniconjou, equally numerous; the Brûlés, and last of all the Hunkpapa and those smaller groups who camped with them. White Bull said there must have been more than two thousand lodges in that camp, with from one to three warriors for each lodge. Of these warriors, perhaps rather more than half were fit to bear arms in a hard fight. White Bull estimated the number of such warriors as around twenty-five hundred.

When all these people (many of them strangers to each other and to the country) came dragging down the valley of the Greasy Grass, they found old heralds posted along the trail to direct them to their respective campgrounds, shouting: "The Cheyennes have made camp downriver on the flat; the Sans Arc are down yonder, too, but nearer the water; you Minniconjou will find your camp circle forming near the river, just below here; the Oglala must turn northwest, farther from the stream; Hunkpapa and Blackfeet, Santees and Two Kettle, camp here!"

All the way, scouts were riding far ahead and behind and on both

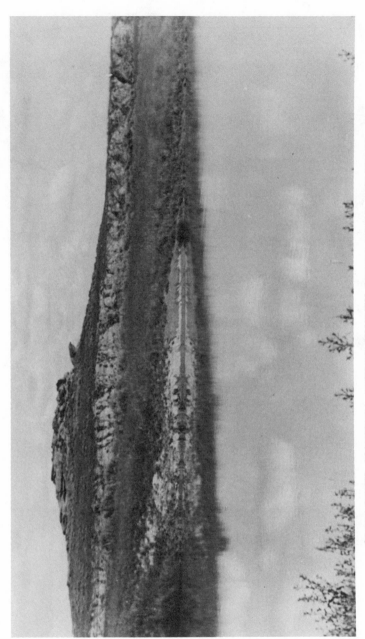

CROW ROCK, MONTANA, WHERE THIRTY CROWS WERE KILLED IN 1869.

(*Montana State Historical Society*)

SEVEN SIOUX WARRIORS WHO PARTICIPATED IN
THE BATTLE OF THE LITTLE BIG HORN.
Left to right, top row: Iron Hail, age 90; High Eagle, age 88;
Iron Hawk, age 99; Little Warrior, age 80; *bottom row:* Comes
Again, age 86; Pemmican, age 85; John Sitting Bull, age 80.
(Illuminated Foto-Ad Service, Sioux Falls, S. Dak.)

flanks, and at night young men would ride around the camps singing, to let people know that they were on the watch, that there was no danger of surprise. Each tribal camp took its turn sending out these scouts and guards.

So they all rolled into the broad, flat valley of the Greasy Grass in clouds of dust that June evening, and within half an hour the whole valley was filled with smoke-browned lodges, circle on circle, and all was as peaceful and as orderly as though they had been there for a month. Each circle was in its appointed place; each band had its allotted place within the circle; each tent its relative position within the band. Every Indian had his known address in that great city of the buffalo hunters.

There for two days they rested, dancing social dances, getting their horses into condition, burying the dead, caring for the wounded. The men took it easy, cleaning their guns, and whetting, cleaning, and greasing their knives and lance heads. Nobody was scared now: they were all set to stick together and fight it out.

Yet some were uneasy. A Cheyenne prophet, Box Elder (otherwise known as Dog-on-the-Ridge), sent a herald to announce that the people had better keep their horses tied up beside the lodges. "In my dream I saw soldiers coming," he said. But nobody paid any attention to him. Another Cheyenne howled like a wolf, and a wolf howled back at him twice from the hills; he knew that meant meat—for the wolves! In the Sans Arc Sioux camp, also, there was a herald who kept warning the people every day that enemies were approaching. On June 24, about noon, he shouted, "Soldiers are coming; they will be here tomorrow. Be ready!" Of course, everyone knew that soldiers were supposed to be looking for them, but they did not expect them so soon. Their scouts kept reporting that "Three Stars" Crook was still going away and that other soldiers were on the Rosebud. They were ready to fight, if attacked. But they danced no war dances, they sent no young men against the white men. Their preparations were purely defensive. As Sitting Bull said, "Even a bird will defend its nest."

Sitting Bull, with the forethought characteristic of the man, was not idle or heedless like so many of his people. His vision had yet to be fulfilled, and he knew that another battle must soon follow: he had seen many soldiers falling from the sky. Yet he was sorrowful to think of the Indians who must die in that battle; the fight with "Three Stars" only a week behind kept that melancholy menace in his mind. And Sitting Bull not only loved his nation; he had also all the Indian captain's dislike for casualties on his own side. But what could he do?

There is no ceremony known to the Sioux which a man can make to insure success to his side in a battle. All he can do is to make a vow or perfect a charm beforehand for his own personal success. Some of the books say that Sitting Bull made medicine during the battle of the Little Big Horn, and took no part in the fighting. But—as all students of Plains Indian religion have long known—the Sioux had no ritual which would serve such a purpose. Even if there had been, Sitting Bull would not have used it, because he had already received divine assurance of the victory. All that story is pure falsehood, intended to discredit Sitting Bull after his surrender. He had no doubt that his side would win. All that worried him was the loss of his warriors, those who must die in the fight. He was sad at heart for them. He had no power to avert that tragedy. There was only one thing he could do. He could pray.

On the evening of June 24, he stripped to the breech cloth, painted himself, loosened his hair, and, taking his pipe and buffalo robe, stepped out of his tipi.

Sitting Bull's tipi stood at the southwest side of the Hunkpapa camp circle: old men still point out its site, fifty yards south of the lane which leads east from the main road to the cottage on the riverbank near the slough. There he was living with his two wives, his brother-in-law, Gray Eagle, his sons, his two daughters, and the newborn twins. The tipi of his nephew, One Bull, stood close by on one side, and on the other the tent of his old mother. Uncle Four Horns, Crawler, Long Bull had their tents close by, and only a little way nearer the river was Inkpaduta's painted lodge.

From his door, Sitting Bull could see the flats to the north thronged with smoking tipis. To the south stretched flat, open bottoms and the slough near by with only a little water showing where the river bed had been long ago. To the west the higher green-brown benches covered with grazing ponies were rolling away to a far blue horizon where the sun was sinking behind the snow-patched rampart of the Big Horn Mountains. But Sitting Bull turned toward the east, facing the ash-gray bluffs which towered above the green cottonwood timber along the river. Leaving his camp, he waded the stream, and, climbing northeastward along one of the dry ravines, came out upon the hilltop not far from where the monument now stands. Already the light was fading.

From that dominant point he could see to the north a far-off ridge with the green timber below it; to the east, barren hills, scabby with sagebrush; to the west, steep slopes and lapping ridges leading down to tufts of green cottonwood foliage where the river lay under the bluffs at his feet, and beyond these the glowworm triangles of tipis lighted by the home fires of his people. The hum of that great encampment came faintly to his ears—the singing and drumming, the high-pitched, gnatlike cry of some old herald making his announcement: all the familiar sounds of home. Darkness fell, and all but those firelit tents faded from his vision.

That same night, General "Long Hair" Custer talked with his Ree scouts, and revealed to them hopes and ambitions which he had never dared utter until that hour. How he was staking everything upon this fight, on conquering the Sioux. How, if he won, he would be president of the United States—the Grandfather.[2] And how, if the Rees did as he told them and made off with the Sioux ponies next day, he would look out for them when he came into power. He was then in disgrace with President Grant because he had dared expose the corruption of his administration; it had almost cost him the command of the Seventh Cavalry in this campaign. But now, if he could only win—only kill enough Sioux—beat Sitting Bull—Grant would not dare meddle with him. Nothing could stop him then. So Long Hair talked that night to hearten his Rees, for they were always telling him he would find more Sioux with Sitting Bull than he could handle. He did not believe them; his heart was full of plans and hopes and ambitions. He was hungry for battle. If he found the Sioux, he would strike them hard; they would run from *him*. If they did not get away, he would shoot them down. The more he could kill, the better.

But Sitting Bull, that night, was not thinking of himself, nor of killing. Standing on that hilltop, so soon to be made bloody in the fight which "Long Hair" was seeking, the chief raised his hands to the dark sky and wailed and prayed to Wakan' Tanka, Who had promised him the victory: "Wakan' Tanka, pity me. In the name of the nation, I offer You this pipe. Wherever the Sun, Moon, Earth, Four Winds, there You are always. Father, save the people, I beg You. *We wish to live!* Guard us against all misfortunes and calamities. Take pity!"

Sitting Bull went home then. He left up there small offerings of tobacco tied to wands stuck in the ground. Next day the hooves of Custer's troop-horses knocked them down. But, the Sioux say, those offerings were not in vain.

23. Custer's Last Stand

Sitting Bull and I were at the point where Reno attacked.   —GALL.

NEXT MORNING, June 25, the day broke clear, hot, and almost windless. It had been very dry for some time, and the trails were dusty.

At dawn, One Bull and Gray Eagle turned loose the family stock, which had been picketed close by the lodges all night. Then they mounted and drove the herd to water at the near-by river. They had to pick and choose carefully to find a watering place, because the banks were soft and steep and four or five feet high. There they sat, their bare legs dangling, while the ponies thrust their noses deep into that cold water rushing over its pebbled bed. The stream was only about twenty yards wide, and not deep enough to swim a horse in most places. When the ponies would drink no more, and began to splash and squeal and nip each other, the young men drove them out upon the grassy benches west of the camp. They had to go some distance, for the multitudes of animals in that great camp had already (in two days' time) grazed off all the prairie close at hand. When the ponies had settled down to feeding, the two young men went back to camp and had breakfast. Later they returned to have another look at the herd, for their horses were their most precious possessions. Sitting Bull had only twenty head (war horses, racers, buffalo runners, pack animals, mares, and colts), but they were choice animals. The Cheyennes often had more than the Sioux; Two Moon, for example, then had twice as many as Sitting Bull, while one of the Minniconjou—Wounded Hand

—had a hundred. There were too many calls upon Sitting Bull's known liberality to permit him to grow rich, and by custom a chief could not demand a return when he made a present.

It was hot on the prairie, and after a time One Bull and Gray Eagle came home again. It was not yet time for the midday watering.

Sitting Bull was then in the council tipi in the middle of the Hunkpapa camp circle, talking with friends. That morning he wore his ordinary clothes: a fringed smoke-tanned buckskin shirt embroidered with green porcupine quills, with tassels of human hair on the long decorated shoulder straps. Leggins and moccasins to match, red breechcloth, and a single eagle feather upright at the back of his head. His long braids, wrapped in sleek otter fur, hung down his chest. Framed by those braids, his broad face, with its firm jaw, piercing eyes, and the whimsical twist at the left corner of his thin-lipped mouth, was painted red, for luck, as was usual among men resting in camp. At his belt he carried his knife—a curved butcher knife with a brown wooden hilt—which rested in a shiny black sole-leather sheath studded with three rows of brass tacks. At that moment, Sitting Bull was gently waving a buffalo tail mounted on a short stick—a fly-brush—for the flies were a terrible plague on the Greasy Grass that summer.

It was a lazy day. In spite of the warnings, people did not expect enemies. Some of the young men were fishing, and the hills west of the river were dotted with women digging tipsin.

Just then Fat Bear dashed up to the council tipi. Brown Back had brought the news, he said. That morning early, two young Hunkpapa boys were out looking for stray horses. They crossed a soldier trail, and in it found a lost pack. Curious to see what they had found, they broke it open. It was full of hard bread. Hungry as boys will be, they sat down and began to eat. While they were eating, some soldiers came back on the trail, saw them, and began to shoot. The soldiers killed Deeds, but Hona's brother made his getaway!

Sitting Bull sprang up and, throwing aside the door flap of the council lodge, limped as fast as he could toward his own tipi, not far off. It was nearest to the soldiers. While he was hurrying, there was a yell of alarm. A man was pointing, yelling, and everyone turned to look where he pointed—south—upriver. There in the bottoms they saw a tower of dust coming, and in it, as it came, the blue shirts of soldiers, the heads of horses! While they stared, the column of soldiers widened into a line, smoke bloomed from its front, and they heard the snarl of the carbines.

Sitting Bull hurried into his tipi to get his arms. He had a revolver, calibre .45, and an 1873 model carbine Winchester, .44, center fire, with one band. Both weapons were gifts from his nephew, White Bull. In the tent he found One Bull bent on the same errand. One Bull had a muzzle-loader, but he knew it would be useless in hand-to-hand fighting. He caught up his stone-headed war club, and offered the gun to Sitting Bull. Already the bullets were whining overhead, and one of the tent poles was splintered above them.

One Bull was just twenty-three. "Uncle," he said, "I am going to fight."

"Good," said Sitting Bull. "Go ahead. Fear nothing. Go right straight in."

Taking his own shield from its buckskin case, he flung the carrying-strap over One Bull's head, so that it protected his chest. Together they ran out of the lodge. Sitting Bull was buckling on his cartridge belt. Already someone had caught up his war horse—the famous black with white face and stockings given him by Makes-Room. Sitting Bull leaped upon its bare back.

All around him was confusion. Old men were yelling advice, young men dashing away to catch their horses, women and children rushing off afoot and on horseback to the north end of that three-mile camp, fleeing from the soldiers. They left their tents standing, grabbed their babies, called their older children, and hurried away, frightened girls shrinking under their shawls, matrons puffing for breath, hobbling old women, wrinkled and peering, with their sticks, making off as best they could, crying children, lost children, dogs getting in everybody's way and being kicked for their pains, nervous horses resisting the tug of the reins, and over all the sound of the shooting. First of all, Sitting Bull saw that his old mother was safely mounted and on her way.

Four Horns was there, old as he was, on a mixed roan-and-bay horse, armed with a bow and arrows. No newfangled firearms for that old-timer! And now White Bull, out with his horses to the north of the Sans Arc camp, had seen the soldiers coming, mounted his war horse, and, carrying his Winchester, came dashing down to his uncle's camp. Every man able to fight was mounted and ready by that time, and White Bull could hear Sitting Bull's resonant bellow: "Be brave, boys. It will be a hard time. Be brave!"

The Hunkpapa stood their ground bravely, covering the retreat of their women and children down the flat. Veterans of that fight say, "It was sure hard luck for Major Reno that he struck the Hunkpapa camp first."

White-Hair-on-Face had had to run and catch his pony. Now he came galloping back to take part in the fighting. He could see Sitting Bull out in front of all the warriors, shouting to them. Everybody was yelling and giving orders; nobody was listening. White-Hair-on-Face met his mother-in-law running to safety; she was dragging one child by the hand. He gave her his horse. She put the little fellow behind her, the big girl in front, and away they all went—three of them on one horse.

As fast as the Sioux were mounted, they rode out to meet the soldiers on the flat. Those who had guns fired occasionally, falling back slowly, trying to cover the retreat of the women streaming to the north. Every moment reinforcements came up, and the firing grew constantly heavier, until there were enough Indians to stop the soldiers in their tracks. While this was going on, the Sioux on the right flank swept down on the Ree scouts, recaptured the pony herd they had taken, and sent the Rees flying. Some of those Rees were so scared of Sitting Bull's Boys that they did not stop running for two days! Circling Hawk was in the thick of this part of the fight.

And now the soldiers stopped sure enough, got off their horses and began to shoot and fight on foot. The Sioux took courage. The women and children were safe. They charged on the soldiers from the west side, as well as from the north, and the soldiers began to give way and drop back eastward into the timber. Pretty soon their line was behind a cutbank among the trees, where the river bed used to be, and they were facing southwest. The Sioux were all around them then.

Bob-Tail-Bull had come out of his tipi when the fighting began. Somebody shot at him and he dodged back. But by this time he had caught his pony, got his gun, and was out in front with the other men. Said he, "The first person I saw there was Sitting Bull, yelling encouragement."

Sitting Bull was puzzled by Reno's behavior. He had come against that huge camp with a handful, and then—instead of charging, the only way he could hope to fight his way through—he had dismounted his men and was fighting them afoot. Sitting Bull thought Reno was acting like a fool. But Sitting Bull was much too intelligent to underestimate his enemy. He wondered what was up. Therefore he remained with the warriors to the north of the troops, between the camp and the enemy. "Look out!" he yelled, "there must be some trick about this."

Meanwhile, One Bull was over on the west side of the soldiers with other young men. As Sitting Bull's nephew, wearing his shield, he considered himself their leader. As the troops fell back toward the cutbank and the timber, these young men charged the soldiers. One Bull, young Kansu, Swift Bear (Crow King's brother), young Black Moon, and a lad named White Bull (not Sitting Bull's nephew) led that charge. While the troops on the flanks ran for the trees, the troop in the middle held its ground and kept shooting for a while. Then they fell back, too.

The young men swung past them and started back for the Indian line. They lay close to the necks of their ponies to avoid being shot. But it was no use. Good Bear Boy was shot from his horse, then Black Moon went down, and right away White Bull was killed. One Bull saw Good Bear Boy fall, and told Looking Elk to save him. Looking Elk paid no attention. Good Bear Boy was not dead, he was trying to crawl back to his friends. One Bull turned back, got off his horse, helped his friend up across the animal, and mounted behind him. The wounded man was bleeding freely, and very soon the whole front of

One Bull's clothes was covered with blood. Good Bear Boy was shot through the thighs, both legs, the left being broken.

When One Bull had reached what he thought a place of safety, he dismounted and got ready to help his friend down. As he did so, the horse turned broadside to the soldiers and was shot in the hind leg. One Bull led the horse to the rear, keeping in front of it. He was in a bad place, right between the soldiers and the Indians. He kept in front of the horse because he thought the soldiers had more ammunition than the Sioux. As soon as he had placed Good Bear Boy in the hands of friends, he hurried back to the battle.

By that time the soldiers in the timber had mounted their horses, dashed from the trees, and were galloping up the west bank of the river as hard as they could go, all strung out, looking for a place to cross. The moment Sitting Bull saw them running like that, without order, every man for himself, he knew that Reno's attack on the village had not been inspired by unusual bravery. He guessed the answer to his puzzle then: those soldiers had been *waiting* for somebody to come and help them; that was why they fought on foot and took cover in the trees. Right away Sitting Bull surmised that there was another war party of enemies somewhere around. After that he did not urge the young men to rush the soldiers.

But they needed no urging. They were all over those fleeing troopers, killing them with war clubs and the butts of their guns, shooting arrows into them, riding them down. "We killed the soldiers easy; it was just like running buffalo. One blow killed them," said the old men. "They were shot in the back; they offered no resistance." Away they went, plunging through the river, and up the steep, sprawling ridges of that high bluff, to find a breathing space on top. Thirty of them lay dead and a few had been left in the timber. It was an utter rout, due to bad leadership. Reno had never fought Indians before.

In this part of the fighting, Dog-with-Horns was killed and Chased-by-Owls mortally wounded. The Indians chased the soldiers right to the bank of the river, and some of them rode their ponies over. Sitting Bull could not stop them.

"In this fight there was no leader; all were brave," they told me.

"There was no need to give orders; everybody knew what to do—stop the soldiers, save the ponies, protect the women and children." And so every man did as he thought best. Everybody shouted suggestions and encouragement; nobody paid much attention. No one was in command. "I was not standing around looking on; I was shooting." That is what they told me. There must have been a thousand warriors against Reno's three troops. Benteen, who saw them chasing Reno, estimated nine hundred.

Just then One Bull came up with others and reached the bank of the river. Some of the warriors had crossed, and the last of the soldiers were scrambling up the steep bluffs. Last of all went four horse holders who had been left behind. One Bull and his comrades, hot with victory, started to plunge into the stream, ford it, and kill these. But Sitting Bull objected. "Let them go!" he yelled. "Let them go! Let them live to tell the truth about this battle." He wanted the white men to know that this fight had been begun by the soldiers, not the Sioux. They came shooting and fired the first shot. He was sick and tired of being blamed for the sins of others. Everything that went wrong in the Sioux country was laid at his door.

One Bull obeyed. He turned back, and his uncle saw that he was all covered with blood. This was the blood of Good Bear Boy, but Sitting Bull did not know that. He said, "Nephew, you are wounded. You had better go back and have someone attend to your wounds."

One Bull laughed, explained that he was unhurt. Then Sitting Bull, with that anxiety lifted from his mind, at once reverted to the suspicion raised in his mind by Reno's strange behavior. Said he, "Then you had better go back and help protect the women and children." Those women and children had run a long way north by that time; they must be stopped, rounded up, and guarded. They might need protection. Sitting Bull mounted and rode north toward the abandoned camp.

As he approached the end of the brush near the prairie-dog town, he came upon the Negro, "Teat" Isaiah Dorman. Two Bull, Shoots-Walking, and several others rode up at the same time. "Teat" was badly wounded, but still able to talk. He spoke Sioux, and was well-liked by the Indians. He had joined the troops as interpreter because, he said, he wanted to see that western country once more before he died. And now, when he saw the Sioux all around him, he pleaded with them, "My friends, you have already killed me; don't count *coup* on me." He had been shot early in the fight.

Sitting Bull arrived just then, recognized "Teat" and said, "Don't kill that man; he is a friend of mine." The Negro asked for water, and Sitting Bull took his cup of polished black buffalo horn, got some water, and gave him to drink. Immediately after, Isaiah died. The warriors rode away. Afterward, some spiteful woman found the Negro's body and mutilated it with her butcher knife.

Sitting Bull rode north through the abandoned camps, one after the other. The tents stood empty and forlorn, their gaping doors open to the hungry, prowling dogs which sneaked in looking for meat, hardly able to believe that their good luck was real, and running off guiltily when they heard the hoofbeats of the black war horse. Here and there lay a dead horse where some stray bullet had found it. Sitting Bull hurried on up the flat to the north and west. He could see the women and children gathered there, boys and old men trying to keep them together. By this time they had learned that the soldiers had been routed upriver and were streaming back to their tents again.

But just then another war party of enemies was seen upon the bluffs across the river to the east, Custer's five companies trotting along the ridge, apparently looking for a place to cross. Sitting Bull's hunch was justified: there *was* a second war party!

Instantly, the women who had started back to the tents ran out on the prairie again, and were gathered together on the flat opposite Custer, but somewhat to the southwest, perhaps half a mile from the river. Sitting Bull and other men tried to hold them there. There were plenty of men to do this; though every able-bodied man who could get there in time had defended the camp against Reno, not half the warriors in camp joined the attack on Custer.

Meanwhile, One Bull was dashing downriver on the east bank with the other young men to meet this new danger. They had just killed many soldiers, they were confident they could kill many more. Away they went, whipping each other's horses, riding like mad.

But suddenly One Bull remembered the orders of his uncle, Sitting Bull. Reining up, he splashed his pony through the stream to the west side, and galloped northward to the horde of women on the flat, not far from the Cheyenne camp circle. They had stopped running now. Sitting Bull was there with a number of other warriors. He sat on his black war horse, his quirt dangling, looking on at the battle across the river.

The white soldiers were trotting along the hilltop in a cloud of dust, making toward the ford. Four Cheyennes rode out to face them, only four at first. But those four—Bob-Tail-Horse was one—seemed to daunt them. At any rate, the soldiers stopped. Shooting began. The smoke rolled down the hill in a dense cloud. The Indians were all around, more and more of them. What with the dust and the smoke there was not much to see.

One Bull was eager to go and join the fighting. He urged his uncle to go with him. But Sitting Bull replied: "No. Stay here and help protect the women. Perhaps there is another war party of enemies coming. There are plenty of Indians yonder to take care of those." By "those," of course, he meant Custer's immediate command. Once Sitting Bull's suspicions were aroused, they did not readily sleep again. Having been greatly puzzled by Reno's strange behavior, he was even more puzzled by Custer's. Why, *why*, had he halted just when he should have charged? Unless he was waiting for someone. Once more, Sitting Bull's hunch was right. If Benteen had not been delayed, he might have struck the village from the west side.

Such skill in forecasting the enemy's movements, such canny sizing-up of a situation, were what made Sitting Bull peerless as a leader of the warlike Sioux. Brave men were plenty in their camps: but a man who combined intelligence and skill and courage as Sitting Bull did was hardly to be found. He knew, as Napoleon knew—and said—that "battles are won by the power of the mind."

Sitting Bull was too seasoned a warrior to become excited when there was no need. He knew what would happen. Over beyond the river, up on the tumbled ridges, under that haze of smoke and dust, it was happening very swiftly. Cheyennes and Sioux were making quick work of Custer's tired troopers.

Some of the cavalry units were still mounted and moving when the horde of mounted Indians caught up with them, and the warriors at their backs had them at a great disadvantage.

Among others, Sitting Bull's nephew, White Bull, side by side with Crazy Horse, Iron Lightning, Owns-Horn, and others were jerking soldiers off their horses, counting *coups*, capturing guns and horses and dashing between and around the troops in bravado.

But once all the soldiers had dismounted and let their horses go, it was quite the other way around. Then the soldiers' fire power quickly blasted the Indians out of their saddles.

Then for a time it was all shooting, and after the Indians captured the soldiers' horses and found pistols and ammunition in their saddlebags, the firing increased in volume. Then some of the soldiers were killed, or retreated, and the Indians obtained carbines and cartridge belts, advanced up the coulees and ravines and the firing grew hotter and hotter. But as the number of Indians' guns increased, the number of troopers diminished, and the Indians rushed in to fight hand to hand. White Bull had circled around the last group of soldiers until he was on the east side just where the monument stands now. There were only about twenty soldiers on their feet.

At this time White Bull, though only twenty-six years old, had already taken part in nineteen engagements. Ten of these were with white men,[1] one with government Indian scouts,[2] and the rest with other Indian enemy tribes.[3]

He had counted seven *coups*, six of them "firsts", and had taken

[1] Killdeer Mountain, July 25, 1864; Battle of the Badlands, August 19, 1864; attacks on Powder River Expedition, summer of 1865; Fort Phil Kearny "massacre" or Fetterman Fight, December 21, 1866; the Wagon Box Fight, August 2, 1867; the Baker Fight, April 14, 1872; raids on the white buffalo hunters near the Big Bend of the Yellowstone, and on a railroad train in Nebraska in 1876.

[2] On the Bozeman Trail at Pumpkin Buttes near Fort Reno.

[3] Crows, Rees, Flatheads, Assiniboins, Shoshoni, Metis or Bois Brûlés (Red River half-bloods).

168

two scalps, killed three enemies, wounded one, shot three enemy horses, rescued six wounded comrades and recovered one dead body under fire. He had captured and spared an enemy Assiniboin woman and her husband, had stolen forty-five head of enemy horses, and been hit twice in battle by bullets, and had had a horse shot under him.

Three different warrior societies had invited him to become a member, and he had been elected Drum Keeper of the Fox Soldiers. On two occasions he had undergone the voluntary tortures of the Sun Dance. Also he had thrice been given a new name because of brave deeds.

He had the assurance of a successful warrior, the son and nephew of great chiefs. In addition to these distinctions, young White Bull had killed twenty-three bears, some of them grizzlies—the first at only eleven years of age. By the time of the Custer fight, he had been married nine times and had a number of children. His naturally strong, aggressive character is shown by the fact that the sacred vision he had as a boy was a dream of the Thunder. And he had just finished striking four *coups*.

Of course, White Bull had no idea what regiment or soldier chief he was fighting with. He had never seen Custer—whom the Indians called *Pe-hin Hanska* (Head Hair Long or Long Hair)—in his life.

On the day of his death General Custer was considered the most dashing and successful cavalry officer in the army. During the Civil War, he had distinguished himself repeatedly, and his division had led the van in the pursuit of General Lee's forces. It was to him that the Confederates brought their white flag just before Lee's surrender. General Sheridan reported, "I know of no one whose efforts have contributed more to this happy result than those of Custer." To Custer was given the table on which Grant wrote the terms of surrender. He was celebrated as "the boy general" who had never lost a gun or a color. "Custer's luck" was a proverb in the army.

And so far there was none to match him as an Indian fighter. Though in disgrace with President Grant at that time, his services had been deemed indispensable in the campaign against Sitting Bull. He understood Plains Indians because, like them, he loved glory.

169

He had been the second strongest man in his class at West Point and remained to the end a man of extraordinary vigor. Lithe, slender, with broad shoulders, he was a fine horseman and good shot, standing six feet in his boots and weighing about 165 pounds. He could ride all day, carry on his duties until midnight, then scribble long letters to his wife—one of them running to eighty pages—and still be "r'aring to go" in the morning.

Like White Bull, Custer was naturally hardy, daring, aggressive and self-confident. Neither man touched liquor. Custer did not even use tobacco; White Bull sometimes smoked his pipe. Custer was taller than the Indian—who stood only five feet, eight inches in his moccasins—and probably outweighed White Bull. But the Indian was fully ten years younger, and had had a good night's sleep. Custer had been marching much of the night in the vain hope of surprising the Sioux.

Custer was stronger than White Bull, but the Indian had far more experience of hand-to-hand fighting than the officer. Here is how White Bull described their struggle:

"I charged in. A tall, well-built soldier with yellow hair and mustache saw me coming and tried to bluff me, aiming his rifle at me. But when I rushed him, he threw his rifle at me without shooting. I dodged it. We grabbed each other and wrestled there in the dust and smoke. It was like fighting in a fog. This soldier was very strong and brave. He tried to wrench my rifle from me, and nearly did it. I lashed him across the face with my quirt, striking the *coup*. He let go, then grabbed my gun with both hands until I struck him again.

"But the tall soldier fought hard. He was desperate. He hit me with his fists on the jaw and shoulders, then grabbed my long braids with both hands, pulled my face close and tried to bite my nose off. I yelled for help: 'Hey, hey, come over and help me!' I thought that soldier would kill me.

"Bear Lice and Crow Boy heard me call and came running. These friends tried to hit the soldier. But we were whirling around, back and forth, so that most of their blows hit me. They knocked me dizzy. I yelled as loud as I could to scare my enemy, but he would not let go. Finally I broke free.

THE VALLEY OF THE LITTLE BIG HORN
(Roahen Photograph)

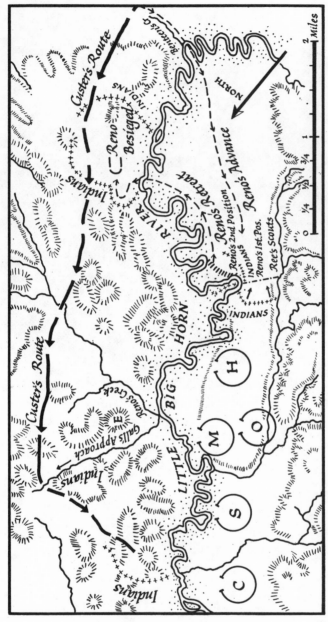

MAP OF CUSTER'S LAST BATTLE

The principal camp circles of the Indians are shown as given by Chief Joseph White Bull. H—Hunkpapa Sioux circle, in which some Blackfeet Sioux and Two Kettle Sioux were also encamped (300 lodges). M—Minniconjou camp (400–500 lodges). O—Oglala Sioux (400–500 lodges). S—Sans Arc Sioux (400–500 lodges). C—Cheyenne circle, containing some Arapaho (300–500 lodges). E—Hill where Sergeant Butler was killed.

"He drew his pistol. I wrenched it out of his hand and struck him with it three or four times on the head, knocked him over, shot him in the head and fired at his heart. I took his pistol and cartridge belt. Hawk-Stays-Up struck second on his body.

"*Ho hechetu!* That *was* a fight, a *hard* fight. But it was a glorious battle, I enjoyed it. I was picking up head feathers right and left that day.

"Now I was between the river and the soldiers on the hill. There were not many left. All at once ten of them jumped up and started down the gully where I was, shooting all the time. In front, two soldiers were leading, one of them wounded and bleeding from the mouth. I and a Cheyenne waited for them. When they came close I shot one. The Cheyenne shot the other. We both ran forward to count the *coups*. I struck first on one soldier, but the Cheyenne beat me to the other one. I got only the second *coup* on that enemy. The eight soldiers left kept on coming. I had to get out of the gully onto the ridge. Taking the dead soldier's gun, I started up the hill. Suddenly I stumbled and fell. My leg was numb. I looked for wounds but could not find any, until I saw that my ankle was swollen. The skin was not broken, only bruised. I must have been hit by a spent bullet. I found a shallow ditch, crawled into it and lay there till all the soldiers were killed. At the time I stopped fighting, only ten soldiers were on their feet. They were the last ones alive. The fight began before it was time for the midday watering of the ponies and only lasted about an hour. There were very few cartridges in the belts I took from the soldiers."

White Bull laughs at the yarns about the soldiers committing mass suicide. Said he, "The soldiers looked tired, but they fought to the end."

"I waited where I was until my friend With Horns came along and found me. He put me on his horse and led it back across the river. The people were some distance west on the flat, they had not had time to move their tipis."

After White Bull had rested awhile and had his wound dressed, he asked for his horse and rode across the river to get his leggings and saddle. He then rode over the battlefield to see the dead. By that time most of the bodies had been stripped, but he saw no one mutilating the dead. It must have been relatives of the young men killed in the fight who went up there afterwards and did that.

"On the hill top, I met my relative Bad Juice [Bad Soup]. He had been around Fort Abraham Lincoln and knew Long Hair by sight. When we came to the tall soldier lying on his back naked, Bad Soup pointed him out and said, "Long Hair thought he was the greatest man in the world. Now he lies there.""

"Well," I said, "if that is Long Hair, I am the man who killed him." Nobody scalped Long Hair, because his hair was cut short.

It was not until some time after the battle that Sitting Bull learned who had led the soldiers against him. We have his own statement for this, and all his old Hunkpapa friends and relatives say the same. This yarn is one of the many legends which have grown up about the mystery of Custer's death. As the old-timers put it, "There are too many tongues."

The story goes that all the Indians knew Custer (just when or how is not explained) and that they failed to strip or scalp or mutilate him because they respected him so. The yarn shows a complete ignorance of Sioux customs. For its was precisely the bravest enemy who was most likely to be cut to pieces—if only because he made the most trouble. That day, moreover, the Sioux had no cause to single out any one man as particularly brave—all the soldiers were brave, and fought hard to the last. The only man mentioned as braver than the rest is Sergeant Butler, who ran out to one side and stood off the Indians singlehanded for a long time. That man, with the three stripes on his sleeve, they say he was the bravest of all.

Moreover, the dead soldiers were so grimy with powder smoke and dust that their own friends could hardly identify them when they reached the battlefield, and Custer had his hair cut. And seeing that he was the man who had opened the Black Hills to white settlement, he was the last officer in the army to be admired or respected by the Sioux. He was the man who, as Swift Bear put it to the Commission, made "that thieves' road." Besides, Custer *was* stripped. And nearly half the bodies found around him were also unscalped, unmarred. It was only down near the Hunkpapa camp, where the women returned after Reno was routed, that all the enemy bodies were mutilated.[4]

Many stories are current about Custer's horse, also. One day, not long after this fight, White Bull drove his ponies to water. At the watering place he saw a fine sorrel in the bunch of Sounds-the-Ground-as-He-Walks, a Santee, and a son of Inkpaduta. White Bull asked if it was a good horse. The Santee answered, "I know it is a good horse, for it used to be Long Hair's."

When the fighting was over, Sitting Bull rode across the river and asked, "Are they all killed?" Someone answered, "Yes."

Sitting Bull said, "Let's go back to camp."

The dead horses and soldiers at the south end of the camp became so offensive in the heat that the Hunkpapa moved downriver, and some of the Indians went over on the grassy benches west of the bottoms and rigged up temporary shelters there. The wounded had to be cared for and the dead laid away. As soon as this work was well under way and the camp was full of warriors again, Sitting Bull galloped off with others to have a shot at the soldiers entrenched with Reno on top of the bluff. He found the soldiers had dug rifle pits and put their horses and mules in the middle. Earlier in the day some of the mules had run down the bluff and the young men caught them, finding ammunition in the packs. But Two Moon said that they did not catch all these runaways, as they would get scared when they smelled the Indians and run back up again. When Sitting Bull arrived, the Indians were assembled on the south and to the northeast of the whites. The chiefs had ordered the young men to leave a lane open on the east side, in case the soldiers wished to leave the country.

White Bull, the chief's nephew, was with the Indians to the northeast—quite a way from the soldiers, on higher ground. Sitting Bull was with those to the south, a good deal nearer. There was some charging back and forth that day, and Sitting Bull charged with the rest. Two soldiers got separated from the others, and Sitting Bull's men killed them. Shell-Ear-Ring and Snake Creek ran out to them and counted *coup*. In the group with White Bull there was a man named Dog's-

[4] For extent of mutilations, consult Byrne, *Soldiers of the Plains*, 106 ff., 245–46.

Back-Bone. He kept warning his comrades, "Look out, now, boys. Those soldiers are a good way off, but their bullets are coming over mighty fierce." Just as he finished saying this, a ball hit him in the forehead; he was shot dead.

All that evening the Indians kept up a hot fire on the soldiers, and official reports show that they did not shoot in vain: Reno lost eighteen killed and forty-six wounded. The young men kept on shooting until it got dark, and Sioux and Cheyennes hung around all night, and scared Reno's scouts back when they tried to get away.

Sitting Bull returned to camp. The soldiers on the hill imagined they heard scalp dances going on down in the bottoms; but by all accounts they were in a very anxious and excited condition. There were no scalp dances that night; old Sioux are indignant at such an indecent suggestion. Too many Sioux warriors had fallen; there were too many mourners in the camps. That was no time for rejoicing. It was never the custom to hold a victory dance, under such circumstances, until after four days had elapsed and the mourners had given permission. Sitting Bull mourned with the others. Said he, "My heart is full of sorrow that so many were killed on each side, but when they compel us to fight, we must fight." And he commanded, "Tonight we shall mourn for our dead, and for those brave white men lying up yonder on the hillside." So it was done.

The racket those frightened soldiers on the bluff heard that night was the wailing of the mourners, and the shouting and hallooing of people collecting their belongings and moving camp in the dark, the songs of mourning, and all the noisy grief to which the Indian mourner abandons himself. A great many women were gashing themselves and wailing that night. Added to this was the hullabaloo made by some agency Indians, who had got drunk on the whiskey found in the dead soldiers' canteens; they fired wanton volleys at the stars.

Sitting Bull had other reasons for grief that evening. The Indians had not obeyed his warning, they had taken the spoils, had carried off the guns, horses, clothing, everything. His own immediate following touched nothing, but those of other bands did; no man could have controlled them in the excitement of that victory. A stubborn and stiff-necked generation. Sitting Bull said, "Because you have taken the spoils, henceforth you will covet the white man's goods, you will be at his mercy, you will starve at his hands." And he added, "The soldiers will crush you."

Few of Sitting Bull's band have any souvenirs from that battle. But One Bull, his nephew, afterward married a woman of another band, and she brought into his home a saddlebag taken from the soldiers. For nearly fifty years it was used as a valise in her family. It is now in my possession.

They had to make haste with the burials that evening. It was so hot and the flies were so fierce that even during the little time they were fighting with "Long Hair," the bodies of those killed at the south end of the camp had become flyblown.

Next morning, as soon as it was light, the Indians gathered in great force and began pouring a terrific fire upon Reno's entrenchment. The Indians could see that the horses were no longer saddled, but the troopers had dug such deep rifle pits that the men were out of sight. Sitting Bull was with his "boys" up there. The young men were delighted with the guns and ammunition they had captured. Many of them had never used a breech-loader before, or fixed ammunition. The shiny cartridges pleased them. Altogether, they had taken the carbines and pistols of more than two hundred dead soldiers, and perhaps fifty rounds for each gun from the saddlebags and cartridge belts. Custer's men carried one hundred rounds each into the fight. It appears that Reno's men used up more than half their ammunition in the bottoms, since they begged Benteen's men to supply them when he arrived soon after they reached the bluff. Custer's men had only what they carried in their belts, after their horses stampeded with the saddlebags. Probably the Indians took about ten thousand rounds: some of this was used up in fighting Custer, some in celebrating the victory or shooting into the dead after the fight. But they had plenty left to make Reno's position uncomfortable. He, of course, had all the twenty-four thousand rounds brought in by the pack-train.[5]

[5] For these figures I am indebted to Colonel Charles Francis Bates, the Custer historian.

About the middle of the morning, some of the Indians rushed the trenches from the south, up the steep slope, right across the open. It was nearly as steep as a house-roof, and there was not a shred of cover. Long Road reached the trench, struck a soldier with his *coup*-stick, and started back. Right there they shot him. He was a brave man: one of Lieutenant Gibson's men killed him. There is a marker on the battlefield where he fell.

The soldiers were in a tight place. Everybody, both whites and Indians, agree that, if the Indians had charged all at once from all sides, a retreat must have followed, and a second retreat under Reno must have become a rout. There was no place to run to: every soldier would have been rubbed out. Many have wondered why the Sioux let these soldiers go. The books say that they stopped fighting because they feared the troops coming with "Red Nose" Gibbon and "Star" Terry. But that is nonsense: the Indians could easily have killed all of Reno's men before the infantry arrived, and then have run away on their fleet ponies. Long before noon the women were already striking the tents.

The truth has never been told about this: it was Sitting Bull who saved Reno.

About noon he came to the Sioux line again. He told the young men to stop shooting. "That's enough," he yelled, "let them go! Let them live, they are trying to live. They came against us, and we have killed a few. If we kill them all, they will send a bigger army against us."

Sitting Bull sent Knife King to carry this order all along the Indian lines. While Knife King was shouting Sitting Bull's commands, a soldier suddenly rose up, fired, and shot Knife King through the body. However, Knife King survived.

The young men were tired, thirsty, hungry; they were glad to go. White Bull had already gone back to camp and was taking a nap after his night's work. When the women took the tipi down, he woke up, and with two other young men rode north to raid the coming soldiers' horse herd. They were successful; they captured seven horses. When he got back, he found the camp gone, but followed the trail, and overtook it near the Big Horn Mountains. There the Indians held their first victory dance. By that time the prairie was all ablaze, sending up great volumes of smoke visible for many miles around. As usual after a great victory the Indians had, as they say, "set the prairie afire." This great smoke signal informed every Indian in that region that Sitting Bull was victor.

The Custer battle was over. No captives had been taken, there was no torture. A whole library of fantastic romance has been woven about this disaster to American arms. But the only men who *knew* what happened that day were the Sioux and Cheyenne survivors. Their testimony is abundant, and in agreement, so far as the stories of eyewitnesses can be. All the details I have given here could be proved by from two to twenty eyewitnesses.

The mystery of Custer's disaster naturally enough gave birth to many legends. Most of these have already been discounted by the judicious, but inasmuch as most of them have some bearing on Sitting Bull, it may do no harm to discuss them here.

Journalists made wild surmises, and palmed them off on the public as facts; they elaborated some Indian's chance remark into a chapter, though it may have been half-comprehended or wholly misunderstood. Many of these legends were—very naturally—to the discredit of Sitting Bull, General Custer's archenemy. Otherwise, they would not have been popular during the Sioux campaigns.

Thus, they said he was making medicine during the battle, "skulking in the hills." Those defamers could not foresee that the science of ethnology would be developed and explode their lie. They said that he ran away from the fight, that Gall was in command, and so on for pages and pages. They said that he was so excited that he forgot to take his small son with him, and that the child was therefore named The-One-Who-Was-Left.

All this is poppycock. The boy's name, properly translated, means Left-on-the-Battle-Field. It was given him by Four Horns, Sitting Bull's uncle, in commemoration of the time when he himself had been left for dead on the field during a fight with the Crows, an event so famous that it was used to mark the year 1843 in the Hunkpapa calendar.

SITTING BULL

Even if Sitting Bull had run away from the fight (as he could not, being lame), even if it had been the custom to name children for events in their own personal lives (as it was not), can anyone believe that Sitting Bull would have named his own son in commemoration of his cowardice? Anybody who knows the old-time Sioux knows that, if a man does one disgraceful deed, he is thereafter dropped like a hot brick. A coward could no more have gone on leading the warlike Sioux and Cheyennes than a man who cheated at cards could be Prime Minister of England. It is a sheer impossibility.

The popular legend of Sitting Bull is about as much like the real thing as that highly colored lithograph of *Custer's Last Stand* which in the good old days used to hang on the wall of every barroom in the United States. Gaudy, but highly inaccurate.

As for Gall and Crazy Horse, reputed generals of the Indian forces, they were undoubtedly brave soldiers, first-class fighting men—none better. But neither of them was equipped to plan a campaign or lead a nation. When they saw an enemy, they charged: that was the whole of their strategy. Moreover, Two Moon was chief of the Cheyenne contingent, not Crazy Horse; Sitting Bull, not Gall, of the Sioux. Such authority as there was was vested in these men. Gall was a man of action, merely. Old Hunkpapa—Gall was a Hunkpapa—are startled into laughter when they learn that the white men's histories say Gall was commander in that fight. Not one in five of my informants even knew that he was on the ground.

Of course he was there—bold as a lion; of course he led some charges, led his own group. But in a defensive fight like that on the Little Big Horn, there could be no commander, no director: every man fought for and by himself, or with a small group of friends. There were too many bands to follow one leader, and things moved too rapidly.

There was no trap laid, no strategy. Gall, at the south end of camp when Custer came, naturally took the nearest way, up the ravine, to meet him. Two Moon and Crazy Horse, with their own camps in mind, rushed up to meet Custer at the north end. Nothing could have saved Custer from such a battle-hungry horde—after he stopped.

Had there been anything like generalship on the part of Gall and Crazy Horse they would surely have captured the pack train, laden with twenty-four thousand rounds of ammunition, a rich prize, before it could join Reno on his hill. It will not do to explain the actions of Indians or frontiersmen (who adopted their methods) by the science of warfare as taught at West Point. It took no more science to destroy Custer than it did to destroy Braddock. It took courage, men: and the camp of Sitting Bull was full of both.

Plains Indians could not wage war by plan. They had no officers of definite ranks and functions, no service of supply or communication, no ordnance, no commissary or transport, no discipline, no pay chest, no courts-martial. It is noteworthy that they *never* awarded any honors for staff work: the only way to win honor was to ride in and strike the enemy, capture a horse or a weapon, or rescue a friend in distress. On the rare occasions when they did have a plan, some ambitious young man was sure to launch a premature attack, and win all the honors away from the older men. And if the young man succeeded, no one dreamed of censuring him for disobeying orders. In a sudden defensive battle like that on the Little Big Horn, no planning was possible.

It so happened that Gall was asked to go over the field ten years later and narrate his story of that fight. He did so—quite honestly—and the officers who listened to the man's story of his own deeds were apparently unaware that an old-time Indian's account of a battle inevitably takes the form of an autobiography; the moment he departs from firsthand knowledge or ventures upon generalizations or suppositions he risks being branded a liar by his fellow warriors. It is a safe bet that, had any other leading man been asked to speak as Gall was, his name would now adorn the history books as the great Indian leader on that fatal day.

Not that it matters. Sitting Bull's fame does not rest upon the death of Custer's five troops. Had he been twenty miles away shooting antelope that morning, he would still remain the greatest of the Sioux.

Another matter about which there has been some controversy is the number of Indians killed during the fighting on the Greasy Grass. Estimates vary. Chief White Bull, who long kept records (in the Sioux language) of the casualties of Indian forces in the fights in which he took part, gave the following list of names of Indians who fell there.

Early that morning away from the camp young Deeds was shot. In the fight with Reno in the valley two Minniconjou, Three Bear and Dog-With-Horns, were killed; also two Hunkpapa, Swift Bear and one White Bull; a Two-Kettle Sioux named Chased-by-Owls; an Oglala named White Eagle; Elk-Stands-on-Top (Standing Elk), a Sans Arc Sioux, and a Cheyenne, name unknown.

In the fight with Custer's immediate command: Of the Sans Arc Sioux, Long Dog, Elk Bear, Cloud Man, Kill-Him; of the Hunkpapa Sioux, Guts, Red Face, Hawk Man; of the Oglala Sioux, Many Lice, Bad-Light-Hair, Young Skunk; of the Cheyennes, Left Hand (son of Chief Ice), Owns-Red-Horse, Flying-By, Black Cloud, Swift Cloud, and Bearded Man (Mustache).

Two men were killed in the fight with Reno on the bluffs that afternoon: Dog's-Backbone (Minniconjou) and Long Road, a Sans Arc. Also the Sioux Young Bear, Black Fox, and Bear-With-Horn were killed (tribes not given). There were thirty in all.

Not all the bodies of Custer's men were found on the battlefield when the relief column arrived. It was long supposed that they had been lost in the quicksands of the river. But perhaps that is not the whole story. Willis Rowland told how, some years later, he and another Cheyenne found the bones of a man in a thicket fifteen miles east of the battlefield. No buttons, buckles, or other traces of clothing were with these bones. Rowland concluded that these were the bones of some soldier, who, having been knocked out and stripped by the Indians, revived, wandered away by night, and died of exposure or from the wounds he had received.

24. Council of War

THE NEWS of Long Hair's death sped to the agencies by moccasin telegraph and smoke signal. An Indian named Freighter rode day and night to carry the news to Standing Rock. Indians up and down the Missouri knew of the victory a week or ten days before white men heard of it. Young men swarmed away to join Sitting Bull's banners, and he was kept well informed of the vigorous preparations being made to crush him. The country was filling up with pony soldiers, walking soldiers, wagons and cannon. But Sitting Bull was ready to fight, if necessary. He told his new recruits, "Since spring we have killed a thousand whites; now we are done counting them. Let us strike again." He knew—none better—what must be the end of that struggle. *That* was why he had summoned the warriors in April—"to have one last big fight with the soldiers!"

To read the military reports, one would suppose that it was the operations of late summer, autumn, and winter that drove the Sioux to Canada. But already, in midsummer, Sitting Bull had held councils to plan a way of escape. La Framboise attended these councils; we have his report as well as that of the Indians. And we may be sure that, before the councils, Sitting Bull had prepared the ground by private talks. Some say Holy-Faced-Bear first suggested going to the British Possessions, some say Big Mane. But it was nothing new: the Santees had run there after the Minnesota Massacre, and were happy on the reserves granted them by the Red Coats.

"Friends," said Sitting Bull, "we can go nowhere without seeing the head of an American. Our land is small, it is like an island in a lake.

We have two ways to go now—to the land of the Grandmother [Queen Victoria], or to the land of the Spaniards."

The land of the Spaniards was a long way off—probably none of the Sioux had ever gone so far, though their friends the Southern Cheyennes raided there. Canada, however, was near by. Many of the older men had hunted there, and (only two generations back) all the Sioux had been British subjects. Many of the chiefs had silver medals bearing the image of George III, given to their grandfathers for fighting the Americans. Moreover, they had never had any trouble with the Red Coats.

Sitting Bull said: "We can find peace in the land of the Grandmother; we can sleep sound there, our women and children can lie down and feel safe. I do not understand why the Red Coats gave us and our country to the Americans. We are the Grandmother's children. And when we go across the Medicine Road [the boundary], we shall bury the hatchet. My own grandfather told me that the Red Coats were our people and good people, and that I must always trust them as friends."

There was really no choice: to go to Canada was to go home.

But Crazy Horse was not in agreement. He was a warrior, and nothing else; there was no career for him in Canada. He was not like Sitting Bull, bound to provide and look out for the poor and the helpless; he had no obligations other than to fight. Said he: "My friend, the soldiers are everywhere; the Indians are getting scattered, so that the soldiers can capture or kill them all. This is the end. All the time these soldiers will keep hunting us down. Some day I shall be killed. Well, all right. I am going south to get mine!"

Sitting Bull answered, "I do not wish to die yet."

Crazy Horse rode away toward the Big Horn Mountains, and hunted until his relative, Spotted Tail, came and persuaded him to surrender at Camp Robinson, Nebraska, in the spring. They say he went down there, expecting to be honored and made head chief of all the Sioux by the soldiers, but that they treated him like a captive, not a friend. He was invited to visit an army post, and then the commandant tried to throw him into the guardhouse. Crazy Horse resisted, and while they held him, a soldier stabbed him in the back with a bayonet. Somehow or other, nearly every first-rate man among the Sioux was "eliminated" after he made peace with the white men.

The band of Crazy Horse was one of the most warlike, the best armed. When his three hundred warriors surrendered, they turned in 117 guns.

When the Indians first left the Custer battlefield, the combined camps moved upriver and on to the Big Horn Mountains. There they had a victory dance on the fourth day after. Some white men (Lieutenant F. W. Sibley, Grouard, and others) were surrounded in these mountains, but got away in the night, July 7, leaving their horses behind. After a time the camps moved back again, and passed the place where Custer was killed. The soldiers had gone away, but the hills were littered with the bones of mules, horses, and white men. The Sioux observed that the soldiers had thrown a little earth upon the bellies of these skeletons, and that some of them were laid in pairs. The Indians say that the soldiers must have moved them, that they did not lie so close together when they fell. After hunting on the Rosebud for a time, they went on north to Tongue River, cut across eastward to the Powder, then to Beaver Creek and the Little Missouri. Up to that time (August) they had all remained together. But then they began to split up and drift apart: it was too hard to find meat when they were in such a big camp. Sitting Bull moved his tipis down to Grand River.

One day a stranger, Johnny Brughière (very dark, heavy-set, with long hair, good face, a brave man), rode into Sitting Bull's camp. Brughière was an Indian, but also a white man; he was fleeing from a charge of murder. He gave Sitting Bull his gun and horse, and called him "brother." Sitting Bull adopted him. Because Brughière wore big cowboy chaps, the Sioux called him Big Leggins.

Down on Grand River, Sitting Bull had a sad time. One of his sons was kicked in the head by a mule, and killed. The white men were trying to make a treaty and force the Sioux to cede the Black Hills, but Sitting Bull would have nothing to do with it. And while he was down on Grand River, refugees came running to tell him of the affair at Slim Buttes.

25. Slim Buttes

In that affair, surely, the army were the assailants, and the savages acted purely in self defense. —FINERTY, Warpath and Bivouac.

I T WAS the season when the wild plums ripen, September 9, 1876. All the agency Sioux were drifting back to the agencies with their packs full of dried meat, buffalo tongues, fresh and dried buffalo berries, wild cherries, plums, and all the staples and dainties which tickled the Indian palate. Sitting Bull still had a thousand warriors in his camp near Twin Buttes on Grand River: Oglala under Crazy Horse, Minniconjou, Sans Arc Sioux, and Hunkpapa. Other camps were not far off. Iron Shield (sometimes called American Horse), Thunder Hoop, and Looking-for-Enemy, with forty lodges of Oglala, Brûlé, and Minniconjou, were camped at Slim Buttes. *All these people were within the limits of the Great Sioux Reservation.* The council for the cession of the Black Hills was not begun until September 26, nor was the cession ratified until February 28, 1877. Many of these Indians had certificates of good conduct dated from the Spotted Tail Agency and signed by their agent; their only sin was that they had been unable to get back during the winter to an agency where there was nothing to eat, and that they had defended themselves against Custer. But General Three Stars Crook with two thousand men was plodding through the sticky gumbo of Owl (Moreau) River "to jump them before they could get to the agency."

One morning there was a cry of alarm in the camp of Sitting Bull's people. Someone was yelling, "There is trouble at the camp near Slim Buttes. A lot of people are getting killed."

Sitting Bull prepared for battle. He put on a war bonnet with two buffalo horns and a long mane of feathers down the back, took his carbine, and mounted a fast white horse. With him rode nearly a thousand warriors, as fast as they could go through the mud to Iron Shield. It was all of thirty miles to Slim Buttes.

About noon they met Fleece Bear, who gave more details: "Soldiers struck the camp before it was light this morning. They have killed Holy Eagle, another man and his wife, two old women, a tall girl, taken four prisoners, and wounded many people. They captured half our horses—two hundred or so—and burned the tents. Most of the people ran to the bluffs; some are in a ravine with soldiers all around; when I left they were still shooting."

Sitting Bull and his men rode hard for the Buttes. Very soon they met more fugitives—a man named Making-a-Horse, and his wife, Hawk. Said they, "The soldiers are killing all the children, big and little. They are still fighting down there." They said there were only a few soldiers fighting, two hundred, perhaps. The man's estimate of the number of soldiers (in fact one hundred and fifty) was fairly accurate at the time he left the fight, but before Sitting Bull could arrive—at one o'clock—Three Stars had come plodding through the gumbo with the reserves, and now outnumbered the forces of Sitting Bull two to one. The Sioux came riding up, just as the last of these reserves were dragging into camp.

As soon as the Sioux reached Slim Buttes, they could see the dark blue soldiers standing in a row, "like pine trees." As they advanced, the soldiers began to fire at them. Sitting Bull called out, "Be careful now. Those men are crack shots. Let High Crane go to them."

High Crane was a Minniconjou. He wore the skin of a black-tailed deer, with horns complete. This species of deer lives in the breaks and is very hard to kill; it is almost impossible to hit it. High Crane had the skin of this animal all over him. The skin of the head covered his head, and the legs of the skin were fastened to his elbows and knees. The horns, shaved thin, were braced by strings of red beads. Because he wore the skin of this animal, High Crane was bulletproof.

It was about two hundred yards to the soldier line. High Crane galloped toward it, and passed back and forth in front of the line several times. All the soldiers were shooting at him, but he was not hit. And when they saw they could not hit him, they backed off. They must have been afraid of his power. They moved back about a quarter of a mile. So far nobody had been hurt.

At the tail of the column, dragging along through the mud, were some broken-down cavalry horses, about a dozen, which had been abandoned, but were following along after the troops. Some of the Sioux charged on these, and ran them off. The soldiers shot at them, and they had a hard time making those old plugs run out of rifle-range. But nobody was hit. The Sioux always liked to get those big, strong American horses.

They could hear a woman crying and wailing from among the soldiers. She called to Sitting Bull: "My husband is dead, but my son is only wounded. I dragged him over yonder into that tall grass. Look after him. I am a captive, and must go with these soldiers."

They fought until late in the afternoon, but it was no use. There were too many soldiers. There was quite a lot of shooting going on near the camp, where Iron Shield and some of his people, men, women, and children, were being besieged in a hole in the ravine. Finally that shooting stopped. When the battle was over, Sitting Bull called his men together. "Bunch up now. We'll camp here tonight. Tomorrow we will see our dead relatives." They camped about five miles from the soldiers; it was a wet night.

In the soldier camp that afternoon there had been a bombardment of the ravine where Iron Shield was entrenched. When the attack was made, he and some others had got into a hole which the children had dug for fun in the bank, and, screened by some box elders, had fought off the soldiers, doing considerable damage. Finally, General Crook got the survivors to surrender, and Iron Shield came out, clutching his bowels, which protruded from his belly. The "enraged soldiers" wanted to kill everybody, and Finerty, the war correspondent, in his account of the affair, well indicates the inflamed state of the public mind towards Indians in the West: "Let the country blame or praise the General for his clemency. I simply record the affair as it occurred."

That night Ute John and some of the soldiers scalped the Indian dead.

American Horse (better known to the Indians as Iron Shield) was past all surgery. His woman bound his gaping wound with her shawl, and he sat calmly among his fellow captives, until he suddenly fell backward, dead. Before he died, he warned "Three Stars" that the other Indians would attack. Being an Oglala, he naturally mentioned the name of the great Oglala chief, Crazy Horse. Therefore the books all credit Crazy Horse with having attempted the relief of the besieged at Slim Buttes. But as a matter of fact, Sitting Bull was the leader.

Finerty tells how the Sioux "kept up perpetual motion, apparently encouraged by a warrior . . . who, mounted on a fleet white horse, galloped around the array and seemed to possess the power of ubiquity." Finerty supposed this must be Crazy Horse. It was Sitting Bull.

Next morning, Sitting Bull returned to the attack. The soldiers were moving out to the north, going toward the Black Hills. They crossed the creek and marched along. The Sioux swept around the buttes from the other side, and touched the soldiers as they came to the north of the buttes. Old Bull charged right through the soldier line, between two companies. As he dashed through, he saw Charging Bear and his wife, held captive by the soldiers, going with them. Charging Bear afterward joined the army scouts and fought against Sitting Bull's people. Old Bull was sorry for Charging Bear that morning, but his sympathy was wasted: Charging Bear was going along of his own free will.

The soldiers kept up such a heavy fire that the Sioux could not break their line. Sitting Bull was anxious to look after the dead and wounded left behind, and as soon as the soldiers had moved away from the Indian camp, he called off the warriors. They rode down among the burned lodges, looking for their relatives. That was what they had come for. His warriors—estimated by Finerty as now six to eight hundred—were far outnumbered by the troops.

Sitting Bull found one woman, sitting hunched up, with a blanket over her head. "Are you living?" he asked. There was no answer. He pulled the blanket from over her. It was Red Water Woman, a Minniconjou, sister to Chief Shot-Through-the-Hand. She was dead. Near by was an old man lying dead, and near him an old woman in a blue woolen dress, with her face in the mud, shot dead. In another place a young woman with a suckling child was lying with her baby. Both were dead; the child had been hit in the head. Moses Old Bull, Little Wounded, and others whom I interviewed saw all these things.

Under the cutbank they saw something moving. It was a wounded old woman, crawling on hands and knees. "Who are you?" they asked. She answered, "My brother's name is Swift Bear." She was crying. "I'm shot through the back, and I'm just about dead." Blue Stem, a man, was lying there also.

Under some hay, Sitting Bull found the body of a young girl, nine or ten years old. Dead too.

There was a woman in the ravine whose whole head had been blown off, clear down to the roof of her mouth; they did not know who she was. And right close by was another woman. The soldiers had shot her through the breasts. Little Wounded, a boy of five years, had seen his mother shot dead; he was wounded in the foot himself. When he told about this tragedy, there were tears in the eyes of his listeners.

But the worst thing of all on that battlefield was what they found where Little Eagle's daughter had tried to run away. She was about to become a mother, and when the shooting began, became frightened, and ran. She dropped her unborn child; it was lying there on the muddy ground, cold as the mud itself. But the mother was a Sioux woman, and hard to kill. She survived.

In the abandoned camp they found the captives, whom "Three Stars" Crook had turned loose with a message to their relatives under Sitting Bull. He had told them, first of all, that the "white men did not make war upon women and children." But at that moment, while Sitting Bull stood by with tears running down his cheeks, the humor of that statement was hardly appreciable. Next, they said, "Three Stars" told his captives he would let them go if they would tell Sitting Bull and the other men of the hunting bands that the army would keep on pegging away at all Indians in hostility until the last had been killed or made prisoner; that the Sioux would only be following the dictates of prudence in surrendering unconditionally at once, instead of "exposing their wives and children to accidents."

Sitting Bull said nothing. He was too deeply moved. There was much to be done. They gathered up those who were living, buried the dead, and started home again. The soldiers had found plenty of trophies of the Custer battle in the captured camp: clothing, money, letters, arms, McClellan saddles, and a guidon of the Seventh Cavalry. Sitting Bull had warned those people that, if they took the spoils, the soldiers would crush them. But they had no ears.

All summer long, Sitting Bull had been trying to interest other tribes in his plan for uniting to save their country from the white men —but in vain. All the nations around him were enemies. And in the country of the Grandmother (Queen Victoria) to the north, the Red Coats had persuaded the chiefs of the Blackfeet to make no alliance with Sitting Bull. His great camp was splitting up, his followers becoming tired of the endless fighting. It was clear that the plains to the south were overrun with soldiers. Sitting Bull moved his camp northward, intending to pass the winter in his old hunting grounds along the Yellowstone.

Afterward, he found out that it was his treacherous "brother" Sitting-with-Upraised-Hands (Frank Grouard) who had led the soldiers to the village of American Horse. Probably Sitting Bull wished he had killed the man the first day he saw him, instead of saving his life. But from that day things began to be all mixed up in Sioux country. The Cheyennes and even the Sioux began to go over to the soldiers and fight against Sitting Bull's following.

26. Bear Coat

The art of war among the white people is called strategy or tactics; when practiced by the Indians it is called treachery.—GENERAL NELSON A. MILES.

ALL THIS TIME the Grandfather had been sending more troops into Sioux country, and Colonel Nelson A. Miles, who had been so successful against the tribesmen of the Southern Plains in 1875, was ordered from Fort Leavenworth to command the forces then building the cantonment at the mouth of Tongue River. He reached the Yellowstone about the same time Sitting Bull did—the middle of October.

Sitting Bull's young men found a wagon train going up the river to the new cantonment, and one night a party of them hid in a ravine near the soldier camp, and towards morning opened so hot a fire upon the corral and yelled so loud that they stampeded forty-seven mules from under the noses of Captain C. W. Miner and four companies of infantry. Next morning the crippled train tried to advance, but the Indians made things so lively that it had to turn back. As soon as that happened, the Sioux let the wagons go. But the civilian teamsters were so terrified that they refused to go with the train a second time, and had to be replaced by enlisted men.

Forty-seven mules hardly squared accounts for the two hundred ponies taken from the Indian camp at Slim Buttes. Yet they were better than nothing: they were good army mules. Wherever the soldiers went, they ruined the hunting for miles around. The mules were taken to compensate the Sioux for that inconvenience.

One day soon after, Sitting Bull's nephew, White Bull, heard shooting over the hill. With eight other young men he rode to the sound of the guns. When they reached the hilltop, they saw the wagons, with many soldiers on foot all around them. The Sioux were riding around, trying to get at the wagons, but the soldiers would not let them. All the Sioux were on horseback. White Bull was riding a pinto, reared from a foal by his mother.

The wagons never stopped; they kept right on going. All the time the soldiers were charging back at the Indians, and then running to catch up with the wagons, and the Sioux were all around, circling and shooting and yelling. White Bull saw his friends firing into these soldiers. He did not know why, but he did not wait to ask questions. He charged right into the middle of the fight. Afterward someone told him, "We saw these wagons and rode down to ask them for something to eat, we were hungry. But the soldiers started shooting, and that's the way the fight began."

For a while, White Bull was in the thick of it. He rode up within seventy-five yards of the wagons, looking for a chance to charge in and count *coup*. The soldiers were firing all the time, and there were a lot of them, nearly two hundred. Then the first thing White Bull knew, he was shot. He was hit in the left upper arm. The bullet went clear through, and broke the bone.

The shock of the wound knocked White Bull out. But he stuck on his horse, and right away two of his friends came and led him back to camp. The only other Indian wounded in this skirmish was Broken Leg; he was shot in the sole of the foot. No Indians were killed. The fight did not last long.

Sometime after White Bull returned to the camp for first aid, Sitting Bull arrived on the battlefield. He made Big Leggins Brughière write a note in English, and sent a young man with it. It was left in sight of the soldiers in a cleft stick.

YELLOWSTONE
I want to know what you are doing on this road. You scare all the buffalo away. I want to hunt in this place. I want you to turn back from here. If

191

you don't, I will fight you again. I want you to leave what you have got here and turn back from here.

I am your friend

Sitting Bull

I mean all the rations you have got and some powder. Wish you would write as soon as you can.

That was the letter, ending—like Sitting Bull's speeches—with the essential item in the postscript. His old trick! Colonel E. S. Otis, in command of the escort, sent Scout Jackson with a reply, "stating that he intended to take the train through to Tongue River, and would be pleased to accommodate the Indians with a fight any time." The wagons kept moving, and some of the Sioux fired at them for a while.

But Sitting Bull soon put a stop to that, and sent a flag of truce forward. He said that the Sioux were hungry, tired of fighting, and willing to make peace, "I will meet your chief on the open prairie," he sent word. But Otis would not risk that; he suggested that Sitting Bull come and talk with him.

Sitting Bull said: "These white men are all liars. If I smoke with them, they will start a fight right away, and then I shall be perjured before Wakan' Tanka. I will not smoke with them. I will send somebody else in my name."

Three other Indians went in to talk with Otis. One of these, Kills-Enemy (father-in-law to Moses Old Bull), told the soldiers that he was Sitting Bull. They gave him a lot of rations, bacon and hard bread; he fooled them. Or thought he did.

Otis had no authority to treat for peace. But (although Otis does not seem to have understood Kills-Enemy's brag that he was Sitting Bull), after all that unnecessary shooting, the Colonel *gave* the supplies which the Indians had asked in the beginning, dumping a quantity of bacon and hard bread on the prairie, as he moved off. The Sioux made no further trouble. A gift was always a proof of friendship; to refuse a gift, a proof of enmity. That was the Sioux custom. A good many fights could have been avoided if the army had understood it.

During these skirmishes no Indians were killed, and no soldiers.

This was perhaps due to the fact that the Indians were saving their scanty ammunition for the hunt they were making. Yet all that shooting had scared the buffalo away. Sitting Bull's people had to march two sleeps north before they found their shaggy cattle and killed meat. It was plenty there, they made a big surround, and afterward stayed in camp, feasting. White Bull, with his left arm in a sling, was able to feed with his comrades. Says he, "I drank lots of soup that day." The Sioux were not worrying about the soldiers who might be following them. They camped on a small stream three sleeps north of the Big Dry. There they made another big hunt.

On the fourth day, October 20, 1876, Gall was heard calling the principal men—representatives of every band—to a council in Sitting Bull's tipi. The Hunkpapa called for were Four Horns, Red Horn, No Neck, Long Horn, and Crawler.

All the young men, White Bull among them, crowded around Sitting Bull's tent to hear what was said. Only the chiefs went inside. Long Feather and another Hunkpapa from Standing Rock Agency had come on a mission of peace: the white men were sending agency Indians to all the camps, asking them to come in and settle down. This message, however, was to the soldiers; it may have been sent by the agency Indians themselves. Long Feather said that all the Sioux ought to make peace with the soldiers. Sitting Bull and the other chiefs agreed. They said they would go with the Standing Rock Sioux and hear what the soldiers had to say. Right away they set out. It was only four miles to the camp of Colonel Miles, on Cedar Creek.

One of the two men from Standing Rock carried something white furled on a long staff. Sitting Bull rode with this man in front, and behind rode about two hundred warriors. When they came near the soldiers, they stopped on the prairie. Long Feather unfurled the white thing on the staff, and the young men saw that it was a white flag, with figures or writing upon it. This flag came from Standing Rock. The minute the soldiers saw this white flag, they halted, standing close together. There were about two hundred soldiers, and they had a cannon (a Gatling gun). Long Feather, carrying the flag, galloped right in among the soldiers. There he remained.

193

After a while a soldier came riding a sorrel horse, and as soon as he reached the Indian line, he asked for Sitting Bull. Sitting Bull shook hands with him. The soldier said, "Sitting Bull, the soldier chief wants to talk to you."

Sitting Bull replied, "All right, tell him to come ahead and talk to me, if he wants to."

The soldier galloped back with this message, but soon returned alone. Said he, "Sitting Bull, my chief says for you to come and talk to him."

Sitting Bull smiled. "Well, then, let's talk in the middle, between the lines. If you will leave your guns and ammunition behind, I will." So it was arranged.

The conferences between Colonel Miles and Sitting Bull figure in all the histories of those days, but the only firsthand record of the conversations is the rather sketchy account found in that officer's memoirs, which makes no attempt to quote the actual words spoken. For this reason the Sioux version here following is of unusual interest; it throws much light upon the state of affairs, the motives, and the tone of Sitting Bull and his enemies just after the Custer battle. The account here given is from the memory of men who heard the talks, verified through separate interpreters at times and places far apart. The memory of old Indians is extremely tenacious, and more than one of these old fellows could repeat the entire conversations *verbatim*. Of course, after the council the whole matter was threshed out in the Indian camps, and everyone knew what had been said—even those who were not within earshot. However, I have stuck closely to the report of White Bull, who was present, and have not given anything from the hearsay of men not actually within hearing of the talk between Miles and Sitting Bull.

As soon as the soldier had made the necessary arrangements, here came Miles and his aides. Sitting Bull and his group met them on the prairie, and spread down a buffalo robe for the officer to sit on. Because Miles was wearing a long coat trimmed with bear fur on the cuffs and collar, the Indians immediately dubbed him Bear Coat. He was wearing a fur cap, and other soldiers had long blue overcoats and soldier caps on. It was a cold day, but there was no snow.

Sitting Bull usually wore feathers in his head when on the warpath in those days. But this time he had been called out when hunting. He wore only moccasins and leggins, a breech-cloth and a buffalo robe. He had no feathers in his head, and wore no shirt. He did not mind the cold.

Frederick Remington's well-known painting of this scene is nothing like the real thing. He painted from hearsay, and shows the Chief and General both mounted. Sitting Bull is shown wearing a war bonnet and fringed buckskin shirt.

Sitting Bull sat down opposite Bear Coat; he had no weapons. He was facing south. On his left sat his nephew, White Bull; at Sitting Bull's right hand sat a Brûlé, High Bear; then Jumping Bull, his "brother," last of all on the right end of the line, Fire-White-Man, a Sans Arc. Big Leggins Brughière acted as interpreter, sitting between Bear Coat and Sitting Bull.

The two parties sat there for some moments, studying each other. Miles knew that he was having a rare chance of sizing up the Sioux chief, and took full advantage of his opportunity. He describes him as "a fine, powerful, intelligent, determined-looking man," adding that his manner was "cold, but dignified and courteous." What Sitting Bull thought of Bear Coat has not come down to us. But we know what White Bull was thinking; he was suspicious. Though it had been agreed that weapons should be left behind, White Bull thought that these soldiers probably had concealed some about them, under their long coats. Said he, "I was looking for their knives and pistols." He was not surprised to learn recently that his suspicions were justified. Miles, in his own memoirs, states that he and his men were armed with revolvers.[1]

Pretty soon they began to talk. Bear Coat spoke first:

Bear Coat: Sitting Bull, ever since you grew from boyhood, you have been strongly against the whites, haven't you?

[1] See *Personal Recollections of General Nelson A. Miles,* 221 ff.

Sitting Bull: No. I never thought that I was against the white man, but I admit I am not for him.

Bear Coat: You are against white people, ready to fight white people, and you like to fight all the time.

Sitting Bull: I never had any such idea.

Bear Coat: Then why is it that everybody keeps saying you are so strong against the whites?

Sitting Bull: They are all wrong. I have always been glad to see white men. I like to be friendly. I don't want to fight, if I don't have to.

Bear Coat: All the same, that is what I've heard. They say you are well known to be hostile to the white man.

Sitting Bull: That's all wrong. All I am looking out for is to see how and where I can find more meat for my people, more game animals for my people, and to find what God has given me to eat.

Bear Coat: Nevertheless, that is what they are saying about you all the time.

Sitting Bull: Any white man who comes into my country as a post trader or a traveling trader is welcome. I always try to go to their trade-houses and trade back and forth with them the best I know how.

Bear Coat: If that's the case, which way are you heading now, Sitting Bull?

Sitting Bull: There are more buffalo hereabouts. That is why I came here, to get those buffalo and feed my nation. *(Sitting Bull glanced over Bear Coat's head at the soldiers.)*

Bear Coat: Have you enough meat now?

Sitting Bull: Yes, I've made a hunt twice recently. I've been well fed since I crossed the Yellowstone. While I was hunting, a bunch of your soldiers came and scared my buffalo away, and when I went to meet them they started shooting. I had a little shooting scrape with them just a while back. I know what you came here for. You came to fight me. That's all you soldiers are made for—just to fight. *(A new quality had come into Sitting Bull's voice, and an angry shine into his eye. He made a slight gesture, pointing with pursed lips, and glanced at White Bull. White Bull looked up, and saw that the soldiers had lengthened their line, and that the ends of that line were curving outward, as if they were trying to surround the council. Mr.*

H. C. Thompson, of Miles City, who was present as a sergeant, says the soldiers became restless and fidgety during the long conference.)

Sitting Bull (to High Bear): Get up and yell to the Indians to line up just like the soldiers.

High Bear: Line up now. Line up just like the soldiers! *(The Indians obeyed.)*

Bear Coat (seeing what the Indians were doing, became angry; White Bull looked at him, and he had an angry face): Sitting Bull, why is it your boys line up like that?

Sitting Bull: Your boys lined up first, so I lined mine up afterward. I don't like to start a fight, but you seem to have lined up your soldiers as if you wanted to fight me again. Therefore I lined up my warriors to be ready.

Bear Coat (angrily): Sitting Bull, you bunch up your boys again.

Sitting Bull: You're the man who lined up first, and you will have to close your line up first. Then I will close up mine.

Bear Coat (to one of his officers): Go back and tell those men to back up and form as they were before. *(The officer went back, and the soldiers resumed their old formation. As soon as they had done so, he returned.)*

Sitting Bull (to High Bear): Bunch up those Indians as they were before. *(High Bear obeyed.)*

Bear Coat: Sitting Bull, which way are you going from here?

Sitting Bull (evasively): I haven't got enough meat yet. I will make another hunt, and then I will know where to go.

Bear Coat: Sitting Bull, I wish to take some of your people who are unable to run around over the country, people who have come from the mouth of Tongue River, and carry them back with me. The rest can go on hunting, and come in afterward to join that bunch and be all together. How would you like that?

Sitting Bull (emphatically): No! These are the very people I'm trying to protect, the young and the old and the helpless. I won't give them up. I will hunt, and when I have enough meat I will cross the Yellowstone just where I crossed before—the same old crossing.

Bear Coat: Sitting Bull, now you are hunting. But some day you will find a place where you will have an agency all your own. That will be your place, your agency.

197

Sitting Bull: When I have made my hunt and when I think I have enough meat to carry me through, I will go straight back to the Black Hills and winter there.

Bear Coat: Just what place will you choose to winter in?

Sitting Bull: In the Black Hills where Cottonwood Creek flows into the Spearfish is a place we call the Water Hole. That is the place. Other Indians will of course pick out their own campgrounds, and where it is suitable to have an agency; we will all live in the Black Hills.

Bear Coat: Good. That's very good. Would it be all right with you, if I went along with you on your hunt?

Sitting Bull: Yes, but if you come along, give me some ammunition, powder and ball.

Bear Coat: All right. I'll give you some. All the Indians whose guns will take the same cartridges we carry can have some.

Sitting Bull: After I get enough meat, I'll come back.

Bear Coat: I'll come back with you. After that we'll go straight to the mouth of the Tongue. I'll get straightened out there, and then we'll go to the Black Hills, together.

Sitting Bull: Well. But now it is getting late. We have just about finished our talk. Let's close the council.

Bear Coat: That's all right. But here where I am camping there is no wood or water. So I shall have to move back a little to the east where I can get them. You pack up and come and camp with me, and we'll have another talk tomorrow.

The council then broke up. Bear Coat and his companions rejoined his command, and Sitting Bull and his friends went back and took their Indians back to camp. As Sitting Bull was leaving, Big Leggins Brughière came to him from the soldier camp and said, "You'll be sure to come to talk with Bear Coat tomorrow?" Sitting Bull said, "Yes." Big Leggins carried this word to Bear Coat, and then rejoined the Indians.

That night there was another council of chiefs in Sitting Bull's lodge, and it was decided that the people would do whatever Sitting Bull and Bear Coat agreed upon. Early next morning it was announced that all the warriors must be ready to go and meet the soldiers for this conference. The whole camp turned out—all the bands. The two forces met as before. This time a soldier came riding horseback to meet Sitting Bull. Sitting Bull took hold of his bridle rein and led his horse around through the Indian lines, so that everybody could shake hands with the white man. After that, this soldier returned, and brought Bear Coat out with him, and several others. They met in the middle again, and talked for a good while. There were five or six on each side.

At this second conference, Sitting Bull was accompanied by Old Bull, Good Crow, Good Bear, One Bull (his nephew), and Crazy Bull. Gray Eagle (Sitting Bull's brother-in-law, and until recently judge of the Court of Indian Offenses at Standing Rock Agency) held horses within earshot. White Bull was not present at the beginning of this conference, and, as I am sticking to his story, I shall give no hearsay. Miles, impatient to discuss terms of peace, had apparently had a change of heart during the night. Perhaps he regretted being so agreeable with Sitting Bull; people who talked with Sitting Bull were apt to fall under the spell of his winning personality. Or perhaps Bear Coat's young men had influenced him against the chief. At any rate, the interview soon became stormy.

Sitting Bull was perfectly willing to keep peace and be friendly, but "he spoke like a conqueror, and looked like one." He wanted the military posts in his hunting grounds removed; he wanted the Black Hills cleared of whites. Apparently Bear Coat imagined that he could talk Sitting Bull out of a lifelong policy in fifteen minutes. The Colonel states that Sitting Bull refused to surrender his arms and ponies, and that he declared he intended to continue to hunt for a living. Also, according to Miles, Sitting Bull declared dramatically: "No Indian that ever lived loved the white man, and no white man that ever lived loved the Indian. God Almighty made me an Indian, and not an agency Indian, and I do not intend to become one." But none of the Indians who heard the conversation between their chief and Bear Coat have any recollection of this pretty declamation.

Miles also states that Sitting Bull "finally gave an exhibition of wild frenzy. His whole manner seemed more like that of a wild beast than a human being. His face assumed a furious expression. His jaws were tightly closed, his lips compressed, and you could see his eyes glisten with the fire of savage hatred." Good stuff to feed the troops, but, if Sitting Bull displayed such fury (for perhaps the first time in his life), Bear Coat must have said something pretty nasty to cause it. It seemed to the Sioux who were present that Bear Coat came there to pick a fight with them.

It is possible that Big Leggins Brughière had something to do with the misunderstandings which arose during the talk.

While Bear Coat and Sitting Bull were talking on the flat, White Bull circled the soldiers' camp, making a reconnaissance. What he saw only confirmed the suspicions aroused in him by their conduct on the previous day. The Gatling gun was pointed toward the Indians, and the infantry lined up in readiness, gun in hand. When White Bull came back to the Indian lines, his friend Owns-the-Warrior rode back from the council between the lines and said, "Friend, they are talking too strong over there. You go on over there. I will stay here and then follow."

White Bull rode out to where they were talking, got off his horse, and stood right behind his uncle. The talk was getting strong. This is what he heard:

Sitting Bull: You are telling a pack of lies. Yesterday when we talked, I agreed to all you said, and you agreed to all I said. We got along all right. But today you are changed, you are angry. Why are you marching through this country, and why are you angry about it?

Bear Coat: I have orders from the Grandfather to be here. Awhile back a bunch of freighters came through a little way below here, and some of your Indians took their mules away from them.

Sitting Bull: Yes. You're right about that. Your Grandfather orders the soldiers to do such things to my boys. So we have a right to do the same to you.

Bear Coat: You're speaking frankly now.

Owns-the-Warrior (whispering to White Bull): You had better get your uncle away from this soldier. They are both angry.

BEAR COAT

White Bull (to Sitting Bull): Uncle, I was over by the soldier camp just now. I saw them getting ready: they are pointing their cannon this way, and lining up ready for a battle. You've talked long enough. If you go on like this you might get angry and start something. Look at Bear Coat; he has an angry face.

(All this time Bear Coat was watching White Bull. White Bull was wearing a buffalo robe. He had his revolver strapped to his right hip under the robe, but it was visible; he had forgotten to take it off before approaching the council. Bear Coat seems to have thought that he was trying to slip the gun to Sitting Bull. White Bull's arm was still in a sling. It was natural that Bear Coat should expect treachery; he had a pistol concealed under his own coat.)

Sitting Bull (getting to his feet): Now let the talk be over. You are losing your temper. Your soldiers are preparing to fight us again. Let us dismiss the council.

Bear Coat and his aides went back to the soldiers, Sitting Bull and his companions to the Indians. The books say that Colonel Miles told Sitting Bull he would give him fifteen minutes to get back to his own lines before he attacked, and that he held a watch on him. Big Leggins Brughière did not translate this, if he heard it; none of the Sioux are aware of any such thing being said. In fact, such a message must have stumped Big Leggins; it was untranslatable in the Sioux language of that day. But Bear Coat was so angry that he expected impossible things.

It is probable that Big Leggins would not have translated that remark, even if he could have done so. For, if he had translated such an insult to Sitting Bull, White Bull would undoubtedly have shot Bear Coat then and there; the young man was devoted to his uncle. The Indians were mounted, the soldiers afoot. Bear Coat could never have regained his lines. The Colonel must have been crazy with rage to issue such a reckless order; how else can one explain it? It was not Sitting Bull who lost his temper that day, it was Miles.

Miles was lucky. Later (December, 1879) he got Brughière cleared of the charge of murder, and enlisted him at Fort Peck as a scout against Sitting Bull. Perhaps Brughière was not guilty, and deserved to go free. But the service Miles did for him was small compared to the golden silence of that interpreter, which saved the Colonel's life that day. No one who knows Indians can doubt that, if Sitting Bull and his companions had known that Bear Coat wanted war, they would have attacked him there and then. Old-time Sioux did not maneuver for position before a fight: they either ran away, or attacked at once. Bear in mind that no pipe had been smoked at this council.

Bear Coat went back to his command, and said, "If Sitting Bull wants to fight, I'll give him a fight!"

Of course, Sitting Bull broke off the conference precisely because— as he had said repeatedly—he did *not* wish a fight. But within a few minutes, Miles ordered the soldiers to attack. They fired the first shot. All of them began to shoot at once.

The Sioux were not expecting the attack, but, as they happened to be pretty well scattered, nobody was hit.

When the soldiers fired on the Indians, young White Bull was so furious at their treachery that he went berserk. "Come on, let's go and rub them out!" he yelled. He started on a run for the soldier line, all alone. But no sooner had he rushed beyond the Sioux line than someone dashed up beside him, grabbed his horse's rein, and led him back. It was Sitting Bull. He pointed to White Bull's broken arm. "Hold on," he said, "it is only six days since you were wounded; you're not fit to fight. Fight no more." White Bull's uncle sent him home with some who were going, to get him safely out of the way. He remained there, helping to pack up, and did not go back to the battle that day. Only one Indian was wounded in that skirmish—Iron Wing (Iron Ribs); he died from his wounds. He was hit in the side.

The fighting was continued next day, and the books say that Sitting Bull's camp was abandoned, and that he left behind a quantity of dried meat. The soldiers were so hard beset that they had to form a square to defend themselves.

While Bear Coat and Sitting Bull were busy on the Yellowstone, commissioners at the various agencies were forcing the Sioux to cede the Black Hills and the Powder River country. The Sioux had no option, for Congress had provided (August 15, 1876) that no sub- sistence would be furnished the Indians until they relinquished all claims to those lands, and to the hunting grounds along the Yellow- stone. The starving chiefs at the agencies had no choice, they signed the ready-made treaty: Red Cloud welcomed the commission, saying, "You have come to save us from death." Only head men were asked to sign; the pretense of getting the signatures of three-fourths of the adult males was dropped. Treaties with the Sioux were no longer mere scraps of paper to the Grandfather, they were confetti.

Says the commission, "Our cheeks crimsoned with shame."

At Standing Rock Agency the chiefs took a very humble tone. John Grass, Running Antelope, Two Bears, Mad Bear, and Big Head signed away their birthright without delay; the council occupied only one day. Their only plea was for clemency for Kill Eagle, the Black- feet Sioux chief, who had been forcibly detained in Sitting Bull's camp in June, and was now imprisoned as a "hostile." When the paper was signed, Bull Ghost voiced the real question at issue: "We have now agreed; when do we eat?"

Sitting Bull and Gall and the Hunkpapa went on with their hunt- ing: they still had plenty of ginger. But some of the hunting bands were tired of being chivvied around the country by the troops, and when Miles sent Big Leggins Brughière to talk to them, they crossed the Yellowstone and had a talk. They agreed to make peace.

The official report calls this agreement a "surrender." The Sioux did not understand it so at the time.

Bear Coat was plausible. He said, "Now we will get on a steamboat and go to the agencies downriver, and the families of those on the boat can go overland." Accordingly a number of head men went on the steamboat: Bear-Stop (Red Shirt) and White Hollow Horn, both Minniconjou; Black Eagle and Moon-Comes-Up, two Sans Arc head men; perhaps there were others.

Those who went overland reached Slim Buttes, and then learned that their friends and relatives on the steamboat were being held as prisoners, and might be killed if they themselves did not come in and give up their arms and horses. They loved their horses. All night they wailed and cried, and the next day held council. At this council it was left to White Bull to decide what they should do. For he was Sitting Bull's nephew; his opinion had weight; he was, moreover, a famous warrior with thirty brave deeds to his credit, though only twenty-six years old. They listened to hear what he would say:

"Uncles and Brothers, not long ago I was taking part in a fight with Bear Coat's soldiers, and my uncle Sitting Bull came and stopped me and led me off the field. He said I was not to fight in a war again. That was why I made peace, it was his orders. And so Bear Coat got some of our men to go on the fire-boat, and now he is holding them prisoners. Those men are our relatives, we cannot let them down. We must go to the agency. From this day on the Grandfather will take over the nation that used to be ours; he will take our guns, our knives, our horses—*everything*. Therefore, I am going to give you a chance to go in with me. Those who do not wish to go may remain."

White Bull took his outfit in to Cheyenne River Agency, the soldiers took their guns and horses. They passed a hard winter there. The Black Hills were gone forever. "And that," says White Bull, "was the end."

Up on Powder River and around the Big Horn Mountains it was not yet the end. Sitting Bull, though not wishing war, and (as we have seen) advising his close relatives against it, was by no means willing to go in and give up his hard-earned guns and horses, only to starve at an agency. Miles got all the credit for the "surrender" which White Bull had made at his uncle's orders. But Sitting Bull did not know or care; he was too busy hunting, and trying to keep out of the way of the soldiers.

Once, long before, when he was out alone after antelope, he had had a strange communication. He heard someone singing over the ridge, and peeped over to see. Sure enough, he could still hear the singing. It was a wolf, and it ended the song with a long howl, "Hiu! Hiu! . . ."

BEAR COAT

The wolf was telling Sitting Bull how he must live, what he must do. Sitting Bull memorized this song, and sang it himself at times.

I am a lonely wolf, wandering pretty nearly all over the world. He, he, he!
What is the matter? I am having a hard time, Friend.
This that I tell you, you will have to do also.
Whatever I want, I always get it.
Your name will be big, as mine is big. Hiu! Hiu!

Yes, that song was Sitting Bull's own. For he had now become indeed a lonely wolf.

27. Indian Summer

The Sioux have behaved remarkably well ever since they crossed into Canada. —SIR JOHN MACDONALD, Minister of the Interior, 1878.

AFTER THE SKIRMISH with Bear Coat, Sitting Bull's mounted warriors easily ran away from the walking soldiers, and the story went that Sitting Bull was engaged in a "mad flight" to the British Possessions. Canada lay two hundred miles due north—a matter of five or six sleeps for a man in a hurry. Yet Sitting Bull did not arrive there until seven months later, May, 1877. In fact, his flight was so "mad" that apparently he mistook his direction, for he "fled" southeast, and was rambling up and down the Yellowstone from the Big Horns to the Powder and eastward, most of the winter. Some Tetons did go to Canada. There, they had been told, an Indian could be friends with white men without having to pay all he possessed for the privilege.

On December 7, 1876, and again on December 18, First Lieutenant F. D. Baldwin struck at Sitting Bull.[1] Nobody was killed in these

[1] War Department reports state that Baldwin "overtook Sitting Bull's camp of 190 lodges, followed and drove it south of the Missouri near the mouth of Bark Creek." But none of my Indian informants had any recollection of such an attack on their camp at this place. Since going to press, I am happy to learn, through the kindness of Brigadier General William C. Brown, U.S.A., retired, that Baldwin's unpublished diary corroborates the story of the Indians, and proves the records of the War Department mistaken. The diary shows that Sitting Bull was in camp on Porcupine Creek, December 3, and that on December 6, the chief, evidently hearing of the approach of Baldwin with three companies of infantry, retired of his own volition across the Missouri, put his women and children safely in camp on Bark Creek, and waited with his

brushes, though the Sioux lost sixty head of horses and mules. Once more Sitting Bull "fled madly"—this time southeast to the Powder, upriver to the Big Horns, looking for his friend Crazy Horse. He could not find him. Moving eastward again through that bitter weather, he found little meat, and turned northward to the country of the Crows and Hohe. There the wolfers had been busy, and when the Sioux found a buffalo freshly killed, and tasted the flesh, they found that it had been poisoned! After that they were afraid to eat such meat. Moreover, it seemed that the poison drove other game away. They killed nothing. Camping in the Missouri bottoms, a spring freshet swept away their tipis. They had nothing to eat. Wearily, the chief and his forlorn band dragged into the country of the Red Coats.

But before they crossed the line, Sitting Bull took one last crack at the Americans. At the Shallow Crossing on Milk River, he led a party of young men against a camp of white men, fired into them, and ran off some horses. Turn about is fair play. He was riding a buckskin horse belonging to his brother-in-law, No Teeth. Moses Old Bull, Iron Dog, Looking Elk, Bear Eagle, Shield, Gray Eagle, Four Horns, and White Horse were among those present: there were twelve in all. Old Bull brought home a mouse-colored horse.

That first year in the Grandmother's country was a spell of fine weather in Sitting Bull's troubled life. Now, for the first time in years, he could eat plenty, sleep soundly, and give himself to the pleasures of family life and friendship without fear. Of late years he had been singing all the time of war and danger and wolves wandering over the world: *"Friends, hardships pursue me; Fearless of them, I live."* Or: *"All over the earth I roam, all alone I've wandered; Love of my country is the reason I'm doing this."* Or, in memory of a comrade killed on the field of honor: *"You Heralds, a Fox Soldier has not returned, did you hear? Red Boulder has not come back, did you hear?"*

But now in the land of the Grandmother, under the firm though

warriors in an impregnable position for Baldwin's attack. Baldwin, being outnumbered, wisely withdrew until he could meet the Indians on equal terms. His chance came on December 18, at the head of Red Water. The Indians say he struck their camp when most of the men were away hunting.—S. V.

just government of the "Mounties," Sitting Bull could think of gentler things. He composed a song in honor of his mother. The word "Father," of course, here means Wakan' Tanka; in the first two lines the mother is supposed to be speaking. The second two lines are spoken by the poet himself about his mother, and celebrate her function as such. Sitting Bull's mother was then named "Her Holy Door," believed to be a reference to his entrance into the world.

> *The Father to earth He has sent me;*
> *Along with the buffalo He has sent me.*
> *My mother to earth she was sent;*
> *With offspring with her, she was sent.*

Sitting Bull had more time now for his children, and especially for the newcome twins. They say he used to carry one of them around pick-a-back, singing the following jolly little thing. Owls were the bugaboos of the Indian child; there was a legend about a mother who said she wished an owl would carry off a fretful child one night, and what do you think? When she turned around, her baby was gone! And so babies feared owls, because owls—as a rule, you understand— did not spare babies! Hence the poet's teasing reference to the friendly little owls here. The song is addressed to the child.

> *Only One, Only One, loved by everyone,*
> *Only One speaks sweet words to everyone,*
> *Hence the Only One loved by everyone.*

> *The little owls, the little owls—even by them!*
> *Only One, Only One, loved by everyone,*
> *Hence the Only One loved by everyone.*

Sitting Bull made peace with all the tribes up there. And his good feeling was not merely for his own kin. He used to go through the camps of the Sioux loudly advising the people: "Be cheerful now; have a holiday spirit. Do not have special friends; be friends with everybody." He would stop and admonish boys to be brave, and generous in their games. And often, when he found some poor child neglected by its parents, with chapped lips and sores, a running nose, and ragged, dirty clothing, he would lead it home to his tipi, have his wife clean it up, give it food and some new clothes, braid its hair and paint its face nicely. Then he would send the child home to its parents, saying, "Tell your folks that this is the way you should be taken care of." And yet, though generally so tender and kindly to his own people, Sitting Bull was a soldier, and could be hard as nails when he thought it necessary—even to them.

When the bands had divided and scattered, in the autumn of 1876, Sitting Bull seems to have felt the need of an organized body of fighting men to protect and police his camp. The old warrior societies were too loose and their members too independent. Accordingly, he picked one hundred Hunkpapa young men and organized them for service: they were known as "Sitting Bull's Soldiers." Brave Crow and Runs-His-Horse were chosen as leaders, and One Bull and Morris Bob-Tail-Bull were Sitting Bull's aides. Elk Nation also was a member of this force.

Sitting Bull called these young men to his tipi, which stood inside the camp circle on the north side. He told them their duties: "Keep your gun handy, and plenty of ammunition. Have a fast horse that will carry you. Protect the camp, and when you hunt, remember to kill meat for the old and helpless; there are always many who need help." He ordered these young men to report every morning at his tent. The Hunkpapa were much impressed by these young men—a hundred strong—who paraded every evening around the camp circle, inside and out. They listened when Sitting Bull gave an order.

When Sitting Bull held council with the Red Coats, one of the things they tried to ram home to him was that his people *must* obey the law, or get out. "There must be no horse stealing," they told him. "You cannot camp in the land of the Grandmother and make raids upon the Americans across the line," they said. "We shall hold you responsible for the deeds of your young men." Sitting Bull tried to make his people understand that he and the Red Coats meant business; there must be no more horse stealing!

Now this was a hard thing for the adventurous younger generation to grasp. Ever since they could remember, capturing horses had been considered a highly creditable deed; it was difficult to adjust the mind to these strange notions of the Red Coats. It all seemed so unreasonable, novel, and arbitrary. Why, in the name of common sense, must a man give up stealing horses, just because he had crossed north of an invisible line marked here and there by little cairns of stone? *Hehan!* Only a year before, Sitting Bull had been sending these same young men far and wide to steal horses; only a few moons before, he had led them himself, on Milk River! But ever since the new order was announced, the young men had to hunt all the time; it was getting to be a terrible bore, an unbroken routine. Peace was all very well for old boys like Sitting Bull with plenty of good, strong feathers; "but where do we young men come in?"

That summer of 1877, Sitting Bull held a Sun Dance on the slopes of Wood Mountain, near a village of Slota, French Indians. These people had a race horse which won everything; it made the young men's knees ache with desire to grip his sleek sides. It was an irresistible temptation. During the dance, about one hundred head of horses disappeared, and among them the racer. M. Poitra was not slow in making complaint to the Red Coats, and soon after the Mounted Police came to Sitting Bull's tipi. They rightly regarded him as the most important chief among the Sioux. He inquired what young men had been absent from his camp, and to his surprise found that the culprit was his own brother-in-law, Gray Eagle!

"These young men must be punished," said the Red Coats. "Shall we do it, or will you?"

Sitting Bull replied, "What punishment do the Red Coats inflict for this offense?"

It is too late now to find a white man who can tell what the Red Coats answered, or how the interpreter twisted their words. But the answer, as Sitting Bull understood it, was: "We have an iron horse with a sharp back. We shall mount these young men on that iron horse, and split them in two."

Sitting Bull, wishing to save the life of his brother-in-law, said, "I prefer to punish these men by the law of my nation." The Red Coats said, "Good."

When Gray Eagle returned to the camp at Wood Mountain, Sitting Bull called his hundred soldiers together. That day his nephew, One Bull, was in command. Sitting Bull ordered: "Saddle a gentle horse for Gray Eagle, and start him right off after those missing horses. If he does not bring them back, he can take the consequences." One Bull led a gentle horse to Gray Eagle's tent, went in and brought him out, and told him to mount. Sitting Bull told his brother-in-law, "These Red Coats were going to kill you." Then he commanded the Sioux soldiers: "Run him to the top of that bluff, keep after him, and if he falls off, shoot him. If he sticks on his horse, let him live."

One Bull and five others, Brown Eagle, Bob-Tail-Bull, Little Horse, Brave Crow, and Killed-Plenty, took their guns and rode after Gray Eagle, herding him straight for the edge of that high, steep hill. They ran him as hard as they could go to the edge of the bluff. There he threw his pony on its haunches—right on the brink—and saved his life; he did not fall off. The Soldiers therefore emptied their guns into the air above his head. After that, Gray Eagle went out and brought back some of the missing animals. Not all—the chiefs had to make the others good from their own herds.

When Gray Eagle came in with these horses, Sitting Bull said, "Who else was in this? How many were you?"

Gray Eagle gave three names: Good Crow, White Bird, White-Cow-Walking. The Soldiers arrested them. Sitting Bull then gave instructions as to their mode of punishment: he was in dead earnest. When Sitting Bull's wives heard those orders, they began to wail and cry and plead for mercy for their brother, Gray Eagle. Sitting Bull then decided that, inasmuch as Gray Eagle had been shot over and driven from the camp by the Soldiers, his punishment was already severe enough. The other three, however, had to take their medicine. It was a strong dose.

The Soldiers cut two poles for each of the culprits and set them upright in the ground. The poles were just far enough apart to allow a man to stand between them, and as tall as a man could reach up, with a fork at the top of each. The young men were hung on these poles, their hands lashed in the forks, and their ankles to the bases of the poles. Their toes barely reached the ground, they were naked, and the mosquitoes were many and fierce that summer. The three young men were allowed only water, and over each one was a guard of two Soldiers. If a guard failed to do his duty, or allowed the relatives of the guilty to free them, Sitting Bull ordered, the guard was to take the place between the poles of the man who was freed. For a week these young men hung there in the camp all day, where the people could see them. At night they were allowed to go to their tents; or, if the camp moved, the Soldiers left them free by day, and hung them up at night. They had no chance to escape, for the Soldiers rode in two lines on either side of the moving camp, and by day paraded around the camp in columns of twos. The Hunkpapa were afraid of those Soldiers of Sitting Bull: there were a hundred of them; no faction could hope to resist them.

When the punishment of these young men was ended, Sitting Bull and his Soldiers came together and invited them to a feast, to show that there was no ill will. Every Soldier gave something for a present to the young men, and they all received an entire new outfit: leggins, otter robes, new moccasins with porcupine-quill embroidery, necklaces —everything. Gray Eagle, not having suffered with the others, received nothing.

Having endured their punishment without complaint, the young men were now in good standing again. It was considered that they had expiated their escapade; that ended the matter. Afterward, all these young men were among the most honorable men of their nation: Gray Eagle was later appointed judge of the Court of Indian Offenses at Standing Rock, and in that capacity served for a generation with unblemished probity.

It was a severe ordeal, but Sitting Bull considered it necessary. For unless the people could obey the law, and so remain in Canada, they would be at the mercy of Bear Coat and the soldiers across the line. He had to be hard, once. Once was enough; that lesson was not forgotten by his people. But there are those who say that Gray Eagle, also, could not forget the shame which his brother-in-law had thrown upon him.

28. The United States Commission to Sitting Bull

If they wanted me to live with them, why did they run me out?
—SITTING BULL.

D URING ALL these months, the Dominion government kept urging the United States to arrange the return of Sitting Bull and his refugees to their own country. It appears that the Grandfather was not anxious to have him back, though a number of priests and scouts crossed the line to talk to him about it. But at last the settlers in Montana became so insistent that something had to be done. Up to that time the correspondence had consisted of "Why don't you call your Sioux home?" countered by "Why don't *you* drive him back?" But in 1878 a special commission was sent to interview Sitting Bull, and Major "Long Lance" Walsh, in his red coat, came to summon Sitting Bull to the conference.

He arrived just a few months after Chief Joseph had been trapped by General Miles at the Bear Paw Mountains; about one hundred Nez Percé Indians had escaped the troops and were still in Sitting Bull's camp.

It was not an auspicious time. Sitting Bull and the Sioux were deeply stirred by the story of the Nez Percé, by the wailing of their women, by the blood and the wounds—all fresh evidence of the cruelty of the Americans, and of the fate which might be theirs if they returned.[1]

---

[1] For the Nez Percé account of how they joined Sitting Bull in Canada, see "Chief Joseph's People Join Sitting Bull, September, 1877," in my *New Sources of Indian History, 1850–1891*, 240–45.

To go south then would be to "go south," indeed, they thought. Long Lance had a hard time talking Sitting Bull into going to the fort. Sitting Bull's people knew that the American soldiers were many and the Red Coats few; they could not understand what it was that kept the troops from following him into Canada, and the plight of the Nez Percé frightened them. All the way in, the party kept stopping to smoke and reconsider their decision to accompany Long Lance, and it was not until Commissioner James F. MacLeod, of the Mounted Police, joined his voice to that of Long Lance that they finally came in. He reassured them, though Sitting Bull said: "There is no use in talking to these Americans; they are all liars, you cannot believe anything they say. No matter what terms they offer, we cannot accept them, because we have no faith in their promises." When they arrived at Fort Walsh, Sitting Bull refused to enter. Said he, "I have never been inside a fort; I would rather camp outside."

But after MacLeod had told him there were no Americans inside, and had made all the Mounties come out and shake hands with Sitting Bull, he and his twenty Sioux entered the fort.

The commission from the States was delayed, and it was all the Mounties could do to get Sitting Bull to wait for them. But on the afternoon of October 17, the council convened in a room at Fort Walsh. The following Americans were present: Brigadier General Alfred H. Terry, U.S.A. (known as "Star" to the Sioux); the Honorable A. G. Lawrence, of Rhode Island; H. C. Corbin, brevet lieutenant colonel, U.S.A., secretary; Jay Stone, stenographer. Lieutenant Colonel James F. MacLeod, Major Walsh, and other officers of the Royal Northwest Mounted Police, represented Her Majesty's interests. Sitting Bull was accompanied by some twenty sub-chiefs, including Bear's Cap (Bear's Head), Spotted Eagle, Flying Bird, Whirlwind Bear, Iron Dog, Crow, Little Knife. Each party had brought its own interpreter.

Sitting Bull came in and shook hands warmly with the Red Coats, but "passed the commissioners in a most disdainful manner." He and his chiefs sat on the floor opposite the chairs of the commissioners, and he demanded that the table between them be removed and that all spectators be shut out. The stenographer must have labored under some difficulty without a table, but, as it turned out, his labors were of very brief duration.

"Star" Terry opened the meeting, explaining the wishes and promises of the Grandfather. Briefly, these were (1) peace with the Sioux, (2) a full pardon to those who surrendered, (3) the same treatment as that given to other surrendered Sioux then at the agencies, food and clothing, and cows to the value of the surrendered guns and horses. The General spoke in a kindly, conciliating, if somewhat patronizing manner, apparently under the impression that the Sioux would be glad to come back on such terms, and gain a "pardon" for past offenses. But he very soon had his eyes opened and his ears set burning when Sitting Bull began to talk. That old cripple had a heart full of accumulated indignation. So the Grandfather would pardon *him*, and suggested that *he* "march on foot to the reservations"—a thousand miles or so! It is hard to understand how Sitting Bull was able to get along with a language which contains no profanity.

Sitting Bull: For sixty-four years you have kept me and my people and treated us bad. What have we done that you should want us to stop? We have done nothing. It is all the people on your side who started us to making trouble. We could go nowhere else, so we took refuge here. It was on this side of the line that we first learned to shoot, and that's why I came back here again. I would like to know why you came here.

I did not give you my country, but you followed me from place to place, and I had to come here. I was born and raised here with the Red River mixed bloods, and I intend to stay with them. I was raised hand in hand with these people, and that is why I shake their hands [shaking hands with the Red Coats]. That is the way I was taught. That is the way I intend to go on doing. See how I live with these people.

Look at me. I have ears, I have eyes to see with. If you think me a fool, you are a bigger fool than I am. This house is a medicine house. You come here to tell us lies, but we do not want to listen to them. I don't wish such language used to me, nor any such lies told to me in my Grandmother's house. Don't say two more words. Go back home where you came from.

216

THE U.S. COMMISSION TO SITTING BULL

This country is my country now, and I intend to stay here and raise people up to fill it. I shake hands with these people [shaking hands again with the Red Coats]. You see me; that's enough. The country that belonged to us, you ran me out of it. I have come here, and here I intend to stay. I want you to go back, and take it easy going back. [Taking a Santee Indian by the hand.] These Santees—I was born and raised with them. He is going to tell you something about them.

There followed a number of brief speeches evidently inspired by Sitting Bull, who introduced the speakers. Much that was said repeated his own remarks, but a few statements may be given here which show the situation more clearly, and reveal the background of Sitting Bull's thought:

We did not give our country to you; you stole it. . . . You come here to tell lies; when you go home, take them with you. . . . Sixty-four years ago you got our country, and you have kept us fighting ever since. . . . You promised to take care of us, but did not. . . . These people are good; I intend to live here. With bullets here we intend to kill meat and hurt nobody. . . . We have sense enough to love one another. . . . They let me trade here; everything I get I buy from the traders. I steal nothing. . . . Sitting Bull here says that whenever you found us out, wherever his country was, why, you wanted to have it. . . . Fourteen years ago I came over here to escape you. For fourteen years I have not had to fight with your people—that is all I have lost by staying in this country. . . .

Sitting Bull's stage management of this council was admirable; he overlooked nothing. One of the most effective speakers was a woman, whom he brought in to present the case of the Sioux mothers: she was The-One-That-Speaks-Once, the wife of Bear-that-Scatters. Said she: "I was over in your country. I wanted to bring up my children there, but you did not give me time. I came here to raise my family and have a little peace. That's all I have to say. You go back where you came from. These Red Coats are the people I am going to stay with, and raise my children with."

It was not over pleasant for the United States commissioners, to sit and listen to the frank reproaches, almost abuse, of these "savages" whom they had condemned and despised and had come so far to "pardon." More especially, it was unpleasant because all was spoken in the presence of the officers of the British government, with which Americans were none too friendly in feeling just after the Civil War. Particularly, as both the Americans and the Red Coats knew very well that Sitting Bull's stand was thoroughly justified by the corruption of the Indian Bureau, the unnecessary Indian wars, the abuses of the Indian trade, and the indiscriminate killing of Indians, including not a few women and children. There sat Terry, who had been in command of the troops when Custer fell, and when thousands of American soldiers could not keep the peace on the frontier. And in the same room sat the Red Coats who—with a mere handful of policemen—controlled the Indians of a territory far larger than the country of the Sioux, and all without any bloodshed whatever. And there sat Sitting Bull, the man whose warriors had inflicted the most complete disaster to American arms in the history of the nation, pointing the difference in the two groups of officials in the most dramatic way, his whole attitude a tribute to the justice of the Red Coats and a proclamation of the corruption and inadequacy of the frontier government of the United States. It must have been a relief to Terry when Sitting Bull rose to leave the council.

However, "Star" spoke once more:

Shall I say to the President that you refuse the offers that he has made you? Are we to understand from what you have said that you refuse those offers?

Sitting Bull: I could tell you more, but this is all I have to say. If we told you more—why, you would pay no attention to it. I have no more to say. This side of the boundary does not belong to your people. You belong on the other side; I belong here.

Crow added a few remarks, telling the Commission that "These people that don't hide anything, they are the only people I like. . . .

Here I have plenty to eat, and everybody respects me." The council adjourned.[2]

Afterward MacLeod had a conference with the Sioux, at the request of the commission. He urged Sitting Bull to consider well his answer; that the Red Coats would not admit his claim to be a British Indian; that his only hope was the buffalo, which would not last forever; that the Queen would protect them only while they behaved themselves, and never feed them; that they could not cross the line with hostile intent; that the young men must be controlled: that, if trouble once began, it might involve all.

Sitting Bull replied at length, protesting his own innocence, dwelling upon the way his people at the agencies were abused, telling how many Sioux had been killed by the soldiers, how the game had been driven away by the smell of blood south of the boundary, and insisting that he only wished peace and a chance to trade. The Sioux had never sold their country, nor taken annuities in payment; the Americans stole their country, and the gold in the Black Hills. "We will pay for what we want here: we asked the Americans to give us traders, but instead they gave us fireballs [shells]. All of them robbed, cheated, and laughed at us. They never tell the truth. They said they did not wish to fight, but they began it. Everything bad began with them; I have never heard a good word of them. . . . If they liked me, *why* did they drive me away?"

That puzzled Sitting Bull. For what earthly reason did the Americans want him to come back, unless to kill him? But he would not budge from his position. His people had come to Canada crying: now they were happy. He intended to stay.

MacLeod promised the Sioux that traders were free to travel anywhere, that they might have ammunition for hunting, and gave them some presents and tobacco. They went off well pleased, and the Com-

[2] See *Report* of the Commission, appointed by direction of the President of the United States under instructions of the Honorable the Secretary of War and the Secretary of the Interior to meet the Sioux Indian Chief, Sitting Bull, with a view to avert hostile incursions into the territory of the United States from the Dominion of Canada (Washington, 1877), and the Canadian records found in *Sessional Papers,* 3 to 4, No. 4, Vol. XI, No. 5, 41 Victoria A. 1878, Appendix D.

mission went back to report that Sitting Bull would not be returning to the States for some time to come, if at all.

That council let everyone know where Sitting Bull stood. It gave the Red Coats some worry, because they expected other Sioux to come in his wake. It gave the United States cause for concern, since the agency Indians (relatives of Sitting Bull's Sioux) might be constantly moving back and forth across the line. All these considerations affected the chief's life later. But none of them had such an effect as the frank terms applied by him to the commissioners: "Liars!" The officials of the Indian Bureau did not forgive those words. And the day would come when Sitting Bull must endure their retaliation.

For the time being, he was well content. At any rate, he was better off than Crazy Horse, who had been stabbed in the back by a soldier, and put safely out of the way. So long as buffalo ran, Sitting Bull would stick to his job of feeding the remnant of his nation.

The trouble was, most of the game ranged south of the international boundary, and Sitting Bull continually had to risk the attack of Bear Coat's soldiers when hunting buffalo on Milk River.

One day in 1879, when he was camped on that stream, one of his Sioux was out looking for stray horses when he saw eight strange Indians riding toward the camp. He quirted his pony, dashing off to save himself. But one of the strangers called after him in Sioux, saying, "Stop! Wait! We want to enter your camp." Then the Sioux recognized the voice and figure of "Big Leggins" Brughière, whom Sitting Bull had adopted. With him were seven Cheyennes; they were all scouts serving under Bear Coat Miles.

The lone Sioux said, "If you go into that camp, you will never come out alive." All the Sioux were angry at Big Leggins and the Cheyennes for joining the soldiers to fight them. Big Leggins said he was going in, and one of the Cheyennes who could speak Sioux went along. With them went Bob-Tail-Horse, one of the four Cheyennes who had ridden out to face Custer alone that day on the Little Big Horn. These three advanced, while the other five scouts remained on the hill, watching, so that they could take back word if the three were killed.

Big Leggins and his two comrades rode to the Sioux camp. As soon as they reached it, they jumped off their horses, entered the first tipi quickly, and sat down on one side, with their Winchesters in their hands. There was a woman in the tent; she gave them one look and ran out.

A moment later, a big Sioux came in, rifle in hand, and sat down opposite. Right behind him came another Sioux, similarly armed, and sat down beside the first. Then a third entered, carrying a war club, to join the others. The two parties sat silent, watching each other. After a few minutes, Sitting Bull came limping hurriedly in, unarmed, and sat down between the two Sioux with the Winchesters. He began to talk: "Where are the soldiers? Are they following you to attack us and kill our women and children? Did you bring an army with you?"

Sitting Bull ignored Big Leggins Brughière, his turncoat "brother" who had gone over to the enemy. He spoke to the Cheyennes. The one who could understand Sioux spoke up: "No army is with us. Just eight of us, sent here to ask you to surrender. We Cheyennes have done that, and we are happy. We were told to come here and ask you to do the same."

Perhaps Sitting Bull knew the speaker and distrusted him, or perhaps he was wary because the man was a stranger. At any rate, he paid no attention to his words, but suddenly stood up, looked fixedly at the third man and spoke:

Sitting Bull: You're the man they call Bob-Tail-Horse?

Bob-Tail-Horse: That's me.

Sitting Bull: These two men are going to speak Sioux, but do you use the sign language. And take care to tell the truth. We want to keep away from the soldiers. If you lie to us, we'll kill you.

All the Sioux were very menacing and angry, and a good many had gathered outside the tent.

Bob-Tail-Horse: There are only eight of us here; we can't do anything. I know you can kill me. I knew that when I brought my body into your camp, that my body would be food for dogs. I threw it away before I came here.

Sitting Bull: When a man is out to do mischief, he can expect to be killed. It is my duty to live here on my own ground and protect my people.

Sitting Bull spoke angrily, yet the courage of Bob-Tail-Horse touched him in the vulnerable spot; he could not fail to be impressed by the man's unflinching valor. Thereafter he talked only with him.

Bob-Tail-Horse: I came here not to lie, but to tell you the truth, and to give you a chance to save your women and children. That's all we want to do. If you surrender, they will treat you the same way they treated us. They'll give you a reservation, and you'll have peace. You remember how you and we Cheyennes used to fight side by side? They have pushed us pretty hard the last few years. We gave in, and that's what we want you to do. Bear Coat captured some of us and sent them to Two Moon's band. He surrendered, and that's how I come to be here.

Sitting Bull: Once you Cheyennes were leaders in war, big fighters! Why did you put away your guns? If you had not, if you had stuck to me, the soldiers would go away, they would not have the courage to attack us all.

Bob-Tail-Horse: This is your last chance. Go down and surrender, and save your families, or the soldiers will chase you all over the country. Bear Coat will be here when the plums are ripe. And if I get away from here alive, I'll go straight to him, tell him where you are, and bring him here. And the first man you'll see will be *me!*

Sitting Bull: We'll not surrender, not for a year or two, anyhow. But we are not going to do any more running around. We're going to stay right here, outside the post.

Bob-Tail-Horse: We used to fight the soldiers, too. But now it is up to you to fight or to surrender.

Sitting Bull respected that brave Cheyenne, but the challenge in his words roused the old chief's dander. Perhaps, had Bob-Tail-Horse been less reckless, Sitting Bull might have destroyed him then and there as a traitor. But now he scorned to take advantage of this man who threatened him, lest others should say he was afraid. He could be as disdainful of danger as any renegade Cheyenne. His next words showed the contempt he felt for the man's threats—

Sitting Bull: When are you men going home?

Bob-Tail-Horse (doubtless relieved, but pushing his advantage): We're not going until you move camp and start in some direction.

Sitting Bull (proudly): I'm not going to run away. I'm going to stay right here.

Bob-Tail-Horse: Then you had better look out when the plums are ripe. I don't care what happens to me, I tell you you will have to fight then.

Sitting Bull said no more. He went out of the lodge, and the three scouts rode away with whole skins. Let them go back and tell Bear Coat where the Sioux were camped. What of it? Sitting Bull wanted peace, wanted to hunt south of the line. But he could not bring himself to surrender to that turncoat Big Leggins, or give up his gun and his horse at the demand of men who had formerly fought under his orders. He had been foremost man of the greatest nation too long now; his pride would not permit it.

Bob-Tail-Horse was as good as his word. Soon after, he led Bear Coat's soldiers to Sitting Bull's camp on the Beaver, and chased him across Milk River and back into Canada.

29. Thrown Away

NORTH OF THE LINE WERE, for Sitting Bull, peace and safety, the friendship of Major "Long Lance" Walsh, the hope of a reserve to be granted by the Grandmother. South of the line were hunger, the threat of Bear Coat's troopers, and the ultimate humiliation of surrender, the giving up of his arms and horses, and all that made a man a man. Yet, as time passed, the pressure increased, forcing him to return and go on the dole at the agency, a captive of the white men. Plenty gave way to famine, fires swept away the prairie forage, deep snows and mange ravaged the Sioux pony herds, and his followers drifted away, band by band, under the steady persuasions of Major Walsh and the even more insidious tactics of Superintendent L. E. F. Crozier, who ignored Sitting Bull's claim to be chief, dealt with all Indians alike, and so undermined the old man's influence. Scout E. H. "Fish" Allison came from the States to urge the Sioux to surrender, Black Robes came on the same mission, and agency Sioux. And at last he was left with only a handful of his followers.

Yet so long as his friends, the traders, would credit him for food and supplies, Sitting Bull delayed his going. For surrender meant no mere temporary disgrace, no mere personal danger. It meant the end of the Sioux nation and of his own career. Who could tell? Perhaps, another season, buffalo might come swarming over the hills again, tribesmen come swarming up from the south. Perhaps—if only he could hang on for a bit.

But his friends, the traders, quickly tired of feeding him. For years they had dealt with him at outrageous advantage, growing rich at his expense. But now, like all the other whites, they turned against him. So long as buffalo ran and he could fill their warehouses with shaggy robes, how glad they were to shake his hand! There are those who say that he was encouraged to stay in Canada because of the influence of certain men interested in the Indian trade who could sway the Dominion Government. But now, in 1881, they were only too glad to kick him out and sell him down the river.

The principal trader in the Wood Mountain District was Jean Louis LeGare.[1] As early as 1878, Scout Howard from the States had told him there would be money for the man who could get Sitting Bull to turn in his gun at Fort Buford. Now came the golden chance. LeGare called a council at his store at Willow Bunch, and made a speech.

The man LeGare, born in France, was a most remarkable and picturesque personage. He was illiterate, but shrewd, of immense physical vigor, with "eyes that could count a man's vertebrae from the front!" He was not usually loquacious, and knew Indians like a book. In manner he showed an inflexible imperturbability. The Sioux had never heard him talk; they listened.

He advised them to surrender, told them that the Red Coats and mixed bloods in Canada were tired of them: that they were poor, and would have to surrender soon. "I will try once more to help you. Take my words. Surrender."

Sitting Bull answered. "I trust you, but not the Americans. They are only waiting to get us all together, and then slaughter us."

LeGare countered by proposing that a party go with him to Fort Buford and talk to the commandant. LeGare would feed them, arm them, and mount them for the trip, and talk for them. "If you get no good answer, I will bring you back—every one of you."

"But if he keeps us there, what will you do?"

"I will stay with you."

Thirty men agreed to go with LeGare. But Sitting Bull, seeing his camp melting away, left the old and sick and helpless at Willow Bunch, where LeGare could feed them, and started northeast to Fort Qu'-

[1] For LeGare's story see F. C. Wade, K. C., "The Surrender of Sitting Bull," *The Canadian Magazine*, Vol. XXIV, No. 4 (February, 1905), 336 ff.

Appelle to make one last desperate plea to the Grandmother to let him stay in Canada, to grant him a reserve. He started on April 27. LeGare took his thirty Sioux and struck out for Buford the next day, an eight days' trip, with carts.

Sitting Bull did not reject LeGare's words. He knew well enough that a price had been put on his head; the newspapers said it was as much as twenty thousand dollars. He suspected that there was profit in this for somebody; he had never known a trader to do anything except for profit. He sent five men after LeGare. One of them, his nephew, seized the trader and shook him violently, saying, "We know what you are up-to, taking that party to Fort Buford. You want to take all the big ones down there, and sell them by the pound!" After that, all but sixteen of the Sioux turned back.

Sitting Bull, however, had said that he "would see about it" for himself. He did. He sent Moses Old Bull, his aide, and Catch-the-Bear, a close friend, to Buford to find out how his people were getting along. At that time his camp was on White Mud River. These two men went to Buford, and were so well treated and given so many presents that they hastened back to get their relatives and carry them down to the agencies. Finding Sitting Bull gone, they left their message with Long Horn, who faithfully relayed it to their chief.[2]

Meanwhile, Sitting Bull and his young men were at Fort Qu'-Appelle, pleading with Superintendent Sam B. Steele, of the Mounted Police, to give them a reserve in Canada, as had been done for the refugee Santees after the Minnesota Massacre. The Santees had behaved well in Canada, and there was no reason to expect any worse conduct from Sitting Bull's shrunken following. But the Grandmother had made up her mind. No reserve was to be given him. Superintendent Steele telegraphed Lieutenant Governor Dewdney, who promptly came and talked to Sitting Bull: "There is no use asking us for a reserve here, when you have a reserve of your own south of the line, all ready and waiting," he said. Then the officers read aloud the report of Sitting Bull's former speeches to the representatives of the United

[2] For "The Sioux Account of How Sitting Bull's Surrender Came to be Made, 1881," see my *New Sources of Indian History, 1850–1891*, 245 ff.

States, in which he had refused to throw away the Black Hills and the country of the Sioux south of the boundary. They asked him if that was a correct statement of his views, if the paper was true. Sitting Bull answered, "Yes, it is true; it is just as you have it written." Then the officers clapped their hands.

"Now that you are returning home, we want you to think of these words," they said. "In future this will be a matter for consideration."

Governor Dewdney suggested sending Sitting Bull to the States via Pembina at once, offering to ration him and supply an escort. But Sitting Bull, who pinned his faith to the traders—and of the traders to one man only—replied, "No. I will go with LeGare."

At the close of this interview, the interpreter, whom One Bull described as a French Indian named "Li-ka-yo" (McKay?), warned Sitting Bull. "When you return to the Grandfather's country, you will be killed." The interpreter said this, and wept.

The Governor rationed Sitting Bull's party to Wood Mountain, but the way was long, they were tired and discouraged, and the rations gave out before they reached it, on July 2. And when they got there, Sitting Bull discovered that LeGare, who was being eaten out of house and home by the Sioux, had carted off another party of families to be surrendered at Fort Buford.

To LeGare he said: "I heard you were carrying my camp to Buford in my absence. I have come from Qu'Appelle with the same purpose, to surrender, if you give me time for it."

LeGare did not press the chief. Said he: "If you like, you can go with me now. I am starting day after tomorrow."

But Sitting Bull had been riding two days without food. He said: "No, I am all in. I am going to visit my friends and rest. Wait ten days. Then, when we are rested and fatter, maybe I will go with you." But LeGare would only wait seven days.

Sitting Bull took a week to think it over. All his Indian friends and acquaintances—Sioux, Nez Percé, Cree, Cheyenne, Arapaho, Saulteaux, Hohe—say that he was a man who weighed his words and considered well before he made a decision or declared himself. He was a great listener. So now he rested, smoked, and thought it over.

Sitting Bull's camp then consisted chiefly of older people. The young, adventurous warriors, who were always eager for new dangers, had dared to go in and face the Americans first of all. The old folks had hung back, though they were homesick and pathetically eager to return. They had not the energy to act without the guidance of their old leader, who had piloted them through war and famine and exile. It was for him to decide. That devoted handful would go or stay with him.

Sitting Bull loved these people, his relatives, his blood kin most of them, who had stuck to him through thick and thin. No white man has any conception of the strength of the blood tie among Plains Indians. And Sitting Bull, even had he been less thoroughly a Sioux than he was, would necessarily have considered the wishes of his people, if only because—all his life long—he had made so many sacrifices for them. Out on the lonely hills he had fasted and prayed for them; in the tortures of the Sun Dance he had shed his blood for their success and safety; in battle and in the hunt he had risked his skin and covered himself with sweat and dust to keep them supplied with horses and hunting grounds. It was no simple problem he had to face.

It might be better for the old folks to go home and settle down and be happy for the few years that remained to them, back in their old homes, among their children and grandchildren. He himself was not unstirred by that nostalgia.

But no man, however generous and public-spirited, can overlook entirely his own self-interest. Sitting Bull never had and did not then believe one word the Americans uttered. He had heard their smooth talk again and again, and he had told "Star" Terry what he thought of it. There is no doubt whatever that Sitting Bull fully expected to be murdered after he fell into the hands of the Americans.

And why not?

He remembered Ash Hollow, Sand Creek, the dead women and children at Slim Buttes, Killdeer Mountain, and General Sully's alleged attempt at massacre at Fort Rice. He knew all the old story of broken treaties, cheating traders, and thieving Indian agents, the cruel wrongs of the Santees before the Minnesota Massacre, the dead cow at

Laramie, and the rank injustice which had driven Chief Joseph's Christian followers to fly to him for refuge. He had seen Gall's gaping bayonet wounds, and heard how Crazy Horse was lured to surrender and afterward stabbed from behind. He recalled how Dull Knife's people had been locked up at Fort Robinson and starved for eight days, and then shot down as they staggered away over the moonlit snow. And within six months a portion of his own camp had been fired into at Camp Poplar, while they were negotiating for surrender.

Sitting Bull was tough minded; facts loomed very large and objective in his thought. It was useless to tell him that these things were not intended by the great American people, who—like himself—were God-fearing, honest, and peaceable in the mass. The Red Coats had said these things, told him that the abuses he complained of were accidents.

But who could be sure that, if Sitting Bull surrendered, just such an "accident" might not happen to him? No man in his situation, with his knowledge, could have failed to distrust the people south of the boundary. For most of these "accidents" had been brought about by soldiers, agents, licensed traders—*all of them official representatives of the Grandfather*. And now he was asked to put himself into their hands!

He knew that Jumping Bull was in irons, and on returning to Wood Mountain had been told that his elder daughter, Has-Many-Horses, who had recently gone to the States with her new husband, had been seized and shackled there. How could he brush aside such a chronicle of bloodshed and deceit in one day, and forthwith accept the smooth words of strangers? He knew very well that LeGare was selling him— by the pound, he supposed. No doubt it was with grim humor that he increased his weight at LeGare's expense. So long as LeGare would feed him in Canada, he was in no hurry to "go south."

But LeGare was paying forty dollars a day for rations for the Sioux. He pressed for action, and at last Sitting Bull turned once more to the Red Coats. He asked them for rations.

Inspector A. R. MacDonnel was "a somewhat erratic but absolutely fearless and fair-minded man." He had his orders; he refused to feed the Sioux. In desperation, Sitting Bull said, "Then I will bring my warriors and take the food."

MacDonnel could not be bluffed that way. "Go ahead and try it," was his answer.

Then Sitting Bull threw up his arms and cried out, in despair, "I am thrown away!"

30. Surrender

"Let it be recorded that I was the last man of my people to lay down my gun."

NEXT DAY, July 10, 1881, LeGare started south with forty lodges, having taken the precaution to load *all* the supplies in his warehouse upon the thirty-odd wagons and Red River carts which formed his caravan. There being nothing left to eat at Willow Bunch, most of the other Sioux followed. There were 187 souls, all told.

That was a melancholy journey. The creaking carts rolled along single file through the old ruts cutting that green expanse of endless prairie dotted with the blood-red cups of the orange lily, the fire of cactus blossoms, and primroses yellow and white. Among these flowers, in all directions, far as the eye could see, lay the bones of slaughtered bison: broad skulls with empty eye sockets still tufted with brown hair and shriveled skin, or heads still hairy, with shrunken nostrils; half-skinned mummied legs stretched helplessly upon the turf, the arching ribs between them white as chalk. All day they held the eye, and at night the grim and ghastly skeletons gleamed in the darkness and the silence. Sitting Bull might have reflected that his own bleached bones would soon be lying with those of the buffalo, on whom he had formed his life. The virtues of the two were the same. There was no room for them any more.

When about fifty miles from Buford, wagons hove in sight. Sitting Bull reined up his horse, struck his chest, automatically snarled a brave

231

grunt, calling out, "Americans are coming!" But he soon saw it was half-bloods, and grew quiet.

At high noon, July 19, Sitting Bull and his little party of mounted men rode into Fort Buford, and were led to a camping place between the post and the boat landing. At that time there was nothing said. Sitting Bull told the soldiers that he was tired and hungry, and would talk when he had rested and eaten.

While the Indians were going into camp, the officers gathered to see the famous chief. Colonel William H. C. Bowen, U. S. A., retired, then a young officer at Fort Buford, writes that Sitting Bull was in plain clothes, no gaudy trappings. He "did not appear to be a well man, showing in his face and figure the ravages of worry and hunger he had gone through. He was getting old. Since the sixties he had been the hero of his race. Giving in to the hated whites and the final surrender of his cherished independence was a hard blow to his pride, and he took it hard. He was much broken."

It was hard to give up those fast horses which had carried him through so many hunts and fights and endless journeys, but he had to let them go. And when the men lined up to turn over their weapons, Sitting Bull was said to have handed over his own through the hands of his son Crowfoot, then eight years old. Said he, "My boy, if you live, you will never be a man in this world, because you can never have a gun or pony." Note that phrase—"if you live"!

Afterward, Sitting Bull talked for his people to the assembled officers. "The land I have under my feet is mine again. I never sold it, I never gave it to anybody. If I left the Black Hills five years ago, it was because I wished to raise my family quietly. It is the law of the Grandmother to have everything quiet in that place, but I thought all the time to come back to this country, and now, as LeGare was bringing my friends here (I heard one of my girls was with him), I determined to start from Qu'Appelle and come with him to Fort Buford. And now I want to make a bargain with the United States—a solid one. I want to have witnesses on both sides, some Red Coats, some Americans."

Accordingly, there was an agreement. Sitting Bull gave up his arms and horses and in return received a "pardon" for his past. He was promised a soft bed to lie on, and rations. He had understood that he was to have a reserve in the fertile Little Missouri Country, but now it appeared that all his people had been sent to the Standing Rock Agency at Fort Yates, and he was to go there and join them. However, he showed no great disappointment. He was pleased at his treatment by Major Brotherton, and a kindly newspaperman of the St. Paul *Pioneer Press* assured him that his daughter was free, well, and happy. Telegrams were sent to all the Sioux agencies announcing his surrender, in the hope that all Indians who might wish to join him in Canada would think no more about it. The settlers along the border in Montana and Dakota breathed more freely, and immigration into Saskatchewan began.

And so Sitting Bull surrendered, and the War Department of the United States and the Royal Northwest Mounted Police both went on record as having accomplished this long-desired event. "Fish" Allison prepared to write his book,[1] claiming all the credit, and LeGare brought suit for $13,412 in the United States Court of Claims.

That same week the burial detail ordered to the Little Big Horn was at work gathering up and interring the remains of Long Hair's troopers about the base of the new monument there, and John Mulvaney was still busy, after nearly a year's work, upon his much-advertised painting (twelve by twenty-two feet), "Custer's Last Rally."

Newspapermen did themselves proud on Sitting Bull's surrender. They knew how a great man should make oration on such an occasion. "Let it be recorded that I am the last man of my people to lay down my gun."

Unhappily for this gorgeous legend, Chief One Bull, who stood next to Sitting Bull when he handed over his weapon, insists that his uncle said nothing at all. There were still thirty-five families of Sioux in Canada, who might come in at any time and surrender, for all Sitting Bull knew. Such theatricality was not like him, and it is abundantly clear that he took no stock in paper records. Is it likely that this shabby, distrustful, sullen man, hungry, tired, and sick at heart, would

[1] E. H. Allison, *The Surrender of Sitting Bull.*

make any flourishes at such a time? He was interested only in his "bargain."

On July 29, he and his people boarded the Steamboat *General Sherman*. The paddles began to turn, the whistle blew, and the prow swung out into the muddy Missouri. It was three days' trip downriver to Fort Yates and Standing Rock.

III. Captive

31. High Hat

I don't want a white man over me. I don't want an agent. I want to have the white man with me, but not to be my chief. I ask this because I want to do right by my people, and cannot trust anyone else to trade with them or talk with them.   —SITTING BULL.

AFTER HIS SURRENDER, Sitting Bull's life was one long struggle to maintain his authority as chief. It was a long, hard, bitter, relentless fight with the Indian Bureau—a fight to the death.

For two years, however, he was hardly aware of the trouble ahead. For he was not permitted to rejoin his people, as he had been promised, but was sent to Fort Randall and held prisoner of war. As he had expected, the Americans deceived him, just as they had Chief Joseph.

At Fort Randall he had little to complain of. The officers liked and admired him, they allowed him to administer his little camp. Sioux chiefs came from all over Sioux country to ask his advice, and he was deluged with "fan" mail from the four corners of the earth.

Lieutenant Colonel George P. Ahern, 25th Infantry, in charge of Sitting Bull's mail, describes him as "a very remarkable man—such a vivid personality . . . square-shouldered, deep-chested, fine head, and the manner of a man who knew his ground. He looked squarely into your eyes, and spoke deliberately and forcefully. . . . For several months I was in daily contact with Sitting Bull, and learned to admire him for his many fine qualities.

"He would visit me in my quarters when I failed to show up in

237

camp. He would enjoy leaving his card; in fact it was my card which I had left purposely in his tipi, and he would return it with his own name written on the reverse side. The nearest he came to being jovial was when he dropped the card on my table with a smile and a twinkle in his eye. . . . Even then I had become acquainted through older officers with some of the great wrongs done the Indian, and I marvelled at the Indian's patience and forbearance!"

But at last, through the kindness of an old soldier, Andrew DeRockbraine, who explained that Sitting Bull was *not* the "murderer" of General Custer, the chief was sent home to Standing Rock, May 10, 1883. He arrived full of plans and hopes for his people, and with the expectation of being made head chief of the whole agency. But when he met the agent, Major James "White Hair" McLaughlin, he found him a creature very different from the colonel of an infantry regiment. The agent dashed all his hopes, put a hoe in his hand, and informed him that the Grandfather at Washington recognized as the greatest chief that Indian who worked hardest and set the best example to his people. Sitting Bull accepted the conditions, and immediately went to work. McLaughlin, misunderstanding that action, thereupon reported that Sitting Bull was "thoroughly subdued." But if McLaughlin imagined that Sitting Bull had abdicated his chieftaincy so readily, he was soon undeceived. The only way to destroy his chieftaincy was to destroy him.

The Reverend T. L. Riggs, of the Dakota Mission at Oahe, had called public attention to the disgraceful manner in which the agreement of 1882 had been forced upon the Standing Rock Sioux, and the scandal had to be investigated to save the face of the administration.[1] So, not long after Sitting Bull began to work his garden at the agency, five stuffed shirts arrived from Washington, making an elaborate pretense of listening to the many grievances of the starving Sioux. These were the Honorable H. L. Dawes, of Massachusetts, the Honorable John A. Logan, of Illinois, the Honorable Angus Cameron, of Wisconsin, the Honorable John T. Morgan, of Alabama, and the Honorable George G. Vest, of Missouri—a "select committee of the Senate

[1] See 48 Cong., 1 sess., *Senate Ex. Doc. No. 70*, Part I, 34–68, and Part II, 1 and 2.

sent to investigate the condition of the Indian tribes of Montana and Dakota."[2]

The council room was crowded with Sioux. The spokesmen were three: John Grass, chief of the Blackfeet Sioux, and two Hunkpapa, Running Antelope and Sitting Bull. The Upper and Lower Yanktonais at Standing Rock had no spokesmen. For, as McLaughlin puts it, "Were it not for the intimidation of the arrogant and aggressive Hunkpapa and Blackfeet of this agency, the Yanktonais could soon be brought to anything required of them." Such yes men could have no grievances; there was no point in letting them talk.

The report of this Select Committee is one of the funniest documents in all the files of the minutes of Indian councils—and that is saying a good deal. It reads like the Trial Scene in *Alice in Wonderland*. The Senators snapped out one question after another, questions entirely unrelated to the answers previously given, and they soon had poor John Grass bewildered. The Indians went into their grievances at some length, and the committee as steadily ignored their remarks and kept hounding the Sioux as to whether or not they wished to earn the money (already due them), and whether they would try to earn it, *if* the Grandfather ever sent them the tools and seed and machinery promised them so many years before. It is quite clear that the committee cared nothing whatever for the Indians or their troubles, but were merely preparing a document for printing which would read well on the frontier and whitewash the commission of 1882.

That agreement of 1882, however, was one of the grievances, and before he became utterly confused by the irrelevant questions of the committee, John Grass managed to tell the Senators some very pungent truths as to the manner in which the Indians had been handled:

Those men talked a great deal, and we were bewildered. It was not with willing hearts we signed. . . . Those men fairly made my head dizzy, and my signing was an accident. . . . The white men talked in a threatening way, and the crowd of Indians behind me got frightened and rushed up and signed

[2] See 48 Cong., 1 sess., *Senate Reports Nos. 148 to 348*, inclusive, Serial No. 2174, No. 2, especially pages 71, 79, and 81 ff.

the paper. . . . Bishop Marty stood before us and told us if we did not sign it, we might as well take a knife and stab ourselves. . . . That is what frightened the Indians. And he told us also if we did not sign we would be displeasing God. . . . All these men here *know* that was the reason they signed. . . .

That sort of thing might not read so well. And so the Senators hurried the Indians along, confusing the issue. Others of the agency group caught their spirit, and when Red Fish, a dignified old man, got up to explain matters, a sergeant of the Indian Police told him he "looked as if he had been drinking whiskey, and had better sit down." Red Fish sat down. No member of the committee rebuked that sergeant.

Sitting Bull had not been told of the purpose of this committee. Then, as always, the agent "kept him blind." It was all part of the recognized process of "breaking" a chief. Therefore, when Sitting Bull saw the commissioners dodging the issue, talking at random, and confusing John Grass, he concluded that they were there to fleece his people once more. Their manner did not suggest friendship.

Running Antelope saw the chief becoming restive, and expressed the hope that "whoever talks to these men from the Grandfather, will talk quietly and in friendly terms. . . . I want everybody to use such language that no fault can be found with any of us hereafter." He knew it was time for Sitting Bull to speak.

So did the chairman. And he also knew how Sitting Bull had heckled "Star" Terry in Canada. That rankled in the official heart. And so the chairman tried to browbeat Sitting Bull. He did not know what he was biting off.

Here is the official report, *verbatim:*

Chairman (to the interpreter): Ask Sitting Bull if he has anything to say to the committee.

Sitting Bull: Of course I will speak if you desire me to do so. I suppose it is *only* such men as you desire to speak who must say anything.

Chairman: We supposed the Indians would select men to speak for them. But any man who desires to speak, or any man the Indians here desire shall talk for them, we will be glad to hear if he has anything to say.

Sitting Bull: Do you not know who I am, that you speak as you do?

Chairman: I know that you are Sitting Bull, and if you have anything to say, we will be glad to hear you.

Sitting Bull: Do you recognize me; do you know who I am?

Chairman: I know you are Sitting Bull.

Sitting Bull: You say you know I am Sitting Bull, but do you know what position I hold?

Chairman: I do not know any difference between you and the other Indians at this agency.

Sitting Bull: I am here by the will of the Great Spirit, and by His will I am a chief. My heart is red and sweet, and I know it is sweet, because whatever passes near me puts out its tongue to me; and yet you men have come here to talk with us, and you say you do not know who I am. I want to tell you that if the Great Spirit has chosen anyone to be the chief of this country, it is myself.

Chairman: In whatever capacity you may be here today, if you desire to say anything to us we will listen to you; otherwise we will dismiss the council.

Sitting Bull stood there, proud of his high office, of his great nation, facing these pretentious representatives of the people which had cheated his Sioux children so often. He saw they cared nothing for the Sioux, and he thought they had a trick up their sleeves. And nothing convinced him of their duplicity so much as the fact that they refused to recognize as chief the only Sioux who could not be hornswoggled and swindled, the only Sioux alive who could stand up to an official, look him in the eye, and tell him he lied. Running Antelope—all soft soap and smoothness; John Grass, easily bewildered and stampeded into signing a paper against his better judgment; the yes men Yanktonais, who would do anything required of them. Sitting Bull naturally supposed that anyone who would not treat with him *as chief* must wish to do the Sioux a mischief; there could be no other explanation.

And so they denied that he was chief, said he was just a common Indian, did they? They said they would dismiss the council unless he spoke as a private individual? *Hehan!* Well, well! He would have to *show* them who was chief.

The official minutes go on:

Sitting Bull: Yes, that is all right. You have conducted yourselves like men who have been drinking whiskey, and I came here to give you some advice. *(Here Sitting Bull waved his hand, and at once the Indians left the room in a body.)*

The Select Committee were left alone with their interpreter, stenographer, and clerk. Major McLaughlin was also present, and if he had imagined himself dominant on that reservation, he had his eyes wide open now. It was a bad quarter of an hour for the Major, with disgruntled senators all over the place.

However, he was able to bring the Yanktonais to a second council: they were "good" Indians; they always did as they were told. And this was highly gratifying to the committee. Their chairman began by saying, "If these Indians are going to be controlled by Sitting Bull, we do not wish to have any further talk with them. . . . We do not want to talk with such men as Sitting Bull, *who makes war upon the government*"!

Meanwhile, Running Antelope and others were pleading with Sitting Bull to make amends to the committee. One of these white men, it was rumored, would be the next Grandfather. It would never do to offend him. Besides, Sitting Bull had been mistaken; these men were not trying to steal Sioux lands. All the chiefs pressed Sitting Bull to apologize.

When Sitting Bull was in the wrong, and knew it, he was always ready to make amends. "I will speak," he said. And so another council was convened.

Sitting Bull: I came in with a glad heart to shake hands with you, my friends, for I feel that I have displeased you; and I am here to apologize to you for my bad conduct and to take back what I said.

I heard that you were coming from the Grandfather's house some time before you came, and I have been sitting here like a prisoner waiting for someone to release me. I was looking for you everywhere, and I considered that when we talked with you it was the same as if we were talking with the Grandfather; and I believe that what I pour out from my heart the Grandfather will hear.

What I take back is what I said to cause the people to leave the council, and I want to apologize for leaving myself. The people acted like children, and I am sorry for it. I was very sorry when I found out that your intentions were good and entirely different from what I supposed they were.

Now I will tell you my mind and I will tell you everything straight. I know the Great Spirit is looking down upon me from above and will hear what I say, therefore I will do my best to talk straight; and *I am in hopes that someone will listen to my wishes and help me to carry them out.*

I have always been a chief, and have been made chief of all the land. Thirty-two years ago [1851] I was present at councils with the white man, and at the time of the Fort Rice council [1868] I was on the prairie listening to it, and since then a great many questions have been asked me about it, and I always said, "Wait." And when the Black Hills council was held [1875], and they asked me to give up that land, I said they must wait. I remember well all the promises that were made about that land, because I have thought a great deal about them since that time.

Of course I know that the Great Spirit provided me with animals for my food, but I did not stay out on the prairie because I did not wish to accept the offers of the Grandfather, for I sent in a great many of my people and I told them that the Grandfather was providing for them and keeping his agreements with them, and I was sending the Indians word all the time I was out that they must remember their agreements and fulfill them, and carry them out straight.

When the English authorities were looking for me, I heard that the Grandfather's people were looking for me too. I was not lost. I knew where I was going all the time. Previous to that time, when a Catholic priest [Bishop Marty] came to see me, I told him all these things plainly. He told me the wishes of the Grandfather, and I made promises which I meant to fulfill and did fulfill; and when I went over into the British Possessions he followed me, and I told him everything that was in my heart, and sent him back to tell the Grandfather what I told him.

And General Terry sent me word afterwards to come in, because he had big promises to make me, and I sent him word that I would not throw my country away; that I considered it all mine still, and I wanted him to wait just four years for me; that I had gone over there just to attend to some business of my own, and my people were doing just as any other people would do. If a man loses anything and goes back and looks carefully, he will find it; and that is what the Indians are doing now when they ask you to give them the things that were promised them in the past. And I do not consider that they should be treated like beasts, and that is the reason I have grown up with the feelings I have.

Whatever you wanted of me I have obeyed, and I have come when you called me. The Grandfather sent me word that whatever he had against me in the past had been forgiven and thrown aside, and he would have nothing against me in future, and I accepted his promises and came in; and he told me not to step aside from the white man's path, and I told him I would not, and I am doing my best to travel in that path.

I feel my country has got a bad name, and I want it to have a good name. It used to have a good name, and I sit sometimes and wonder who it is that has given it a bad name. *You are the only people now who can give it a good name, and I want you to take good care of my country and respect it.* When we sold the Black Hills, we got a very small price for it, and not what we ought to have received. I used to think that the size of the payments would remain the same all the time, but they are growing smaller all the time. I want you to tell the Grandfather everything I have said—that we want some benefit from the promises he has made to us. And I don't think I should be tormented with any talk about giving up more land until those promises are fulfilled. I would rather wait until that time, when I will be ready to transact any business he may desire. I consider that my country takes in the Black Hills, and runs from Powder River to the Missouri, and that all of this land belongs to me. Our Reservation is not so large as we want it to be, and I suppose the Grandfather owes us money now for land he has taken from us in the past.

You white men advise us to follow your ways, and therefore I talk as I do. When you have a piece of land, and anything trespasses on it, you catch it and keep it until you get damages. I am doing the same thing now, and I want you to tell all this to the Grandfather. I am looking into the future for the benefit of my children [the Sioux], and that is what I mean when I say I want my country taken care of for me. My children will grow up here, and I am looking ahead for their benefit, and for the benefit of my children's children, too; and even beyond that. I sit here and look around me now, and I see my people starving. I want the Grandfather to make an increase in the amount of food that is allowed us now, so that they may be able to live. We want cattle to butcher—I want to kill three hundred cattle at a time. *That is the way you live, and we want to live the same way.* Tell the Grandfather when you get back home. *If we can get the things we want, our children will be raised like the white children.*

When the Grandfather told me *to live like his people,* I told him to send me six teams of mules, because that is the way white people make a living, and I wanted my children the Sioux to have these things to help them make a living. I also told him to send me two spans of horses with wagons, and everything else my children would need. I asked for a horse and buggy for my children; I was advised to follow the ways of the white man, and that is why I asked for those things. I never ask for anything that is not needed. I asked for a cow and a bull for each family, so that they can raise cattle of their own. I asked for four yokes of oxen and wagons with them. Also a yoke of oxen and a wagon for each of my children to haul wood with.

It is your own doing that I am here; you sent me here and advised me to live as you do, and it is not right for me to live in poverty!

I asked the Grandfather for hogs, male and female, and for male and female sheep for my children to raise stock from. I did not leave out anything in the way of animals that the white men have; I asked for every one of them. I want you to tell the Grandfather to send me some agricultural implements, so that I will not be obliged to work barehanded. Whatever he sends to this agency, our agent will take care of for us, and we will be satisfied because we know he will keep everything right.

I want to tell you that our rations have been reduced to almost nothing, and many of the people have starved to death. Now I beg you to have the amount of our rations increased so that our children will not starve, but will live better than they do now. I want clothing too. Look at the men around here and see how poorly dressed they are. We want some clothing this month, and when it gets cold, we want more to protect us from the weather. That is all I have to say.

In these words Sitting Bull made amends for his rebuff to the committee, defended his past actions and his present demands, clearly stated the case of his unhappy people, and with all due courtesy called attention to the fact that he was still, as he long had been, chief of the Sioux and their country.

But did the Select Committee meet him man to man and accept his apology in the spirit in which it was offered? Off with his head! From what followed, one might suppose that when the vanity of a senator is ruffled, the pillars of the Republic are about to fall. Logan demanded a word with "that man before he sits down."

The Senator first painted a pathetic picture of the noble committee and their unselfish motives. Then in shocked accents, he declared that Sitting Bull had accused them of being drunk, and announced that this was an insult. He reminded the Chief that this was not the first time he had shown disrespect to representatives of Congress. Next, the Honorable Gentleman from Illinois proclaimed that God Almighty had nothing to do with making Sitting Bull chief. "Appointments," he boomed, "are not made that way."

Then "High Hat" Logan (as the Sioux afterward called him from his headgear) went on to make statements which were false on the face of them: that Sitting Bull was "not a great chief"; that he "had no following, no power, no control, and no right to any control."

Obviously, the Senator imagined that, when he proclaimed Sitting Bull no chief, the poor Indian would automatically cease to be one. If that was not the Senator's belief, he must have been beside himself with indignation, to say such a thing immediately after the demonstration of authority which Sitting Bull had just given. For lack of logic and lack of sense it would be hard to match this speech of Logan's among the most frightful examples of parliamentary balderdash.

But High Hat was only well started. He told Sitting Bull that the government was feeding him, paying all his expenses, and that he owed everything to the government. These statements were, of course, directly contrary to the facts, the law, and the treaties: it was the government which owed Sitting Bull, and owed him far more than it ever paid. But Logan raved on, telling the chief that he was, in effect, a pauper and a beggar, and ought to be thankful when vain, pompous, well-fed senators came to patronize him, while the nation they represented ignored its repeated guarantees and allowed his children to starve. Finally Logan threatened to have Sitting Bull thrown into the guardhouse, if he ever attempted such a thing again—a threat which must have made McLaughlin anxious.

Having completed his fantastic harangue—to the admiration of four senators, one Indian agent, one clerk, and one stenographer—he sat down. Then he discovered that Sitting Bull was still on his feet.

Sitting Bull: I wish to say a word about my not being a chief, have no authority, am proud, and consider myself a great man in general.

Mr. Logan: We do not care to talk any more with you tonight.

Sitting Bull: I would like to speak. I have grown to be a very independent man, and consider myself a very great man.

Mr. Logan: You have made your speech. And we do not care to have you continue any further.

Sitting Bull: I have just one more word to say. Of course, if a man is a chief, and has authority, he should be proud, and consider himself a great man.

32. White Hair

Ever since 1882 there has been gross and continuous mismanagement of Indian affairs. . . . This able, brilliant people was crushed, held down, moved from place to place, cheated, lied to, given the lowest types of schools and teachers, and kept always under the heel of a tyrannical Bureau.
—LIEUTENANT COLONEL GEORGE P. AHERN, U. S. A., Retired.

SITTING BULL was much too honest to be modest. He had lived up to his code and thought well of himself. On the other hand, he extended his impartial honesty to others, even his personal enemies. Though he held McLaughlin responsible for his term as prisoner of war at Fort Randall, and could not regard him as a friend, he none the less praised the young man to the Select Committee. He thought McLaughlin a good agent, and said so.

In this we see one difference in these two men who were to fight for the mastery at Standing Rock for seven years. McLaughlin has not left one good word for Sitting Bull in all the records, books, and private papers that have come down to us. And because of this utter lack of generosity or sympathy on his part, a good many harsh things have been printed and said about the Major. In his defense, however, the example of such men as Senator Logan may be brought forward. McLaughlin was an immigrant of very limited education, consumed with ambition, apt to resent his rivals, and spurred on by the Indian connections of his Santee wife. Like many self-educated young men, he probably judged people by their worldly success, and by such standards Senator Logan was a shining light. If he and his colleagues could

248

publicly and complacently say for publication the silly things they did about Sitting Bull, it is hardly surprising that a petty official should ape their manner toward the chief. Moreover, McLaughlin had been sent out to destroy Sioux civilization. Under the old Indian Bureau, that was his job.

McLaughlin was, in fact, quite superior to the run of Indian agents of his day, a man who—in spite of the odium which fell upon him after the scandal of Sitting Bull's taking-off—rose to be Inspector, a post only a little below that of the Commissioner of Indian Affairs. He fully represented the old Indian Bureau at its best. And being so closely identified with that Bureau, he necessarily shared the defects of its qualities.

Some of those defects will become apparent in the chapters which follow; others lie outside our field of interest. But if anyone wishes to realize what that Bureau was, let him contrast the Teton Sioux of our day (after fifty years of what McLaughlin stood for) with the same Indians under Sitting Bull and Four Horns for the fifty years preceding. By their fruits ye shall know them. Indeed, by 1929 that old Indian Bureau had become such a stench in the nostrils of the nation that a senatorial investigation became necessary, and many reforms have been, and are being, instituted.

Following the clash with Senator Logan, Major McLaughlin set out to break Sitting Bull's influence. He gradually organized a strong force of employees, Indian police, and hopeful aspirants to office, and of course had the backing of the settlers, the missionaries, the traders, and the military at Fort Yates. He created rival chiefs: Gall, the Hunkpapa, was set up as the Conquering Hero; John Grass, of the Blackfeet Sioux, as the Master Mind. These chiefs had been obedient, had tried to curry favor with the agent, yet, whenever a stranger came to Standing Rock, the first man he asked for was Sitting Bull. Sitting Bull had never done anything to seek favor from white officials, had in fact defied them; yet he won all the honors and attention for which other chiefs had worked and struggled, and all without turning his hand over. It drove them frantic. McLaughlin saw that these jealous rival chiefs could not be happy while Sitting Bull was around. Whenever possible, he sent him away.

Sitting Bull was sent to Bismarck to "decorate the progress" of Grant and the notables who came to celebrate the opening of the Northern Pacific, carried the flag at the head of the procession, and sold his autographs from the tail of a wagon, looking, as the *New York Sun* put it, "like a backwoods Methodist bishop." He took part in the last great buffalo hunt in September, 1883. And on September 15, 1884, he made his first appearance on the platform in St. Paul on a tour of "fifteen cities of the United States" under the management of Colonel Alvaren Allen, who had made the highest bid for the privilege of carting the chief around for exhibition purposes, advertising him as the "slayer of General Custer," and interpreting the old man's friendly words of greeting as a lurid account of the battle of the Little Big Horn. "Mrs. McLaughlin and son accompany me," he wrote to the Honorable Secretary of the Interior, who had authorized this amazing enterprise. Sitting Bull went along because he was promised a talk with the President. But in this he was cheated. Next year he went with another show under more friendly and favorable auspices; the summer of 1885 saw him with Buffalo Bill's Wild West Show.

Sitting Bull traveled with the show all summer. In the States he endured with silent dignity the booing and curses and catcalls of the American crowds, sold his autographed photographs like hot cakes, shook hands with the President, and acquired a taste for oyster stew. In Canada he stole the show, received three times the space in the papers given Buffalo Bill, and was toasted and honored by mayors and members of Parliament, who hailed him as "the illustrious Indian general and statesman, ... the beau ideal of a straight-forward and honest Indian." The Canadians had no illusions about the Toms, Dicks, and Harrys of the American Frontier, whose antics north of the line their own Red Coats had so quickly brought to an end; they knew that the gracious and kingly Colonel Cody was not representative of the class he did so much to make romantic and respectable. They preferred Sitting Bull, who was both representative and genuine.

Sitting Bull made money, most of which, as Annie Oakley bears witness, "went into the pockets of small, ragged boys. Nor could he understand how so much wealth could go brushing by, unmindful of

Sitting Bull

CHIEF JOSEPH WHITE BULL
Elder nephew of Sitting Bull

CHIEF HENRY OSCAR ONE BULL
Younger nephew of Sitting Bull

the poor."[1] He formed the opinion that the white men would not do much for Indians when they let their own flesh and blood go hungry. Said he, "The white man knows how to make everything, but he does not know how to distribute it."

At the end of the season, Buffalo Bill gave him a gray circus horse to which he had become attached, and a big white sombrero, size 8, and sent him home with a warm feeling of friendship for the Colonel. Cody knew how to handle Indians: he thought them much easier to handle than so many whites. Said he, "The whole secret of treating with Indians is to be honest with them and do as you agree."

Sitting Bull's horse attracted much attention at Standing Rock; it could do tricks, such as sitting down and then raising one hoof. The hat the Chief wore only on state occasions. In one of his photographs it is shown with a tiny American flag attached to the band—a sign that he had fought against the United States troops. One day one of his relatives wore this hat. Sitting Bull lost his temper, and said, "My friend Long Hair gave me this hat. I value it very highly, for the hand that placed it upon my head had a friendly feeling for me." After that, nobody ventured to touch it.

Sitting Bull brought his horse and his hat back to Standing Rock and camped with his people, but McLaughlin soon found another opportunity to send him traveling.

One day a letter arrived, inviting Sitting Bull and the band which had been at Fort Randall with him to visit the Crows at their agency in Montana. It was understood that the hosts would give ponies to their Sioux guests. Since horses were few on the Sioux Reservation, Sitting Bull's band was eager to go. And as it happened that the invitation was read publicly at a dance, a good many other Sioux volunteered to accompany them. Because of this mixed crowd, an incident occurred which had no little part in bringing about the death of the chief.

The Sioux traveled peacefully along to Lame Deer, Montana, where they stopped at the agency of the Northern Cheyennes to draw their rations. The party was so large that two clerks were kept busy

[1] Consult Courtney Riley Cooper, *Annie Oakley, Woman-at-Arms*.

serving the Sioux. Among these was a Hunkpapa, a friend of Sitting Bull's, named Catch-the-Bear. He had long been one of the chief's bodyguard, a fighter from the toes up. In the same party was a Yanktonais, known to the Indians as Afraid-of-Bear, but better known to history as Bullhead. He was one of McLaughlin's backers, a "man of courage, energy, and determination," who had been a member of the Indian police since 1878, and in the course of his service held the rank of captain (1878–81), lieutenant (1886), and first lieutenant (1889), and for that year (1886–87) was acting as one of the three judges of the Court of Indian Offenses. Bishop Marty thought highly of him, and in his testimonial to Bullhead commends him for "faithful performance of his duty as a judge and officer," states that he set "a good example, obeying and assisting the Catholic missionaries and [*sic*] the United States Indian Agent in their efforts to convert and civilize his people."

At Lame Deer, this champion of Church and State asked one of the issue clerks for an empty flour sack to put his rations in, and the busy white man gave him one. Bullhead left it on the counter while he went to get his groceries. Meanwhile, Catch-the-Bear came in and also demanded a sack. The second clerk stopped his work for an instant, looked around, and saw Bullhead's sack lying on the counter. He did not know that his colleague had already given it away. He pointed to it, and said, "Take that!"

Catch-the-Bear picked up the sack, put his rations in it, and stepped out of the commissary. A moment later, Bullhead came in, missed his sack, and was told that Catch-the-Bear had taken it. He hurried after Catch-the-Bear, overtook him, and laid claim to the sack.

But Catch-the-Bear would not give it up. He said, "This sack is mine; the white man gave it to me."

Bullhead demanded the sack, and, as the other would not give it up, he jerked it out of his hands, and emptied Catch-the-Bear's rations on the ground. Catch-the-Bear protested, but Bullhead struck him on the back, and went off with the sack.

Catch-the-Bear, though a quick-tempered man, controlled himself. He merely called after Bullhead and said: "Today you have insulted me, you have struck me. We have always been friends. But now you have made me angry. Look out in future. I am going to get you."

Others in the party tried to smooth matters over. But Catch-the-Bear could not forget that blow; from that hour there was bad blood between the men. Soon after, Sitting Bull heard of Bullhead's high-handed conduct. He said nothing then.

At the Crow Agency, the Sioux were entertained in fine style. There were feasts and dances, and these festivities were topped off by a big gathering at which the Crows publicly bragged of their victories over the Sioux. Man after man got up and told how he had counted *coup* on the Sioux, how the Crows had whipped them and run them out of their country, and so on. Some of the younger Sioux, like Shavehead and Bullhead, who had lived on the Reservation a long time, grew restless under the taunts and bragging of the Crows. But Sitting Bull sat still and let them talk.

Then the Crows bragged more and more, trying to anger the Sioux, and some of them talked pretty strong. Finally, one of the Crows, Crazy Head, in the heat of his national pride, jerked off his breech-cloth, and going over to the place where Sitting Bull sat smoking placidly, stood right in front of him, and thrust the tokens of his manhood almost into the face of the Sioux chief.

Sitting Bull, who had attended many such powwows and understood the ways of warriors, knew very well that the Crows were trying to make him angry, so that their triumph would be more complete. He knew that Crazy Head wished to test his heart and see how strong it was. He knew also that, when the Crows had finished, the Sioux would have their turn to boast, and that his hosts would make many presents to the Sioux if he could keep his temper. Unless the peace were firm, there could be no gifts. And so he sat there, and never turned a hair.

But the tame Reservation Sioux, who had come with his party, were angry. They thought Sitting Bull should have jumped up and knocked Crazy Head down. They had not had much experience of the ways of warriors, and so that day they formed a false idea of the chief's courage, and faithfully reported it to McLaughlin. They felt that he had shamed them, and one day, when they got back to Standing Rock,

Shavehead had an argument with Sitting Bull in the trader's store and threw this up to him. Said Shavehead, "Well, anyhow, I never sat still and let a Crow wag his privates in my face."

After Sitting Bull had defeated Crazy Head's desperate efforts to make him angry, the Crows and Sioux made peace, and Crazy Head presented Sitting Bull with thirty head of fine horses, to be divided among the men of his party. When they were driven over to Sitting Bull's tent, he gave them to whatever men he pleased.

The Sioux were all eager to have a horse, for the military had confiscated theirs, and many of them were afoot. Bullhead roped a beautiful pony, spotted black and white. It was just what he wanted; and he seems to have thought that, as a policeman, he could take whatever horse he liked. Or perhaps the horse was so beautiful that he could not keep his hands off it.

But Sitting Bull stepped forward and called Catch-the-Bear. "Throw your rope on that black-and-white spotted horse, friend," he said. "That one that Bullhead has ahold of. That is yours."

Bullhead did not like that, he wanted to keep the spotted pony. He stood beside it for a long time. But Sitting Bull was firm; he had already given that animal to Catch-the-Bear. And when Bullhead yielded at last, Sitting Bull presented him with a nice little buckskin. Thus Sitting Bull rebuked Bullhead for his officious treatment of Catch-the-Bear. And so he, too, was drawn into that quarrel, which, as it turned out, was fatal to all three.

33. Nick Cadotte's Stable

I was born near where I stand. I want you to hold these lands. They will be worth far more. Value them at twenty dollars a foot.   —SITTING BULL.

SITTING BULL had been such a drawing card in Canada, that in 1887, when Buffalo Bill was planning to take the Wild West Show to England, there was talk of sending the Chief along. Mrs. McLaughlin had acted as interpreter for him before, and had he gone, she might have gone along with him—to Queen Victoria's Jubilee. Few women west of the Missouri had ever had such a chance, and not since Pocahontas was presented at Court, probably, had an Indian woman known such a glittering prize within her reach. The McLaughlins were ambitious, and mixed-blood women were then not a little sensitive to the exclusions and airs of the military social set at Fort Yates. The Major's enemies called him "squaw-man" behind his back.

But Sitting Bull refused to go. Said he, "It is bad for our cause for me to parade around, awakening the hatred of white men everywhere. Besides, I am needed here; there is more talk of taking our lands." Buffalo Bill's conquest of London society electrified the States; Sitting Bull's refusal to go with him made the Chief no friends at the agency.

McLaughlin had Sitting Bull on his hands again. But it was not the old Sitting Bull of dwindling influence and doubtful title to a vanishing chieftaincy. The goal of the Sioux was public honor, and Sitting Bull had gained such honor as no Sioux had ever dreamed of. Thousands had packed the stands to see him, had paid their dollars gladly for his autograph. He had hobnobbed with Presidents and generals, mayors and members of Parliament, and one and all had called him Chief! Heretofore his title to that office had rested upon the suffrage of the Sioux, and the Sioux were captives. But now, it seemed to him, his authority had the warrant of the greatest of the whites. He settled down at Standing Rock with a prestige and a self-assurance enormously enhanced by his travels. He had plucked victory out of defeat.

And little he cared that the agent, a petty official of the Indian Bureau, refused to acknowledge his greatness. McLaughlin might pretend and preach and elevate lesser men to agency posts; Sitting Bull merely smiled; he knew he was *the* great man, head chief and master at Standing Rock. To Sitting Bull, McLaughlin's assumption of authority over the head chief of the Sioux nation seemed simply ridiculous. Said he, "My people wish *me* to remain chief during my lifetime." And he added, "Once I had a jealous woman in my lodge, named Snow-on-Her. This agent reminds me of that jealous woman!"

And so, when the agent tried to dragoon him into the church and the system there, he found the old man "incorrigible." As to putting away one of his wives, he said, "I like both; I do not wish to treat them differently." When the ban on medicine men was discussed, he answered, "The main thing is to cure the patient; any method that works is a good one." When the missionaries urged him into the fold, he smiled tolerantly: "What does it matter how I pray, so long as my prayers are answered?" And to the demand that he become altogether like a white man, he replied, "I have advised my people thus: when you find anything good in the white man's road, pick it up; but when you find something bad, or that turns out bad, drop it, leave it alone."

Yet Sitting Bull had a program of his own which he tried to carry through: self-support, education, a reunited nation, the old-time religion. As in former days he had used the white man's gun on the buffalo hunt, so now he proposed to use these other devices of the white man for the good of his people. He actually tried to do what the Indian Bureau only pretended to do. He made a new road for his people.

He went down to Grand River, settled near his birthplace, farmed, raised cattle and chickens, lived in a log cabin, and asked to have a day school built there, to which he sent all his children. He was a law-abiding man, trying to lead his people along the white man's road. The "late hostiles" were all more progressive by far than the lazy agency Indians; they were used to working for a living. McLaughlin himself reports that he had never seen any Indians equal to the followers of Sitting Bull, and McGillycuddy of Pine Ridge gave the same praise to the Oglala who had followed the chief.[1] Sitting Bull was happy. But the rival chiefs were not happy. Everything done for Sitting Bull made them jealous.

And yet Sitting Bull was still their master. For in creating these rival chiefs (Gall, John Grass, Mad Bear, Big Head), McLaughlin had failed to break Sitting Bull. Father Jerome Hunt explained the matter: "He thought making little chiefs would break the big one. But he made a mistake. They all put on the importance of big ones." These four chiefs had nothing more to gain from McLaughlin; they had everything to gain from their own people. And so, when McLaughlin looked at these four chiefs and Sitting Bull, he saw simply four ingrates and one malcontent.

When the commission came to Standing Rock in 1888 to swing a cession of eleven million acres of Sioux lands at a fixed price of fifty cents an acre (an outrageous robbery), and break up the great Sioux Reservation into smaller ones, Sitting Bull was able to line up these chiefs against the treaty. Though they were unwilling to have him speak, for fear he would make the commissioners angry (as he had Senator Logan), they were with him heart and soul. He won over all the older Indians, intimidated the younger folks, and made everyone swear not to sign. It was all over but the shouting before the commissioners arrived. They shouted, McLaughlin shouted; yet, whenever John Grass became bewildered, or Gall became angry, or the Yanktonais chiefs became too pliant, Sitting Bull took a hand and kept them in line. For a month the councils went on, until the commissioners were so exasperated they proposed to break the four chiefs McLaughlin had made. Then Father Jerome Hunt told them that Sitting Bull was the mischief-maker and the four only mouthpieces.

[1] See *Annual Report, Commissioner of Indian Affairs, for 1882*, 43–44, and *for 1883*, 34 ff.

John Grass, a chief whom McLaughlin had created after Father Stephan, the former agent, had broken him, came out flatly against the agent. Said he, "This will be the first time since he has been here that we have not done as Major McLaughlin told us to do." McLaughlin was in an untenable position; his prestige with the Standing Rock Sioux was melting like snow on a hillside; he had to beg to be relieved from service on the commission, in order to save his face with the tribesmen. In his book, *My Friend the Indian*,[2] he gives a story to explain this, but it is evident that when he wrote it his memory had completely failed him as to this matter. The official minutes of the council prove beyond a doubt that he strongly urged the Indians to sell their lands for a song, and that they took him at his word and refused to do so.[3] It was Sitting Bull, not the agent, who saved those millions of acres and dollars for his people.

It was a complete victory for the chief. He went off to Washington with a delegation afterward, held them firmly together under the fire of the Secretary of the Interior, got the price offered for Sioux lands raised to $1.25 an acre, shook hands with the President, and came home again in high good humor. His influence was at its height.

In fact, he was so powerful that when General "Three Stars" Crook brought another commission to Standing Rock in the summer of 1889 to buy Sioux lands at the new price, Sitting Bull blocked him completely. Crook found himself up against the same polite stone wall, the same bland, stubborn resistance. He found "the influence of the chiefs as great as ever." Crook threw up his hands, and told McLaughlin to swing the cession.

That put the matter squarely up to the agent. He had no chance to camouflage failure this time. If he failed now, the world would know that Sitting Bull was master at Standing Rock. The agent begged for time, proposed certain concessions. The commissioners made promises (which, as usual, they had no authority to make), and Crook pledged

[2] See pages 273–80.
[3] See the voluminous Report of this commission, in 50 Cong., 2 sess., *Senate Ex. Doc. No. 17*. Pages 1–293 in Vol. I, Nos. 1–59, especially pages 87 and 88.

his personal word that, if the Sioux signed, their rations should *not* be reduced. Even so, no headway was made against Sitting Bull.[4]

But one night Mrs. McLaughlin gave a party for the commission at her home, at which, of course, all the officers and ladies of Fort Yates were present to greet General Crook. Meanwhile, McLaughlin slipped away with his interpreter, Louis Primeau, and drove five miles to the home of Nick Cadotte, brother-in-law of John Grass, to see that chief. But so great was the power of Sitting Bull that John Grass refused to be seen talking to the agent! Cadotte's house was too public; they met in a disused stable near by.

It has been well said that at most agencies the head chief was a thorn in the side of a good agent and the master of a bad one. Let the reader decide who was master at Standing Rock in 1889: Sitting Bull, whose open stand for Sioux rights and Sioux loyalties was known to all and inspired terror even in the warrior Gall; or McLaughlin, who had to sneak by night into an empty stable in order to confer with the very chief he had created, the chief who—he pretended—was the real leader of the Sioux? Everyone must decide for himself on the basis of the facts—and those facts presented by McLaughlin.

And so they met: the representative of the Indian Bureau and the supposed chief of the Standing Rock Sioux, in that empty stable over by Nick Cadotte's—two vain, ambitious men who understood each other. And there, as McLaughlin relates, "we fixed up the speech he was to make." But when it was over, John Grass flatly refused to face Gall with this betrayal, and McLaughlin had to go and persuade Gall too. Gall, mere man of action, helpless in the world of the white man's guile, had not the skill to argue. He saw that John Grass had changed sides, that his own fame lay in the balance; he climbed quickly aboard the bandwagon. With Grass and Gall behind him, the agent had no trouble with the Yanktonais chiefs. All four—so-called leaders of the Sioux—swapped horses secretly, by night. It was a famous victory.

[4] Report of the Commission of 1889: See 51 Cong., 1 sess., *Senate Ex. Doc. No. 51,* 15–308. Also *Magazine of Western History,* Vol. XII, No. 3 (July, 1890). McLaughlin's account: See *My Friend the Indian,* 280–89.

Yet even then, McLaughlin feared the power of Sitting Bull. Says he, "I had Sitting Bull and the so-called hostiles still to deal with, and I knew that, given an opportunity, Bull would make some sort of demonstration." Yes, he knew that, given any opportunity at all, Sitting Bull would protest against that grand betrayal, that transfer of eleven million acres of Sioux lands, which had changed hands in a stable in the dark. Therefore the agent stationed the Yanktonais and the Indian police "in a compact, four-column formation around the semicircle" of the council, so that Sitting Bull's supporters could not enter to protest against the railroading through of that cession. Then John Grass made the speech which McLaughlin had "fixed up" for him, and was thereupon rewarded by Governor Foster with that glowing encomium which has been faithfully reprinted ever since, as often as the name John Grass is mentioned:

"At Standing Rock we met a man whose strong sense would be conceded anywhere, and who struck me as an intellectual giant in comparison with other Indians. He is known to the white men as John Grass and to the Indians as Charging Bear, and by reason of his superior mind is the most prominent Indian on the Reservation. . . . His speech in answer to the proposition we submitted was by far the ablest we heard."

His speech!

How flattered McLaughlin must have felt. Yet he said nothing; he was delighted. For Governor Foster had finally given official warrant for the claim of the agent that John Grass, of all the Sioux, was the Master Mind. So long as it served McLaughlin's turn, he kept that secret. But in his book he takes care to demolish that claim (no longer useful) and to reveal the true author of the address. He could tolerate no Master Mind at Standing Rock but his own.

John Grass was an intelligent man and remarkably eloquent. He knew how to present ideas, once they were given him. It may be presumed, however, that Governor Foster was unduly prejudiced in favor of this speech, which was just what he wished to hear. Or perhaps he had never read the speeches of John Grass, made in 1888. These, in my opinion, are better. They show more sincerity; they were inspired by Sitting Bull.

Sitting Bull came late to the council at which the destiny of his nation was to be decided, and arrived just in time to find that his spokesmen were about to sign. He heard "Three Stars" Crook saying: "Now we have understood that there have been some threats made against the Indians who sign this bill. You need not be alarmed, because no one will be allowed to interfere with you. And if any damage or injury is done those who have signed, we will ask to have it *paid for from the rations of those who do not sign.*[5] So there must be no trouble. Now the tables will be moved down here and those who want to sign can do so."

Soon after, Sitting Bull was on his feet:

Sitting Bull: I would like to say something, unless you object to my speaking. If you do, I will not speak. No one told us of this council today, and we just got here.

General Crook (to McLaughlin): Did Sitting Bull know we were going to hold a council?

McLaughlin: Yes, Sir. Everybody knew it. . . .

It may seem odd that the Hunkpapa should not have known of a council for which both the other tribes turned out in force. But it is quite as strange that Sitting Bull and his supporters should have been absent wittingly from the most important council in the history of their nation, the council at which the cession was to be voted upon— that cession against which Sitting Bull had used every weapon within reach for six years. Indeed, he arrived so late that his followers never did get inside the barrier formed by the Yanktonais and the Indian police. How careless of him, how unlike him! Especially as he had told Mrs. Weldon of his fears that some of the chiefs would sign, as recorded in her letter of July 3, thirty days earlier.

The Silent Eaters never were admitted to the council. For when it came time to sign, and they tried to force their way in and prevent John Grass from stampeding the people, they were blocked. For a moment, indeed, the issue was doubtful. Gall was so alarmed for his

[5] Italics mine.

personal safety that he allowed Chief Bear Face to get ahead of him and sign third—an honor which McLaughlin had promised Gall. But Mrs. McLaughlin was at hand and called out a warning to her husband. He caught up the papers "to prevent their possible injury," urged the people to be quiet, and a moment later Bullhead and his Indian police rushed out and drove the Silent Eaters from the grounds.

The Silent Eaters rode away with their defeated leader. The cession was signed, the great Sioux Reservation was only a memory. It was the death of a nation. Sitting Bull went back to his tipi in the camp below Fort Yates, and prepared to start back to Grand River.

Someone asked him what the Indians thought of the cession. The questioner was startled by the flash and outbreak of the chief's reply: "Indians! There are no Indians left but me!"

34. Sitting Bull's "White Squaw"

Great men are usually destroyed by those who are jealous of them.

—SITTING BULL TO WHITE BULL.

AFTER SITTING BULL'S failure to block the cession of 1889, his enemies closed round him like wolves around a dying buffalo; his rivals took new heart and kept pressing their master, McLaughlin, to let them get at the chief. McLaughlin began to push him to give up his Indian ways. He sent Gray Eagle, just converted to the Catholic faith, to Sitting Bull. Gray Eagle gave him a log cabin and a number of horses, and said, "Brother-in-law, we have settled on the reservation now. We are under the jurisdiction of the government. We must do as they say. We must stop roaming about, and obey them. We must give up these old dances."

Sitting Bull answered: "Yes, you are right. But I cannot give up my Indian race and habits. They are too deeply seated in us. You go ahead and follow the white man's road, and do as he says. But as for me, leave me alone."

Gray Eagle was nettled at the failure of his mission. He retorted, with some heat: "Well, if you're not going to obey, and do as the whites say, you are going to cause a lot of trouble and lose your own life. I have sworn to stand by the government. We have been friends a long while, but if you will not obey the orders of the agent, we shall not be together any more." The talk took place on the spot where the Chief was afterward killed. Sitting Bull was disgruntled; he turned more and more to the customs of his youth, and seldom went up to the agency.

263

In those last days, his old prophetic power was strengthened. One day he publicly prophesied a bad year ahead, that the sun would burn up everything, and the people go hungry. From the day of his prediction, in August, 1889, no rain fell at Standing Rock until June of the following year, and very little snow. The boom with which the new state had been opened broke like a bubble, and settlers fled back to the East, the dust hanging heavy on the white tilts of their covered wagons. The Chief, knowing there would be no crops that year, gave over his farming, and lived upon government rations and the largesse of Catherine Weldon.

Catherine Weldon was a representative of the National Indian Defense Association, who had come all the way from Brooklyn, New York, to see him, and to help him fight the cession. She was a lady, well dressed, and not bad looking, indeed overdressed, with many showy rings and brooches, and fashionable clothes. Her hair was graying, for she was nearing, if she had not already reached, that age at which some women suffer a change and do unaccountable things. A strange apparition at Standing Rock.

Yet this was but the surface of her novelty. For in her there flickered, as steadily as the winds of that sham civilization would permit, a passionate, if somewhat incoherent, flame of enthusiasm for the good life. She was an artist, and being an artist, had no use for shams. And yet, in that pallid imitation of Europe which then passed for American culture, she herself, as an artist, could be only a sham. Her talent was a curse, fit to drive her to absurdities in that world to which it had, and could have, no authentic relation. Added to that baffling, smothering wet blanket was the damning fact that she was a female. What wonder that she was flighty and quick-tempered? When she turned up in the spring of 1889, McLaughlin did not understand her; all he could do was to classify her. She did the same for him.

She had sent a letter asking the Chief to meet her at the agency. At the time he was ill on Grand River, in low spirits, and mourning the death of his favorite daughter. Yet, as soon as he was able to travel, he started for Standing Rock to meet her.

While Sitting Bull was painfully driving the forty miles to the agency, the lady and the Major had an interview. She was surprised to find that he already knew all about her. She had sent, she says, several letters to Sitting Bull, one of them by Harry McLaughlin, the Major's son, and it is possible that the agent knew their contents. In those days agents were little kings and thought nothing of intercepting letters addressed to Indians. Indeed, Mrs. Weldon's account of this interview is taken from a letter sent by her to Chief Red Cloud, intercepted by some official, and forwarded to McLaughlin as a "fair specimen of a letter from a female crank." She reports that McLaughlin "had come up and seemed very friendly, and began at once to talk of Sitting Bull, though no one had mentioned the chief's name. Said he was a coward, a selfish man, no one's friend, of no importance, and a heavy burden on the younger men who were more progressive." McLaughlin also pointed out that Dr. Bland (head of the association she represented) "had no foothold or influence at Standing Rock." McLaughlin knew very well that she had come to oppose the commission then trying to obtain a cession at the lower agencies.

When Sitting Bull arrived, the old man's charm immediately swept Mrs. Weldon off her feet. She had come to see a great man and was not disappointed. In him she saw the integrity, the wholeness that her baffled heart looked for in vain in that travesty of culture which had frittered her talents away. To her he seemed a rock in a weltering sea. She did not foresee that she herself would soon be beating vainly on that rock.

From that moment, she devoted all her erratic energies to him and his people, singing his praises, defending him, acting as his secretary, showering him with gifts. She immediately proposed that he go with her to the lower agencies to bait the commissioners, and he agreed; the wagon was comfortable, his family would go along. But Mrs. Van Solen pointed out that he must have a pass, and of course McLaughlin would not issue it. Mrs. Weldon lost her temper, asked McLaughlin if he feared a woman, and threatened to report him in Washington: "High words passed between us, and I rose indignantly and left the office." She sent word to Sitting Bull to drop his preparations; the Chief came up to see her, was indignant at McLaughlin, who would not see him. Louis Faribault walked him to the guardhouse, hinted at the penitentiary, and accused the Chief of trying to carry Mrs. Weldon off. Sitting Bull was "surprised and pained at these vile insinuations. He said he looked upon me as his own daughter and would have sheltered and protected me. . . . I resolved to leave Fort Yates at once." The Chief drove her down to the river, so that she could cross to Winona, and "straightway a romantic story was printed in the *Sioux City Journal* of July 2. A story full of the vilest falsehoods, stating that I . . . purposely came from New York to marry Sitting Bull, that the agent tried to prevent a meeting, but that Sitting Bull succeeded in seeing me. . . . All this is the agent's work. He fears Sitting Bull's influence among his people and therefore pretends to his face that not politics were the reason for refusing the pass, but my welfare, and he took this opportunity to humble the old chief and make his heart more than sad. In order to lessen my influence as a member of the National Defense Association, he makes me ridiculous by having the story printed. Red Cloud, is there no protection for defenseless women?"

And she adds: "The agent fears my presence, and did all he could to destroy me. . . . Sitting Bull says he will never sign nor will his followers, but that he is afraid some of the other chiefs may sign in order to be popular. . . ."

Thus the enraged widow's heated charges. But she did not stop with words. She was not merely an artist, but an artist with money. She gave Sitting Bull gifts and cash, financed his campaign against the new commission, supplied him with maps and land lists. The agent was annoyed: all this "had a demoralizing effect upon Sitting Bull, inflating him with his importance."

Catherine Weldon had departed to do her worst, fighting the cession from the borders of the reservation from which she was barred, keeping up a lively correspondence with the chief, and "inflating" him with further presents. In the spring of 1890 she returned.

She was not long content to remain outside the reservation. She visited Sitting Bull on Grand River, painted his portrait, lived in his cabin with the rest of the family. There she continued her work for civilization, washing his dishes, sweeping his floors, cooking for him,

SITTING BULL'S HIEROGLYPHIC AUTOBIOGRAPHY (I)

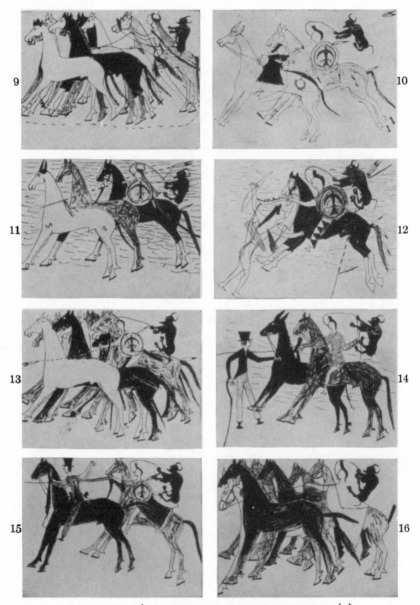

SITTING BULL'S HIEROGLYPHIC AUTOBIOGRAPHY (2)

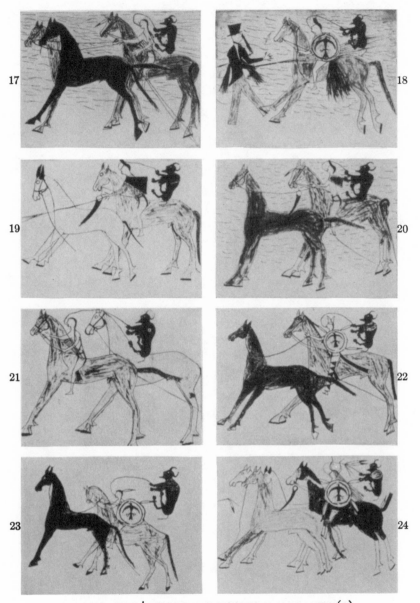

SITTING BULL'S HIEROGLYPHIC AUTOBIOGRAPHY (3)

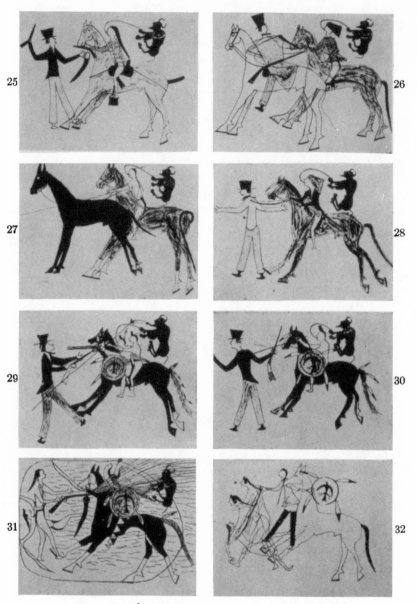

SITTING BULL'S HIEROGLYPHIC AUTOBIOGRAPHY (4)

earning the name Woman-Walking-Ahead. The white women on the reservation, unable to pretend that Catherine Weldon was not just as refined and accomplished as themselves, got back at her by regarding her "infatuation" as a "bitter disgrace" to their sex, a pose encouraged by officials, who looked with distaste upon her "inordinate praise" of the Chief. In no time wild rumors were afloat.

It was said she had actually married the Chief, as wife No. 3, and was with child by him. She had given him presents—a little golden bull, which he wore as a watch charm. His Indian wives, it was claimed, were furiously jealous, had chased her around camp with their butcher knives. She had filled Sitting Bull's head with tales of Alexander, Achilles, and Napoleon, rousing his martial ardor, had given him a revolver and urged him to defend himself. She was learning Sioux, acting as his secretary—a functionary he needed badly. And it was known that she carried on voluminous conversations in Sioux and English, all of which she faithfully recorded on foolscap as a valuable record. Probably it was all that, judging from the fragments that remain to us.

From these it would appear that Sitting Bull, in his straightforward way, took the white woman's extravagant behavior at its face value. The Sioux trail to love is short and straight, and when a woman made moccasins for a man, or performed any wifely service, it was regarded by all as a proposal of marriage. If the scribblings in her handwriting found in his cabin after his death are true records, there can be no doubt that Sitting Bull offered to marry her.

Such a matter-of-fact interpretation of her feeling for him was a facer for the romantic widow. But Sitting Bull's common sense made nothing of her evasions. Said he, "Why not? Chaska [another Sioux] has married a white woman."

Poor lady. His words pierced to her Victorian bosom's core. She cried: "You had no business to tell me of Chaska! Is this the reward for so many years of faithful friendship which I have proved to you? . . ." And then she wrote it all down for us to read.

The old man must have been puzzled to follow the thoughts of this unaccountable woman, who held him in such veneration, performed so many wifely services, and yet would not lie in his bed. He had had nine wives, but Catherine Weldon was something new. She was so sensible at times, and again so absurd. And then, too, she was courageous in her way. She was ready to fight the world for him, and he had had to restrain her forcibly from mounting a bronco which would inevitably have broken her neck.

Precious little sympathy she got from her own race and sex out there. They called her "female crank," or "damned old fool," meddlesome busybody," one "seeking notoriety," who "neglected her dying son for a dirty blanket Indian."

The agency folk had it in for the Chief; he was altogether too observant, too critical, too outspoken. And at last they had him at a disadvantage.

Yet Sitting Bull's rivals had their troubles, too. After the cession, the government built a frame house for John Grass, and Gall (for whom no house was provided) was so angry at this favoritism that he swore to kill Grass, who was then too ill to leave his new home for weeks. People began to say these chiefs had been bought. For, just as Sitting Bull had warned them, the promises made by the commission of 1889 were not fulfilled. No money was forthcoming for the lands ceded, and the rations were not merely not increased (as General Crook had promised), they were actually reduced by 20 per cent! General Crook died in the spring of 1890, and as Red Cloud said, "Our hope died with him." At all the agencies there was hunger, and gaunt starvation at Pine Ridge, where people—especially children—died like flies. For two years the Indians had lost their crops while they were held in council with the commissions of 1888 and 1889. And now the drought made farming impossible. Starvation was followed by epidemics of grippe, whooping cough, and measles (this last almost as fatal to Indians as smallpox). The camps resounded with the thin wails of mourners. The chiefs who had brought all this upon the Sioux took no pleasure in the tune Sitting Bull sang: "I told you so!"

Farm relief in those days usually took the form of an Indian war, and it needed no prophet to foresee what would happen if only suitable propaganda could be started. This, as usual, was provided—by a letter from "a citizen of Pierre," who reported to the Commissioner of Indian Affairs, in May, 1890, that "private information had reached him" that "the Sioux Indians, or a portion of them [which portion not stated] were secretly planning and arranging for an outbreak in the near future." The Commissioner duly referred this rumor to Mc-Laughlin and other agents for investigation and report. McLaughlin, after nineteen days' investigation, reports, "I do not believe that such an imprudent step is seriously meditated by any of the Sioux," and "if such a step was being planned by a few, it could not be kept secret from the rest." All the Sioux agents branded this story as an idle rumor.

But in this questionnaire of the Commissioner, McLaughlin saw a heaven-sent opportunity to get rid of Sitting Bull. He continues: "There are, however, a few malcontents here, as at all Sioux agencies, who cling tenaciously to the old Indian ways and are slow to accept the better order of things, whose influence is exerted in the wrong direction, and this class of Indians are ever ready to circulate idle rumors and sow dissensions among the more progressive; but only a very few of the Sioux could now possibly be united in attempting any overt act against the Government, and the removal from among them of a few individuals, such as Sitting Bull, Circling Bear, Black Bird, and Circling Hawk, of this agency . . . would end all trouble and uneasiness in the future." This report was dated June 18, 1890.

Note that McLaughlin has no charge to make against Sitting Bull and his friends. He aims a vague blanket accusation at a "class" who "are ready to circulate idle rumors." He wanted them "removed" (imprisoned) for that. But, if circulating idle rumors is a crime, why not "remove" the "citizen of Pierre"?

McLaughlin ends his report by declaring that the Sioux "will not be the aggressors in any overt act against white settlers" (a forecast absolutely justified by the event), and adds, "if justice is only done them, no uneasiness need be entertained."

Even had all the Sioux of Standing Rock Agency gone on the war-path, it is hard to see why any uneasiness need have been entertained. For, unless the Dakota boosters padded the United States Census unmercifully that year, the whites in North Dakota outnumbered the Indians (including Rees, Mandans, and Hidatsa, all notoriously peace-

269

ful folk) seventeen to one! Sitting Bull's little band of Hunkpapa on Grand River contained fewer than two hundred souls, men, women, and children. The men in that band able to bear arms did not total fifty, and at no time was there even a remote chance that other Standing Rock Sioux would join in an outbreak. Yet the newspapers played up the "scare"; the settlers began to pull out toward the East, and land values went on falling, down, down, clear out of sight. That idle rumor was having an even worse effect than the drought. The dust on the roads in Dakota which hung above the blistering prairie was raised by departing settlers, not by troops laden with good hard cash. Everything was going to the dogs.

Yet the "citizen of Pierre" had sown the dragon's teeth. Newspapers, frightened settlers, and army contractors cultivated that arid soil. Hunger, Poverty, Pestilence, and Despair watered it with Indian blood and tears. And in the autumn the harvest was prepared. For in October the Ghost Dance came to Standing Rock.

35. The Ghost Dance

Do not fight . . . you must not fight.   —THE INDIAN MESSIAH.

THE GHOST DANCE religion was started by a Pai-ute Indian prophet named Wo-vo-ka, in western Nevada; it swept nearly all the Indian nations in the West. It taught that the Messiah had returned to earth—this time in the flesh of an Indian, since the whites had denied and killed him; that the Messiah was coming from the West with all the nations of the Indian dead, with buffalo and horses; that he would remove the white men by supernatural means, and that all the Indians, dead and living, would be reunited upon a regenerated earth. All that was required to bring about this millennium was to dance the Ghost Dance regularly until he came—only a few moons. Kicking Bear brought the good news to Sitting Bull's camp.

Sitting Bull could not swallow such an improbable story; said he, "It is impossible for a dead man to return and live again." But to the starving, grieving Sioux, the new religion promised the restoration of all they had lost—and they had lost everything. Their nation was only a memory, their own people were plotting against them at the agency. If God also had forsaken them, what had they left but the gaunt scaffolds and the long bundles in the cottonwoods along the river? The white man's road led only to the Indian's grave.

Sitting Bull's people were pagans, entirely tolerant. Faith and devotion were alike alien to their religion; they believed only what they saw. Any prayer that got results was a good prayer. They were ready to try anything once. And in this new dance, they were told, people fell dead (fainted) and saw their dead relatives. And even the most skeptical, even the idly curious, were eager to join the séance and talk, if possible, with their dead. Sitting Bull feared that troops would come and stop the dance, as they had the Sun Dance, but Kicking Bear said he need not fear another massacre. The dancers must wear sacred garments (Ghost Shirts, the white men called them) painted with the sun, moon, stars, the eagle, the magpie, and the buffalo. "The guns are the only things we are afraid of. But they belong to our Father in heaven; He will see that they do us no harm. The sacred garments are bulletproof."

Sitting Bull could not deny that there might be something in that; in his time he had known several men who were bulletproof. As chief, it was his duty to get for his people whatever they wanted, if possible. In 1868 he told Father De Smet how he had gone to war under similar pressure: "My people caused me to do so . . . they have been troubled and confused . . . became crazy, and pushed me forward." It was the same now. As the old men say, "They used him as a shield." The dance was started.

Thus, overnight, Sitting Bull's band became Christianized. Of course the missionaries of long-established sects would not admit that the Ghost Dance was a Christian church. But their claim is absurd. For you cannot believe in the Second Coming of Christ unless you believe in the First. The Ghost Dance was entirely Christian—except for the difference in rituals. However, it taught nonresistance and brotherly love in ways that had far more significance for Indians than any the missions could offer. No wonder the missionaries became alarmed; they were no longer sure of their converts.

Sitting Bull danced with the others, hoping to go into a trance and see the beloved daughter he was mourning. But it was no use; faith was no part of his technique. He could not believe until he saw, though he was pitifully eager to, and listened with close attention to the reports of more favored dancers. McLaughlin himself declares that Sitting Bull did not believe, but allowed his people to dance. Quite true: Sitting Bull was too entirely Sioux to become a Christian overnight and throw away the pagan convictions of a lifetime. He was too old to do so.

It was the custom of dancers to make songs of their experiences in the Spirit Land. Sitting Bull had been making songs all his life, yet he has left no Ghost Dance songs behind him. No better proof of his lack of faith, of his failure to see his dead, could be desired.

When McLaughlin sent the police to drive out Kicking Bear, Sitting Bull stopped dancing. But he could not stop others, and he would not drive out the visitors to his camp; he was too hospitable. And his pride would not permit him to leave home to avoid the dancers; as old men say, "It would have looked *ridiculous* for him to let them run him out of his own camp."

Although the Indian Bureau had, very properly, ignored McLaughlin's request to have Sitting Bull arrested, leading men of the agency faction kept hounding the agent to let them go after Sitting Bull. And at last the agent called a meeting and told the policemen that it looked as though they might have to arrest Sitting Bull. Immediately, the police force fell to pieces. Some felt that the arrest was impossible, others that it was unjustified. Many had relatives down there and were reluctant to start a fight in which blood would be shed, and those who had families demanded who would care for their widows and orphans. They knew that Sitting Bull's followers, though obedient to the white men, would never endure to have Yanktonais and Blackfeet Sioux come and carry him out of a Hunkpapa camp. Crazy Walking, captain of the police, resigned; Grasping Eagle, Big Mane, Standing Soldier, all turned in their guns and uniforms. One Bull was discharged because of distrust; he was known to love his uncle.

McLaughlin tried to enlist men from Sitting Bull's own camp, but they soon returned their guns and blue coats, their shining metal badges: they did not wish to be Metal Breasts and kill their own people. Old Bull, Strikes-the-Kettle, Black Fox, Two Crow, all resigned.

Then Lieutenant Bullhead told the Major, "Let me pick my own men, I'll pick men who will stick." He picked men from Grand River —White Bird, One Feather, Good-Voiced Eagle, Running Hawk, Weasel Bear, Iron Thunder, Black Pheasant, and brave men like that.

He made a strong force. McLaughlin promised these men pensions if they were killed or wounded in a fight with Sitting Bull's followers. Sergeant Shavehead, after this meeting, came reeling like a drunken man to the home of Mrs. Josephine Waggoner beyond Four-Mile Creek. Mrs. Waggoner, then a girl, was with her mother, Woman-of-the-Wind, her Aunt Acorn, and Bear Shield when he came in. Said he: "My relatives, do not be ashamed that I seem drunk. I am a dead man; I am as good as dead. I am here in spirit, but my body is lying on the prairie. We have been ordered to arrest Sitting Bull." His relatives began to cry and answered, "Don't say that."

Among the new policemen was Bob-Tail-Bull, a friend of the Chief, and a former member of Sitting Bull's Soldiers. He was detailed to go down and watch the Ghost Dancers. For McLaughlin had only one thought in mind—to keep out of the mess spreading from Pine Ridge. He foresaw another "scare," another Indian campaign. He was lying low, hoping the storm would pass and leave his reputation unscathed. Said Bob-Tail-Bull: "Some claim that Sitting Bull danced, but I never saw him dance. There were a lot of people dancing for a while. The Major would send tobacco down, and we distributed it among the old people, and told Sitting Bull to take no part in the dance. He said he would not. I kept on going down and looking on, until they all got tired of my coming. I know that Sitting Bull tried to stop the dance, but they were too many and too firm believers. Once, when Father Bernard had talked with him and assured him that the dead would not come back, Sitting Bull publicly announced that he did not believe in the Messiah. He told them to quit, but they had no ears."

All the missionaries took a stand against the dance. And louder and shriller than them all Catherine Weldon preached volubly against this new folly from the West. A long sermon or speech which she prepared in English and had translated into Sioux remains to us. She offered to meet Kicking Bear in open debate! She defied his power to strike her dead. She showed the Sioux electrical toys and magnets to dispose of their fear of the lightning Kicking Bear might call down upon them. She explained that hypnotism was a common thing among white men, and no mystery. She blamed (quite rightly) the white men for the scare over the Ghost Dance then filling the papers. And she blamed (quite rightly) others than Sitting Bull for the continuance of the dance. She knew what she was writing; she lived in the camp while the dancing went on.

But all her carefully prepared speeches were wasted on the enthusiasm of that great camp meeting. She might as well have preached against a Methodist Revival or a meeting of Holy Rollers, or against Shakers, Ranters, Quakers, Flagellants, Jumpers, Adventists, or any other of a hundred Christian sects. Yet the Sioux never laid a finger on this enemy of their faith; they exhibited a most unchristian tolerance. They simply went on with their dancing. Even when she assured them, a flighty Cassandra to whose true prophecies no ears were open, that the white men would certainly take advantage of their dancing to start an Indian war, they paid no heed.

And so she turned, in her extremity, to McLaughlin, and sent him letters, begging him: "Have pity on the Hunkpapa and Sitting Bull, who have been under the influence of Kicking Bear. Do not send police or soldiers! . . . My heart is almost breaking when I see the work of years undone by that vile imposter. . . . If I had known what obstinate minds I had to contend with, I would not have undertaken this mission to enlighten and instruct them. It was money, health, and heart thrown away. . . ."

Sitting Bull took her to Cannonball in his wagon. As they passed Fort Yates on the way up, he went ahead on foot, so that, if the soldiers tried to take him, she would not be harmed. "He was brave to go alone," she says. But to his surprise, all her warnings came to nothing. The officers at the post greeted him and came up to shake hands. Then Sitting Bull (always unwilling to meet a white man with the full hand of friendship) gave them the tips of two fingers.

Yet he was not mistaken about his danger at the agency.

At Cannonball he bade his last white friend good-bye, and set out on the long drive home. He was sad at heart. And as he drove along, the reins lying along the back of the old gray circus horse, he sang to ease his heart of those forebodings.

As the end of his life and his leadership of the Sioux approached, he had been wondering what the song given him by the eagle at Sylvan Lake so long ago might mean for his nation after his death. For a long time he was puzzled about its meaning, but at last solved the riddle. The song was a prophecy that, after Sitting Bull's death, the eagle was to rule this land. And the old men say that song was straight and true, for money rules the land now, and the eagle is stamped on every dollar.

So now, in his hour of sadness and foreboding, Sitting Bull sang the eagle's song:

> *My Father has given me this nation,*
> *In protecting them I have a hard time.*

His enemies were all around him. As he passed Fort Yates that evening, a group of soldiers heard his voice above the rattle of the old lumber wagon. "There he goes, the old son-of-a-bitch, singing his war songs," they said. "We'll get him yet."

Yet the danger was not from the soldiers, but from certain Indians at the agency. At that very moment, three of these jealous enemies were lying in wait for him under the bridge on Long Soldier Creek. By a lucky chance, Sitting Bull took the other road; they failed to kill him that night. Inasmuch as nothing came of this, there is no point in printing the names of those three men.

Sitting Bull had no white friends left, it seemed. In those days the only friends of the Indian were philanthropists in the East, Christians. And when it was represented to these bigots that Sitting Bull was an apostle and priest of the Ghost Dance, even that poor prop was kicked from under. For the missionaries, though they had little to say so long as hunger drove Indians into the church, were loud in protest when it drove them into a church of their own devising.

The Ghost Dance would have died of itself within a few months; the dancers relied upon the Messiah to destroy the white men; they knew they were hopelessly outnumbered, and war was far from their desire. That was what made the bulletproof shirts necessary. Had they intended war, the warriors would have relied upon their war charms; all the men had them, old-timers still have. And, had war been their plan, why put Ghost Shirts on women and children? Women and children do not make war, and never carried war charms. No, the story won't wash; it was only propaganda got up to save the face of a corrupt Indian Bureau, to camouflage an unnecessary Indian campaign. The Indians feared the troops would massacre their families. And they were right; at Wounded Knee, December 29, 1890, about one hundred Sioux women and children, unarmed and fleeing, were shot down by men in uniform.

McLaughlin knew that the Ghost Dance was harmless and dying; all his reports stress this fact. But down at Pine Ridge the new agent, a political appointee, Dr. R. F. "Young-Man-Afraid-of-the-Indians" Royer, got scared and yelped for troops. They arrived there October 19, 1890, and immediately the frightened Oglala fled to the Badlands. As the Indians fled west, the settlers fled east; it was comical. But the Ghost Dance became front-page news, the army had to conceal the ridiculous nature of its errand, and the papers began to say that Mc-Laughlin also had "lost control of his Indians."

At once McLaughlin went down and interviewed the Chief. Sitting Bull disclaimed all responsibility for the dance, which had been brought from another agency, declared it peaceful and harmless, and then, seeing the agent still dissatisfied, made a proposition. "White Hair, you do not like me personally. You do not understand this dance. But I am willing to be convinced. You and I will go together to the tribes from which this dance came, and when we reach the last one, where it started, if they cannot produce the Messiah, and if we do not find all the nations of the dead coming this way, then I will return and tell the Sioux it is all a lie. That will end the dance. If we find the Messiah, then you are to let the dance go on."

A fairer proposition from his point of view could not have been offered. But McLaughlin said he had no time and no funds for such a journey, gave good words to Sitting Bull, and asked him to come to the agency to argue the matter. But the Ghost Dancers would not permit the chief to leave them; they feared for his life. They had heard he was being "laid for" by his enemies of the agency faction.

McLaughlin went home, gave out a story to the papers minimizing the danger of the Ghost Dance at Standing Rock. He did not intend to interfere unless his hand was forced. Things went on quietly as before, for the agent relied upon cold weather to break up the dancing. But Sitting Bull knew that hope was vain. Says Miss Collins, the missionary: "I remember particularly that during the winter of the Ghost Dance he prophesied that the winter would be mild, and said, 'Yes, my people, you can dance all winter this year. The sun will shine warmly, and the weather will be fair.' " It happened as he had foretold.

Sitting Bull did not expect evil from white men. His danger lay elsewhere. For one day, when he was out looking for the old circus horse, which was hiding from him in the breaks, a meadowlark sang a new song to him:

The Sioux will kill you!

That message from his bird friend was a cruel blow to the old patriot. From that hour he expected his own people to destroy him. The meadowlark did not lie.

For ten days matters rested, and McLaughlin's only concern was to keep things quiet at his agency, as is well shown by a letter (hitherto unpublished) from his right-hand man on Grand River, the teacher at Sitting Bull's Day School, John M. ("Jack") Carignan. It is dated November 27:

At a council held at Iron Star's house today, I saw the principal men of the new dance, with the exception of Sitting Bull; if anyone were to leave the reserve, I am confident that some of those at council would have been amongst them. The Indians seem to be very peaceably inclined, and I do not apprehend any trouble. . . . The Indians have been told that soldiers are coming down here, and are badly frightened. If they were assured different, there would be no danger of their leaving. I have done all I could in telling them that the reports they have heard are all lies, and that *no one would try to prevent them from dancing.* I am positive that *no trouble need be apprehended from Sitting Bull and his followers, unless they are forced to defend themselves,* and I think it would be advisable to keep all strangers, other than employees who have business amongst the Indians, away from here, as Sitting Bull has lost all confidence in the whites since Mrs. Weldon has left him. . . .

That states fairly enough McLaughlin's program: let them dance, keep soldiers and strangers away, prevent a stampede of scared Indians off the Standing Rock Reserve. Incidentally, it throws a queer light upon the theory that there was danger for white men at Sitting Bull's camp, if strangers had to be warned off to keep from scaring the Sioux!!

Indeed, the number of dancers at Sitting Bull's camp was much smaller than before, for Male Bear had taken his following away and started a dance of his own on Oak Creek. All was quiet on Grand River. But next day another finger was stuck into the pie.

36. Buffalo Bill Intrudes

When the Seventh Day Adventists get up on the roofs of their houses arrayed in their Ascension robes, to meet the Second Coming, the U. S. Army is not rushed into the field. —DR. V. T. MCGILLICUDDY.

BY THIS TIME the Ghost Dance and the Sioux were front-page news. Buffalo Bill saw a chance to make a grand *coup* and acquire huge publicity for his show. At a dinner in Chicago, he persuaded General Nelson A. "Bear Coat" Miles to give him an order for Sitting Bull's arrest. When Buffalo Bill turned up at Standing Rock, Major McLaughlin tried to frighten him off. But Buffalo Bill was not at all afraid of Sitting Bull; he knew the old man too well. And apparently he did not intend to share the glory of the capture with the military at Fort Yates; he asked for no escort whatever. Instead, he laid in a wagonload of presents, chiefly candy and sweets. As Johnny Baker has put it, "If they had left Cody alone, he'd have captured Sitting Bull with an all-day sucker."

The military at Fort Yates resented Cody's interference. They held that he was only a civilian scout, "just a beef contractor," his rank of colonel had been given him by the Governor of Nebraska, and some thought him more famous than his deeds warranted. They liked McLaughlin; they conspired with him to defeat the orders of the Division Commander. The plan was to get Cody over to the Officers' Club, put him under the table and keep him there, until McLaughlin could get a wire through to Washington and have the General's order rescinded. Captain A. R. Chapin, then assistant surgeon at the post, tells the story:

"The officers were requested to assist. But Colonel Cody's *capacity* was such that it took practically all the officers in details of two or three at a time to keep him interested and busy through the day." And in spite of their best efforts, Cody kept his feet and his head, and was on the road next morning at eleven, with eight newspaper men and a wagon-load of goodies, bound for Grand River. Before leaving, he gave out a news story intended to forecast his valorous achievement, all about "this most dangerous undertaking of my career." But actually he was not in the least alarmed. On the way he stopped at the cabin of William Presley Zahn, a veteran of Custer's command, who had married an Indian woman. Zahn says that Cody was confident of success, and said, "Why, I've got a hundred dollars' worth of stuff in that wagon for every pound old Bull weighs."

Cody was not afraid.

There was no reason why he should have been, considering the number of people Sitting Bull had protected or saved in his time, and how high a regard he had for Cody, who had given him his favorite horse, and the hat he treasured so. Sitting Bull was thoroughly able to protect his guests, as is shown by the failure of the police to arrest Kicking Bear, as ordered. And Sitting Bull was no fanatic. Jack Carignan was constantly at his camp, watching the dancing. And on the very day Cody arrived at Standing Rock, Sam Clover, a Chicago newspaperman, went with Carignan to the camp and took photographs of the dancing from the seat of a wagon. No one harmed him. One Bull believes that his uncle would have gone with Buffalo Bill if his people had permitted it. That, of course, is doubtful. Few of Cody's party were armed with anything more deadly than lead pencils. The worst that could have happened was a disappointment for the famous showman.

McLaughlin wanted no military interference on his reserve; already the papers were calling him incompetent. The only danger in that business was to the agent—the danger that Sitting Bull's Indians would learn that an arrest had been ordered, would take fright, skip, and land the agent in hot water with an Indian commissioner who was known to dislike him already because he was a Roman Catholic and a friend to the military.

And so McLaughlin sent Indian horsemen to meet, mislead, and delay Cody until he could hear from Washington.[1]

Before Cody discovered the trick, McLaughlin notified him that the order for arrest had been rescinded.

Johnny Baker thinks Cody intended to save Sitting Bull. Whatever his motives, his action brought danger to the Chief. The War Department might be balked; it could not be eliminated. On December 1, the Commissioner of Indian Affairs wired McLaughlin: "You will, as to all operations intended to suppress any outbreak by force, co-operate with and obey the orders of the military officers commanding on the reservation in your charge."

McLaughlin immediately tried to reopen the question by asking whether or not he was authorized to make the arrest when he thought best. But this only brought the point-blank command: "The Secretary directs that you make no arrests whatever, except under orders from the military."

Early in December, Sitting Bull received an invitation from Pine Ridge Agency. Short Bull, the leader of the Ghost Dancers down there, had had a revelation that the Messiah was to hasten his coming, since the whites were interfering so much. Now the time was at hand; Short Bull felt that Sitting Bull, as chief, ought to be on hand to greet the Indian Christ. Sitting Bull consulted his people, who voted that he ought by all means to go. He said he would request a pass.

But next day, December 11, an Indian policeman, Running Hawk, brought a letter from the agent to the Chief, who handed it to his educated son-in-law, Andrew Fox, for interpretation. Andrew Fox has given this account of what followed. The letter was peremptory, ordering the dancers home to their farms. Running Hawk also warned the Chief that the authorities were going to disarm the Ghost Dancers and take away their ponies. He told Andrew Fox he had better camp at the agency; that "a fire was to be started in Sitting Bull's camp." But Andrew paid no attention.

Sitting Bull and his circle were amazed at this sudden change on the

[1] The story has been told: see E. A. Brininstool in the *El Segundo Herald*, El Segundo, California, December 28, 1928.

MAJOR McLAUGHLIN'S ORDER FOR SITTING BULL'S ARREST

Besides this and the orders in Sioux there were oral instructions

(Reproduced by courtesy of Mr. A. B. Welch)

ENVELOPE ENCLOSING ORDERS FOR
SITTING BULL'S ARREST

MAJOR McLAUGHLIN'S ORDER FOR SITTING BULL'S ARREST
WRITTEN IN THE SANTEE SIOUX DIALECT
The order is to the same effect as that in English
(*Reproduced by courtesy of Mr. A. B. Welch*)

agent's part from tolerance and gentle remonstrance to threats of punishment.

Sitting Bull decided to ask for his pass and answer the message from the agent in a single letter. The fact that he asked for a pass is a sufficient comment upon the Chief's alleged rebellious and insubordinate spirit. Plenty of Indians in those days went off the reservation without a pass: Short Bull and Kicking Bear, for example, went all the way to western Nevada and were gone six months, without one. But Sitting Bull was obedient to the last. This is what McLaughlin calls "refusing to commit any overt act."

That night the Chief and his advisers sat around a tipi fire, talking and smoking. Blackbird, Spotted Horn Bull, Bull Ghost, and a number of Silent Eaters were there, along with Andrew Fox, then just twenty-seven years old.

To him Sitting Bull said, "My son-in-law, I wish you would write this letter to the agent."

"So," says Andrew, "I said, 'All right.'"

While Andrew was getting his stub of pencil and the piece of folded notepaper on which he was to write, Sitting Bull spoke to the friends sitting beside him: "The agent was here in person lately, and said many good words to me. All the people heard those good words. Therefore I wish to write this letter to him." Said he, "We did not originate this dance. I will not own it, for it was brought here from another reservation."

When Andrew was ready, Sitting Bull dictated the following letter:

To the Major in the Indian Office:

I wish to write a few lines today and let you know something. I held a meeting with all my Indians today, and am writing to you this message [from them]. God made you—made all the white race, and also made the Red race—and gave them both might and heart to know everything in the world, but gave the whites the advantage over the Indians. But today God, our Father, is helping us Indians, so all we Indians believe.

Therefore I think this way: I wish no man to come to me in my prayers with gun or knife. Therefore all the Indians pray to God for life, and try to find out a good road, and do nothing wrong in their life. This is what we want, and to pray to God. But you did not believe us.

You should say nothing against our religion, for we said nothing against yours. You pray to God. So do all of us Indians, as well as the whites. We both pray to only one God, who made us all.

Yet you, my friend, today you think I am a fool, and you gather up some of the wise men among my people on your side, and you let the white people back East know what you think. I know that, but I do not object; I overlook that, because I am foolish enough to pray to God.

Therefore, my friend, you don't like me. Well, my friend, I don't like it myself when someone is foolish. You are the same. You don't like me because you think I am a fool, and you imagine that, if I were not here, all the Indians would become civilized, and that, because I am here, all the Indians are fools. I know this is what you publish in the newspapers back East. I see it all in the paper, but I overlook that.

When you were here in my camp, you gave me good words about my prayers, but today you take it all back again. And there is something else I want you to know. I am obliged to go to Pine Ridge Agency and investigate this Ghost Dance religion. So I write to let you know that.

The policeman told me you intend to take all our ponies, and our guns too. So I wish you would let me know about that. Please answer soon.

Sitting Bull[2]

[2] Here follows what Andrew Fox made (in English) out of the above dictation:

"I want to write a few lines to day & to let you know Some thing. I meeting with all my Indians to day, & writing to you this order. God made you all the white race & also made the Red race & give they both Might & Heart to know everything on the whlod; but white High then the Indians; but to day, our farther is halp us the Indians. Se we all the Indians knowing. So I thing this way. I wish no one to come to in my pray with they gund or knife: so all the Indians Pray to god for life & try to find out good road and do nothing wrong. in they life: This is what we want & Pray: because we did not Say nothing. about your pray. because you pray to god: So we all Indians, while; we both to Pray only one god to make us: & you my friend to day. you thing I am foll; I you take some wise man amongs my people. & you let them know back East. the white people. So I knowing that. but I thing that is all right. because I am foll to pray to God. So you don't like me: My Friend. I dont like my self. when some one is foll; I like Him; So you are the same. you dont like me because I am foll; & if I did not Here. then the Indians will be civilization: but because I am Here. & all the Indians foll, & I know this is all you put down on newspapters back East. So I seeing

While Andrew was busy with his pencil, Sitting Bull said to the others: "This is not our business, this dancing. It was brought here from Pine Ridge to us and started here by outsiders. Therefore I said this business is not our affair, we should not be blamed. The other Indians here also claim it is not our fault."

Then, seeing Andrew struggling with the pencil, the kindly old man added, "Look at my son-in-law. He is writing a letter hard, so we had better all keep still, listening to what he is doing and smoking."

And so the letter was written, and Bull Ghost took it to the agency, handing it to McLaughlin at 6:00 P.M., December 12, 1890.

Earlier that same afternoon, another message had reached Major McLaughlin. It was the military order for Sitting Bull's arrest.

the paper but I thing it is all right: & when you was Here. in my camp. you was give me good word about. my Pray. & to day you take all back from me: & also I will let you know some thing. I got go to [Pine Ridge] Agency & to know This Pray: So I let you know that & t'ıe Police man. told me you going to take all our Poneys, gund, too; so I want you let me know that. I want answer back soo. Sitting Bull"

37. On Guard

In the process of eliminating the big men of the [Indian] race, some stirring events took place.   —MAJOR JAMES MCLAUGHLIN.

HEADQUARTERS DEPARTMENT OF DAKOTA
ST. PAUL, MINN. *December* 12, 1890

To Commanding Officer,
Fort Yates N. Dak.,
The Division Commander has directed that you make it your especial duty to secure the person of Sitting Bull. Call on Indian agent to co-operate and render such assistance as will best promote the purpose in view. Acknowledge receipt and, if not perfectly clear, repeat back.

M. Barber
Assistant Adjutant General

This time there was to be no doubt that McLaughlin, who had balked the Division Commander before, was to co-operate with him in deed and in fact. But he was still able to manage matters to his own advantage: he could still persuade Colonel Drum to let him make the arrest with the Indian police, with the troops in reserve. He could still save his face and the face of the Bureau.

The Indian police were eager enough. Their hands had itched to lay hold of Sitting Bull for a long time. As McLaughlin reports, "Their officers and others of the progressive Indians had been urging me for several weeks to permit them to arrest Sitting Bull and other leaders of disaffection." Their motive, as given by the agent, was that

286

people of their "peaceable" faction could not pass through the Ghost Dance settlement "without being subjected to insults from Sitting Bull and his followers." Lieutenant Bullhead, especially, is mentioned as being "unable to brook with patience the indifference with which the magnanimity [*sic*] of the Government was regarded by Sitting Bull and his followers." And now the time had come; now they could get at him!

The arrest which followed has been much reported, chiefly by the officers (both military and civil) who had a hand in it. Most of these gentlemen make a great to-do over the Ghost Dance, and appear to think that the Ghost Dance made the arrest necessary. *But Sitting Bull's arrest had nothing to do with the Ghost Dance.* That dance was a mere pretext, and a pretext suggested rather late in the game. Mc-Laughlin had recommended the arrest months before the Ghost Dance was started at Sitting Bull's camp.

Had the agent wished to suppress the dance, he might have arrested Shave Bear, who conducted it; that would have been easy, as Shave Bear regularly visited the agency for rations. But in fact, none of the men he wished arrested were shamans or priests of the cult. All along the agent had been lenient, had told the Indians that no one would try to prevent them from dancing. The whole affair was merely the last round of that long bout between the Indian Bureau and the War Department for control of the Indians. Sitting Bull was an innocent bystander, the football of bureaucratic politics.

But the Ghost Dance came in very handily; for McLaughlin, who was so anxious to be rid of him, could think of *nothing* to accuse him of. He complains that the Chief "will commit no overt act," and even the men he was said to be putting up to mischief are not accused of any crimes. McLaughlin could only say, "There is no knowing what he may direct them to attempt." Precisely: had there been any knowing, the agent would have brought it forward. All his reports make light of the Ghost Dance.

But when Sitting Bull was killed, panic swept the Sioux everywhere. From that panic sprang the massacre at Wounded Knee and the subsequent scandal and investigation. Inasmuch as the Indians never did attack the settlements or commit any depredations whatever off the reservation, inasmuch as they only resisted the troops after many of their relatives had been shot down (as they said) "without cause," some pretext had to be found to shield the officials whose graft and folly had caused the wretched business. Eureka! The Ghost Dance! The Messiah Craze! Superstition! Fanaticism! Barbarism! *White-wash!!*

A comparison of the documents prepared by these gentlemen—before and after the event—will convince anyone of the truth of this. When the order for arrest arrived, McLaughlin sent Sergeant Shave Head off with a detail of policemen to join Lieutenant Bullhead on Grand River. His orders were "not to attempt to make the arrest until further ordered, *unless* it was discovered that Sitting Bull was preparing to leave the Reservation."

Lieutenant Bullhead was a most efficient officer. It did not take him long to discover that.

Meanwhile, Bull Ghost brought in Sitting Bull's letter, fixed his one eye upon the agent, and waited for the pass. One can imagine how McLaughlin's excitement mounted when he learned that Sitting Bull wished to leave Standing Rock. He sent Policeman White Bird flying with a letter to Bullhead with the news.

Bull Ghost, of course, got no pass for Sitting Bull. The agent put him off with an evasive answer. Bull Ghost rode home, empty-handed. He reached Sitting Bull's camp about noon next day, December 13, 1890. The news of the order for arrest had preceded him.

This is how it happened. One Elk was going toward Standing Rock, and met his brother Iron Thunder, one of the Indian police. Iron Thunder said: "Brother, Monday they are going to arrest Sitting Bull. Look out. Be ready." They talked for some time, and at last Iron Thunder warned One Elk not to repeat this news. "Tell nobody," he said.

The first man One Elk met was Jumping Bull, Sitting Bull's adopted brother. One Elk liked Jumping Bull; he did not want him to get killed. One Elk said: "Monday they are coming to arrest Sitting Bull. You had better go on home to your wife and children."

But Jumping Bull would not leave the Chief at such a time. He made excuse. Said he: "Some of my horses have strayed away. I shall have to stay where I am until I can find them." He remained in Sitting Bull's camp. He told the Chief and his friends what he had heard. They all knew that the police were coming.

A guard was established around the house of Sitting Bull; for the Hunkpapa were not going to allow those Yanktonais and Blackfeet Sioux to come into their camp and carry off their chief. Such conduct was contrary to all their standards; it made them hot all over to think of it. Bullhead and Gray Eagle and the rest might hold fast to the Grandfather with one hand, as Indian police, but their other hand was clasping the other bands at the agency. The jealousy between these bands was as keen as ever it had been on the plains—keener.

Catch-the-Bear, Lieutenant Bullhead's mortal enemy, was commander of Sitting Bull's bodyguard. Under him were Grover Eagle Boy, Shield, Jumping Bull's son Middle, Blue Mountain, Strikes-the-Kettle, Brave Thunder, Old Crow, and Bull Ghost. They assembled in Sitting Bull's big double cabin, carrying their Winchesters. Crowfoot was with them, though too young to carry arms.

All the night of December 13, they sat in the house with Sitting Bull. The Chief had plenty of kinnikinnick, and they smoked a good deal. Sitting Bull talked of old times. Now that he had fallen on evil days and evil tongues, and the end of the trail was in sight, his thoughts turned back to the good old days of feasting and hunting and valorous deeds, to the old and happy far-off things and battles long ago. He spoke of the good fat meat of wild game which he loved so well, but forbore to contrast it with the agency beef: his mind was unwilling to dwell that night upon the present. He told stories of old-time buffalo hunts he had taken part in: how all the young men raced in friendly rivalry after the lumbering bulls, how such a man was first to reach the herd, and how such another brought down seven fat cows. He talked of the brave fast horses he used to have, and laughed as he narrated anecdotes which illustrated their various characteristics. Also he spoke of raids and fighting with the Crows, Shoshoni and Flatheads. Late that night and again toward morning, he served his faithful handful with food. All night long they were coming and going, two of them standing guard outside in the frosty night, or scouting around the camp and up the trail toward Fort Yates, on the lookout for the police. The gathering was grave, for, in spite of the chief's unruffled bearing, they all felt the pressure of the overhanging doom.

It was too much for Catch-the-Bear. He jumped up, Winchester in hand, and declared: "I stand here as a guard protecting my chief, Sitting Bull. I have a double grudge against Lieutenant Bullhead—once because of the way he treated me over the sack, and another time because he took my beef tongues away from me at the beef issue. If he shows up here, I am going to shoot him. When I sleep, I forget what he did, but when I am awake, I think of it all the time, and if he comes nosing around here, he will meet *me!*"

Sitting Bull said nothing after this outburst. All that night he appeared quite unworried, and showed no concern whatever about what might happen when the police turned up. At daybreak he dismissed the guard. Said he: "You can go home now. I know you sympathize with me. You can go home now and feed and water your stock."

The bodyguard filed out of the cabin into the frosty air, and Sitting Bull walked over to his feeding corral and threw down some hay for the old gray circus horse. As he went back toward the house, the sun was just climbing above the hill downriver. He stood a moment at the door, watching it. That was his last sunrise.

Lieutenant Bullhead's reports led McLaughlin to believe that Sitting Bull and his Hunkpapa would run away. General Custer had made the same mistake.

During the afternoon of December 14, while soldiers and police busily prepared to march on the Chief's cabin, he remained quietly in camp, while the people danced the Ghost Dance. Eagle Boy, the son-in-law of one of Sitting Bull's close friends, took part in this dance. Shave Bear, all dressed up in a long-tailed Ghost Shirt decorated with painted rainbows, horse tracks, and fluttering feathers, was leading the ceremony, calling out, "If you wish to see your dead, I can make you do so."

Eagle Boy had been very fond of his grandmother. She was dead.

He caught Shave Bear's eye and said, "I want to see my grandmother."

Shave Bear held out his closed fists toward Eagle Boy, with extended thumbs turned inward toward each other. Above the sound of the singing, Shave Bear called to Eagle Boy, "Take hold of my thumbs, touch them, and you shall see your dead!"

Eagle Boy obeyed. But somehow, that day, Shave Bear's power wouldn't work. Eagle Boy says, "I tried it, but nothing happened. And so my thoughts fell away. I lost faith and went home. That night the police asked me to join them and help make the arrest. But I couldn't get away. My wife asked me to stay home that night. I refused to go."

Other dancers had better luck than Eagle Boy that day. The dance went on, some saw their dead. And late that night, worn out, the whole camp turned in and went to sleep. Sitting Bull told his tired friends not to stand to their guns that night. He was not afraid. He lay down with his elder wife on their pallet in the big double log cabin, and slept soundly.

Outside on the flat, circling his house, and among the naked cottonwoods along the stream, the conical tipis of the Ghost Dancers, like white steeples of a church slowly rising from the earth, awaited the coming of men in blue coats sent, in the name of Free Government and Christian Civilization, to stamp down that church into the dust.

Long before the members of the new church fell asleep, preparations had been making, and these continued through the night. Of them all we catch brief glimpses: Of a white-haired, likable, self-important, determined man standing on a chair at the agency, speaking to a gathering of stalwart, steady, silent Sioux freshly outfitted with ill-fitting blue uniforms, soft black hats, cartridge belts, shining metal badges on their breasts, and guns of different patterns. . . . Of a Santee woman methodically tearing a bolt of white cloth into strips, to be used as mufflers by the police, so that they would know each other in the darkness. . . . Of Officers' Call at midnight at Fort Yates, the hot coffee and rations in the mess hall, the rumble of wagons and cannon and the creak of saddle leather as the cavalry pulled out to Grand River. . . . Of Jack Carignan and four policemen slipping through Sitting Bull's camp in the darkness, on their way to Bullhead's house, to carry his women and children to a place of safety. . . . Of the gathering of Metal Breasts at Bullhead's place, the reading and interpretation of the order for arrest. . . . Of the long hours spent that night at the house of Gray Eagle, just across the river from Sitting Bull's camp, where the police heartened each other by telling war stories and recounting *coups*. . . . Of Gray Eagle volunteering to go with the police to arrest his brother-in-law. . . . Of a huddle of policemen about a crucifix, while Bullhead led in prayer, some of them anxious for fear the Ghost Shirts might be bulletproof, after all. . . . Of the iron heels of the horses striking fire from the stones of the dry ford, while the coyotes yapped a warning from the hills. . . . Of the quick trot forward, and the swift, galloping charge, like the charge of an enemy, upon that sleeping camp. . . .

38. The Fight in the Dark

The attempt to arrest Sitting Bull was so managed as to place the responsibility for the fight that ensued upon Sitting Bull's band which began the firing. —CAPTAIN E. G. FECHET.

IT WAS the dark hour before the dawn. Suddenly Sitting Bull, sleeping soundly, felt the beat of galloping hooves against the ground on which he lay and was vaguely aware of the loud outcry of barking dogs rushing toward his cabin. The hoofbeats stopped; someone called out. He heard the dull bang of a rifle butt against the cabin door, which flew open, letting in the chill night air. The Chief's wife beside him uttered a startled exclamation: the room was full of men in the darkness, the sandpaper sound of shuffling moccasins all around them. A match flared, lighting up for an instant the rough, chinked walls of the long room, the gray canvas sheeting stretched halfway up all around, the low beds, the stove in the middle of the cabin, the kerosene lamp on its wall bracket, the white mufflers and glinting badges of the Metal Breasts. Sitting Bull sat up.

Immediately after, the Chief felt the hands of several grab his naked shoulders and arms, lifting him from his bed. Another match flared up, and several men pounced upon the carbine, the knife, the revolver lying under the blankets of the old warrior's bed. Someone lighted the kerosene lamp.

Sitting Bull saw that Weasel Bear was holding him by the right arm, Eagle Man by the left. They lifted him up. Lieutenant Bullhead laid his hand upon the chief's shoulder and said, "I am holding you

293

[for arrest].'' Sergeant Shave Head said, "Brother, we have come for you." Red Tomahawk declared, "If you fight, you will be killed here." Red Tomahawk threw his arms around the Chief from behind: the three of them held the old, naked, unarmed man as if he had been a bird which might fly away. To all this Sitting Bull said only, *"Hau* [yes]."

Crowfoot was nowhere to be seen. The two old men who had been sleeping there got up quickly and went out without a word. The Metal Breasts were relieved to find that there were no armed bodyguards in the Chief's cabin. Nobody had much to say for a while. Nobody but the Chief's wife, who stood there, scornful, half-dressed. She spoke her mind freely, "What are all you jealous people doing here?" Mc-Laughlin had given strict orders that no women or children were to be killed.

Sitting Bull, as usual, had been sleeping naked, and now he had to be dressed before he could be taken away. The Metal Breasts picked up such clothes as they could find, an issue shirt, dark blue leggins, and threw them at the chief. But it was impossible for him to put them on, the way they were holding him. They were young men, most of them, new to police work, excited—anxious to get their prisoner away before the whole camp was aroused. Weasel Bear snatched up a moccasin and held it out to the chief. The woman laughed and said, "That is mine!" Weasel Bear saw that it was a woman's shoe, and dropped it. Most of Sitting Bull's good clothes were in the other cabin, and his wife went out after them. Already people had gathered outside; they could hear her calling to her sons, "Boys, they have come for your father; saddle the gray horse."

All this time Sitting Bull was in the hands of the policemen, who were trying to hurry him into his clothes, one pulling on a leggin, another forcing on a moccasin, while the old man, hopping on one foot, swayed to and fro in their arms, protesting: "You need not help me, I can dress myself. You need not honor me like this." To dress a man for any important occasion was an honor: it had been done for Sitting Bull before.

But it was soon apparent that these tactless Metal Breasts were not trying to honor their chief, the way they dressed him. He began to complain. "I was resting easy, and you wakened me. Why not wait until morning, when I would be up and dressed?" It annoyed him, made him angry, they mishandled him so. The door was wide open, the police kept coming and going, everybody could see the way he was being treated, and he heard some of them saying things which angered him. Yet he did not refuse to go. He told them to saddle his gray circus horse for him. White Bird and Red Bear were told off for this duty.

The officers kept hurrying him, and at last he became indignant and balky. He tried to sit down on the bed. But they held him, they picked him up, they started toward the door with him in their hands, half-clad as he was, with one leggin about his ankle. He protested then: "Let me go; I'll go without any help."

They paid no attention: they kept lugging him along toward the door. His dignity would not endure being dragged out in front of his friends and followers like that; he spread his arms and legs across the doorway. That delayed them for a moment. Eagle Man had to kick his legs aside to get him through the door. They carried him outside. Up to this time Sitting Bull had said very little: the Metal Breasts had done most of the talking. They had mishandled him, taunted him, thrown his clothes at him, kicked him.

Yet, they say, the old Chief showed no fear whatever. As Little Soldier put it, "Sitting Bull was not afraid; *we* were afraid." And good reason they had to fear. No Indians had ever gone into a Hunkpapa camp and carried off a chief like that before: it was brave to the point of foolhardiness. Those young policemen knew that Sitting Bull's friends were hard-boiled, seasoned warriors, afraid of nothing: and out there in the darkness they waited—Catch-the-Bear, Strikes-the-Kettle, Brave Thunder, Spotted Horn Bull—desperate men. They pushed Sitting Bull through the door, carried him out into the dark, hazy, starless night.

Once outside, he was allowed to find his feet, and was pushed forward. One of the policemen kept punching the Chief in the back with a revolver, urging him forward, while others still kept fast hold of his arms, and Red Tomahawk embraced his waist from behind. They kept trying to move forward through the angry throng ahead. Sitting Bull did not resist, but kept squirming to avoid the blows, saying: *"Hau, hau!* You have come for me. I have to go, I am going." But the only answer was more punches in the back, and the command, "Shut up! Keep quiet! Do just as we say." They shoved him along, but were able to advance only a few paces from the door; beyond that point they could not go.

Sergeant Eagle Man, unusually noisy that night, kept shouting, "Stand back! Make way! Get out of here!" and shoving against Sitting Bull's deaf-mute son, who—very much excited—pulled and shoved Eagle Man, making horrible noises in the darkness. And as the police forged slowly forward, the terrible wailing of women was mingled with the deaf-mute's unearthly gibberings.

Sergeant Shave Head gave command: "Get round this man; make a circle around him." The police obeyed, but it was no use. The angry mob of Sitting Bull's friends grew in size every moment, as men came running from their tents, guns in hand. The indignant Hunkpapa blocked their path, almost surrounding the Metal Breasts, who were easily recognized in the dimness by the white mufflers they wore. The gray horse had not been saddled; they had to wait while White Bird went after it. Gray Eagle gave him a rope, and he set out: behind every stump and bit of cover he saw a man with a rifle, but he went to the corral and brought back the horse. The police stood still, tried to go no farther. Perhaps they were glad to have the cabin at their backs. It looked like a fight just then, and who can tell how many of those Christian Indians had a lingering fear that, after all, the Ghost Shirts might prove to be bulletproof?

Women were wailing, children crying, men shouting taunts and insults at the Metal Breasts. It was too dark to distinguish the speakers, but the policemen knew many of the voices: "Kill them! Kill them!" shouted Crawler. "Shoot the old policemen, and the new ones will run." Strikes-the-Kettle, that dangerous fighter, was crying, "Let him go! Leave him alone! You're only boys, you're just youngsters, you cannot fight. Let him be!" From the outside of the semicircle, where she was pacing up and down, the shrill voice of Mrs. Spotted-Horn-

Bull leapt high above the babble of the restless crowd, taunting the police: "Here are a lot of jealous men—jealous *women!*" There was the chink and clash of sleigh bells as two of Sitting Bull's Boys rode up, their saddlery studded with bells, to circle that angry crowd, looking for a possible target. So many were in that milling throng in the darkness, so many called out, that no man can remember all that was said. But it was plenty . . . strong words. They stood and wrangled for ten minutes.

Inside the cabin, Bullhead's men had had everything their own way: they would have been wiser to shut the door and await the coming of the troops. But now, outside the cabin, Sitting Bull, though firmly held by both arms and around the middle, was actual master of the situation. They might kill him, but they could not carry him off against his will. As he had always done, he listened to his people before he made up his mind; that was his job, as chief.

One of Sitting Bull's wives chanted a song, which well expressed the expectant mood of his supporters:

> *Sitting Bull, you have always been a brave man;*
> *What is going to happen now?*

When he heard this, some believe, Sitting Bull made up his mind not to go. Meanwhile, White Bird had brought up the gray circus horse, with a cowboy saddle on its back, ready for the prisoner. The police began to urge him toward the animal.

The crowd was more and more angry and noisy, every man encouraging his neighbor. The police, who had been so sure of themselves inside the cabin, now changed their tune. They began to try to pacify the Hunkpapa, and in this they were backed up by some of Sitting Bull's friends and relatives. Gray Eagle, who had volunteered to accompany the policemen to arrest the chief, now came to Sitting Bull and said, "Brother-in-law, do as the agent says. Go with the police."

But when Sitting Bull heard his brother-in-law among those enemies, he would no longer listen: he cried out, "No! I'm not going! Get away! Get away!" Gray Eagle replied, "All right. I'm through.

I have tried to save you." Gray Eagle hurried over to the Chief's other cabin, found his sister, and said, "Cross the river to my house. Do not stick up for your husband. He is wrong." She answered, "Yes." That, said Gray Eagle, was his part in the affair.

Books say that Crowfoot, the chief's son, broke in, "You have always called yourself a brave chief, now you are letting yourself be taken by these Metal Breasts." But none of the living policemen I knew had any recollection of this incident, and it does not figure in the earlier official reports of the affair.

Jumping Bull tried to soothe the indignant Chief; said he: "Brother, let us break camp and move to the agency. You take your family, I will take mine. If you are to die there, I will die with you." He-Alone-Is-Man, policeman, pleaded with Sitting Bull to go peaceably: "No one will harm you. Do not let others lead you into trouble." Others did the same.

The policemen wished to take the Chief with them. It would have been a tall feather in the cap of Bullhead if he could have carried off the chief of those Hunkpapa alive, without a fight. He repeated the message given him at the agency, the bait prepared to lure Sitting Bull to a military prison. Note the nature of the bait held out to the Chief, and then check it by the motives which (McLaughlin says) animated Sitting Bull. Said Bullhead: "Nobody will be killed. We came after Sitting Bull. White Hair, the agent, wants him. White Hair is going to build the chief a house near the agency, so that, whenever any of his people need anything, the Chief can get it for them right away." Shave Head said the same thing.

The policemen behind Sitting Bull kept pushing him toward the saddled horse, saying, "You have no ears." Two of them held him by the arms, and Red Tomahawk, armed with a revolver, held him around the waist from behind. In front of the Chief and a little to his left, facing him and covering him with his rifle, Lieutenant Bullhead stood where he could see his men. All about the Chief stood the Metal Breasts—One Feather, He-Alone-Is-Man, Little Eagle, Shave Head, Hawkman, Magpie Eagle, Weasel Bear, Eagle Man, more than forty in all. White Bird held the horse. Everyone was standing still, and

SURVIVORS OF THE INDIAN POLICE WHO CAPTURED SITTING BULL, DECEMBER 15, 1890.
Red Tomahawk (front center), slayer of Sitting Bull, is in command.

(*Bureau of American Ethnology*)

RED CLOUD

(*Pitt Rivers Museum*)

their steaming breath began to be visible in the graying dimness of that chill dawn. They were ready to go.

But just then the policemen near Bullhead saw him glance sidewise to his right. Someone in a gray blanket, carrying a Winchester, was coming around the corner of the house, growling like a bear. It was Catch-the-Bear, and everyone present knew of his threat to kill Bullhead (Afraid-of-Bear). "Let him go! Let him go!" he was calling. He tossed his gray blanket upon the top of a sunshade or arbor made of poles and brush as he passed, and came on, walking menacingly along the cordon of policemen huddled around Sitting Bull. Catch-the-Bear held his rifle in both hands, slamming it across the belly of each Metal Breast in turn, thrusting his face into each of theirs, looking for his enemy. He passed Weasel Bear by, and others: he was looking for the lieutenant.

Looking Elk, one of the police, grabbed Catch-the-Bear by the shoulder, jerking him back, saying, "Brother-in-law, don't do that; don't say that!" But Catch-the-Bear shook him off, shoved him away. "Don't call *me* brother-in-law," he growled, "Don't say that to *me*."

They heard Catch-the-Bear's seven-shot rifle click, as he threw a cartridge into the chamber.

Sitting Bull looked toward Catch-the-Bear, commander of his bodyguard, chief soldier of his camp. Close beside him were Strikes-the-Kettle, Brave Thunder, Spotted-Horn-Bull, Blackbird, all his fearless warriors, itching to attack these Indians who had turned against their chief. Sitting Bull knew that the fight he had been hoping for and delaying for was bound to take place. How could he bring himself to surrender to a lot of Indians, Yanktonais and Blackfeet, and especially Hunkpapa, who had once been his subordinates? Old friends of his say that his dignity would not permit it, any more than it did when Johnny Brughière and the Cheyenne scouts went after him in 1879. That is what the old men say Sitting Bull must have been thinking. And now here was Catch-the-Bear, and thinking gave way to action. Catch-the-Bear kept coming down the line of Metal Breasts, saying, "Where is Afraid-of-Bear [Bullhead]? Afraid-of-Bear, come here!" Bullhead answered, "Here I am."

Then Sitting Bull suddenly cried out in a loud, resonant voice: "I am not going. Do with me what you like. I am not going. Come on! Come on! Take action! Let's go!"[1] It was the order his friends had been waiting for.

Immediately Catch-the-Bear threw up his rifle. The flash lighted up the startled faces. *Tchow!* Bullhead, hit in the leg, went down on his back, turning as he fell and shooting upwards at Sitting Bull, who was twisting in the arms of his captors. The bullet struck the Chief in the back on the left side, between the tenth and eleventh ribs. As he reeled and staggered from the impact of the Lieutenant's lead, Red Tomahawk shot him from behind. Both shots were close together; either would have been fatal. Sitting Bull, instantly killed, dropped like a stone.

One of his friends called out, "You've been trying to do it, and now you've done it." In an instant police and Hunkpapa were mingled in a general melee.

Strikes-the-Kettle shot down Shave Head, and then the firing was like the hard and rapid clapping of hands. It was all together, the smoke and dust blotted everything from sight, the confusion of that hand-to-hand fight was terrible. Men were shooting and clubbing each other, scuffling and stabbing there in the gray dawn. White Bird and some others flung themselves down the moment the firing began, and rolled back and forth to avoid bullets until they could get round the corner of the house and fire from behind the projecting log-ends there. It was a bloody fight.

And in the midst of all that tragedy, the old gray circus horse, hearing all the shooting, imagined that he was back in the Wild West Show with his master and Buffalo Bill, and began to do his tricks again. He sat down gravely in the middle of all that carnage, and raised his hoof. That scared some of the policemen who saw it worse than the guns of their enemies. They thought the spirit of Sitting Bull had entered into the sitting horse! All around him, bullets were flying like angry hornets, yet the old horse came through without a scratch. He sur-

[1] *Mini kte sni yelo. Tokel eca maya nu kta heci ecun po. Mni kte sni yelo. Hiyupo! Hiyupo! Hopo! Hopo!*

vived, was bought back by Buffalo Bill, and used in the show again. Some of the readers of this book will remember the old gray horse ridden by the man who carried Old Glory ahead of the troop of American cavalry in the Wild West Show at the World's Fair in Chicago. That was the one. He was ridden hard back to Fort Yates with the news that day, and was badly "stove up" for weeks after.

While the horse was putting on his stunts among the dead men, most of the police dodged behind the cabin, for their enemies had taken cover in the timber along the stream, and were keeping up a hot fire from there. Bullhead, shot in the right arm, the right knee, and through the body, said, "Get some quilts and make a bed in that house, so that I can lie down. And cover me up." They carried their wounded into Sitting Bull's cabin—Bullhead, and Middle, and Shave Head, whose bowels protruded from his ripped belly. They carried in their dead also. The floor of that cabin was covered with blood.

While they were moving the mattress to make a bed for Bullhead, the police found Crowfoot, Sitting Bull's son, hidden there. Crowfoot was a schoolboy of seventeen winters. A Metal Breast called out, "There's another one in here." The boy sprang up, crying, "Uncle, I want to live! You have killed my father! Let me go!"

They called to Bullhead where he lay, covered with blood, mortally wounded. "What shall we do with him?" Bullhead answered, "Kill him, they have killed me." Red Tomahawk struck Crowfoot, the blow sent the boy sprawling through the door. Those outside shot him dead. They showed no mercy: their hearts were hot that day.

Those persons who complain that the Sioux would not give the troops a stand-up fight should have seen the field after that mix-up. To the Sioux warrior, the white men were only a side-issue, a nuisance: it was seldom that he took enough interest in them to fight more than was necessary. But, say the old men, if you want a hard fight, a real scrap, pit Sioux against Sioux. Then the fur will fly. The old men's tongues are straight. For when that fight was over, within a few minutes and within a radius of fifty yards, twelve Sioux lay dead, and three more severely wounded, two of them mortally.

Around Sitting Bull's body lay his faithful bodyguard: Catch-the-

Bear, Blackbird, Chiefs Spotted-Horn-Bull and Brave Thunder, his "brother" Jumping Bull, faithful to his promise to die with the Chief; and there, too, lay Jumping Bull's son, Chase-Wounded, and the boy Crowfoot.

Of the police, Little Eagle, Hawk Man, Arm Strong, and Afraid-of-Soldier (Warriors-Fear-Him) were already dead. First Lieutenant Bullhead and First Sergeant Shave Head were mortally wounded, and Private Middle was hard hit, and later had to have his leg amputated. White Bird was hit on his police badge: the badge saved his life.

Sergeant Red Tomahawk succeeded to the command, and sent off two messengers to call up the troops, messengers who reported (first) that all the policemen were killed, and (later) that Sitting Bull's people had them penned up in the house, short of ammunition, and would soon kill them all. Had there been no troops, it is likely that not one Metal Breast would have lived to tell the tale. And when the troops arrived, they began by shelling their allies, the policemen! It was sunup by that time. The police showed a white flag, and the soldiers marched down into the valley.

What happened on the arrival of the troops gives the complete lie to the propaganda that the Ghost Dance was a warlike move against the whites and that these "crazed Ghost Dancers" would have offered any opposition to a military arrest. Sitting Bull had said that he and his people would cheerfully submit to the troops, and that they merely resented being ordered about by other Indians. He spoke truth. For the same men who had given the Metal Breasts such a deadly half-hour, and were even then intent upon wiping them from the face of the earth, offered no resistance whatever to the troops. The arrest of Sitting Bull had not the remotest connection with the Ghost Dance, and the motives which led to the fight (so far as Indians were concerned) were purely personal and intertribal. Many of the Grand River Sioux went back to Fort Yates with the troops, of their own accord.

The friends of Sitting Bull, who had worked such havoc with the Indian police, left the valley as soon as the troops appeared, and retreated without firing a shot at the soldiers, even when some of them scouted on their trail. Not one white man was wounded. Only one demonstration was made after the troops entered the valley. A single Sioux horseman, wearing a Ghost Shirt, paraded back and forth within rifle range, to show off his courage and test out the bulletproof qualities of the sacred garment. He was fired at, but was not hit, and rode off after he had made his little experiment, probably to join Big Foot's band and to fall at Wounded Knee.

Captain E. G. Fechet's report covering this action states: "The Indians fell back from every point upon the approach of the troops, not showing any desire to engage in hostile action against the soldiers." Precisely. But, if the troops had made the arrest, the credit of Major James McLaughlin and the Indian Bureau might have suffered. The Indian police went first—"to avert bloodshed!"

One Bull, Sitting Bull's nephew, had been sent by McLaughlin's orders to haul freight on the Cannonball–Fort Yates road, so as to keep him out of the fracas. The fact that the agent sent One Bull out of reach of his uncle's camp that night is interesting in the light of the agent's repeated protestations that he sent the Indian police after Sitting Bull in order to prevent bloodshed. He must have known, as the Indian police knew and repeatedly said, that any attempt on their part to take Sitting Bull would precipitate a battle. If he did not, why did he promise them and their widows and orphans pensions—pensions which he was not authorized to promise, and which Congress did not grant until nearly forty years after, when the Bullhead faction got votes?

One Bull reached his home, a few miles below Sitting Bull's camp, very early that morning, went to bed, and soon after was awakened by the rifle fire at his uncle's camp—hard shooting. He hooked up his team and went toward the sound of the firing. As he got near, he could see the Indians on the run; one of them told him that the Chief was killed.

As he went on toward his uncle's house, the police leveled their guns at him. He heard Eagle Man telling him to stop. Eagle Man said,

"Come no farther." One Bull halted. Cross Bear was ready to shoot One Bull. But Eagle Man said, "This is our son-in-law, One Bull." To One Bull he said, "We have killed each other on both sides."

One Bull asked, "Have you killed the women, too?" For his wife had been in camp there.

"No," said Eagle Man, "my niece was here a little while ago. Go and get her and go back to your house." So One Bull went looking for his wife along the river, found her, and took her home. He was not allowed to go near his uncle's body, for fear he might lose his temper and make trouble.

One Bull's wife, Scarlet Whirlwind, went home with One Bull. She was great with child. She witnessed the fight. She said that Bullhead fired the first shot, and killed the Chief.

Bullhead evidently wished no one to have any doubt about his share in that affray. As he lay there, mortally wounded, covered with blood, he said to his friend Weasel Bear, "Look after my family in the future, and advise them. Never forget, I killed Sitting Bull." And again, when Turning Hawk came in to see him, he said, "I shot Sitting Bull. Sitting Bull is dead. I killed him."

Then Shave Head, crouching on the quilts like a wounded animal above his broken belly, spoke up, "They have killed me, but I got one of them all right."

Red Tomahawk also claimed to have killed Sitting Bull. The army surgeon said either shot would have proved mortal to the Chief.

The policemen and the soldiers ransacked the Chief's cabins. The extra moccasins said to have been made in anticipation of the Chief's flight were not found, nor was there any Ghost Shirt found in his cabin. However, Bob-Tail-Bull found two in the cabin of his son-in-law, Andrew Fox, near by; he gave them to McLaughlin. All the cabins in the valley for some miles were emptied of their folk that morning, and what the Metal Breasts and soldiers did not take was later carried away by civilian prowlers: no effort was made to protect the property of friendly Indians. They suffered with the others. All the guns found in the camp were broken over a wagon wheel.

When a check was made of the ammunition left to the police, it was found that these forty-three men, some of whom had had not less than 120 rounds to begin with, had altogether only 210 revolver cartridges, and 260 rounds of ammunition for their rifles. Red Tomahawk, Iron Star, Cross Bear, Hawk Man, Weasel Bear, One Feather, Iron Thunder, Black Prairie Chicken, and Spotted Thunder had not a single round. The ammunition of the dead had all been used up, also. These are official figures. It was a hard fight—hard shooting.

Sitting Bull's friends ran off or rode off most of the horses of the Metal Breasts. Three hundred and thirty-three Sioux fled from Standing Rock as a result of this affair. According to the official report, the police were opposed by "160 armed fanatical Ghost Dancers" (certainly not a low estimate), who fled, "leaving their families behind." If the number was so great, it was equal to the troops and police combined, and could have given some trouble, had the "hostiles" wished. Fully half those who fled had taken no part in the fracas, but were quietly sleeping in their homes up and down the river, when the fight began.

By this time, the relatives of John Arm Strong (Broken Arm), one of the dead policemen, had arrived, and finding his body lying in the stable, where he had been shot, began to wail terribly. One of them, Holy Medicine, finding his kinsman dead, was enraged at Sitting Bull, whose followers had killed him. Holy Medicine had acted as tailor, making and painting the sacred Ghost Shirts. But now he was furious. He picked up an old neckyoke lying on the ground, and, going over to Sitting Bull's body, beat it savagely about the head, until the Chief's chin was around under his left ear. The soldiers finally put a stop to that. First Sergeant James Hanaghan of Troop F, Eighth Cavalry, detailed Private A. L. Bloomer to stand guard over Sitting Bull's body.

Said Mr. Bloomer: "Sitting Bull must have weighed 250 pounds, and after it was all over and I was ordered to move the body away from a large pool of blood, I took hold of his arm and tried to drag him away so his body would not freeze to the ground. I thought he weighed a ton. . . . He was lying on his back, with his head toward his cabin. There was no snow, but the ground was frozen. He was ten to fifteen yards from the cabin."

But the malice of the bereaved did not stop with abusing the dead body. They wanted to smash and kill everybody and everything in his camp.

Matthew F. Steele, lieutenant colonel, U.S.A., retired, then a young officer with the troops at Fort Yates, was busy preventing the soldiers and policemen from looting the cabins of Sitting Bull's camp, and also looking for any "hostiles" who might be concealed there. In the smaller cabin he found hanging on the wall a large full-length oil portrait of Sitting Bull, in full regalia, with the signature *C. S. Weldon* in one corner. Said he: "Suddenly one of the policemen, whose brother, another policeman, lay dead on the ground outside, killed by Sitting Bull's band, came into the cabin crying, and saw this portrait on the wall. Quickly he snatched it down and with his Winchester broke the frame in pieces and broke through the canvas. I snatched the portrait away from him and carried it back to Fort Yates." Later, the young officer bought the portrait from Sitting Bull's wives.[2]

Otter Robe, who (after one of his relatives had been wounded) rode boldly in and joined the police in their stand against Sitting Bull's Boys, acted as interpreter for some of the soldiers. He heard Sitting Bull's wives crying, went into the smaller cabin, and found them and some other women seated in a row on the bed. They would not get up, and so the soldiers pulled them off. Under that bed they found Sitting Bull's deaf-mute son and another lad. The soldiers searched these lads to disarm them, found that one of them had a jackknife with a broken blade, and took that. It made Otter Robe laugh. The soldiers also found an old blind woman in camp. Otter Robe talked for her; he protected her.

All this time the lamp in Sitting Bull's cabin burned on. It was still burning when the police and soldiers started back to the fort.

When that happened, there was a dispute among the Metal Breasts. They did not wish to put Sitting Bull's body into the same wagon with their own dead. But Sergeant Red Tomahawk had strict orders to bring in the chief dead or alive, and he said they must do it; there was

[2] This portrait is reproduced in my *New Sources of Indian History, 1851–1891*, 108.

only one wagon for the dead. Then the policemen decided to throw the chief in first, and lay their dead comrades on top of him. This was done. White Bird and Bob-Tail-Bull put the dead into the wagon; when they had finished, they were covered with blood.

The bodies of the men who fell with Sitting Bull were dragged into a cabin and left there. Somewhat later, the Reverend T. L. Riggs, of Oahe, came there with some Christian Indians, and laid the seven dead men away in a common grave. His charitable deed made other sects appear rather heartless, by contrast, and to this day many of Sitting Bull's people are members of that Congregational church, of which he was such a worthy pillar. That grave has never been marked.

About the middle of the day the men in uniform, the wagons and the ambulance, moved out northward on the trail toward Fort Yates and Standing Rock. And thus Sitting Bull was carted like a dead dog toward the stronghold of his enemies, with four dead men riding his mangled, blood-soaked body over the prairie ruts.

At 6:00 P.M. the slow caravan reached the new station on Oak Creek, halting for the night on the site of that pleasant town-to-be, McLaughlin, South Dakota. Next day they went on, and the Chief's body was turned over to the post surgeon at 4:30 P.M. December 16, 1890.

Private He-Alone-Is-Man, one of the police, went home, burned the clothing he had worn in that bloody fight, and took a purifying sweat bath before he would enter his house. Said High Eagle, another policeman, "Well, we have gone to work, and killed our chief."

Thus died Sitting Bull. And, as McLaughlin's obituary states, "The shot that killed him put a stop forever to the domination of the ancient regime among the Sioux of the Standing Rock Reservation."

39. The Only Good Indian

STANDING ROCK AGENCY, S. D., DEC. 16, 1890. . . . *It is stated today that there was a quiet understanding between the officers of the Indian and military departments that it would be impossible to bring Sitting Bull to Standing Rock alive, and that if brought in, nobody would know precisely what to do with him. He would, though under arrest, still be a source of great annoyance, and his followers would continue their dances and threats against neighboring settlers. There was, therefore, cruel as it may seem, a complete understanding from the Commanding Officer to the Indian Police that the slightest attempt to rescue the old medicine man should be a signal to send Sitting Bull to the happy hunting ground.*

—NEW YORK HERALD, DEC. 17, 1890.

THAT "DOMINATION" of Sitting Bull, of which McLaughlin speaks, was resented and feared at Standing Rock long after his resonant voice and slow, emphatic utterance were silenced. Few men have been loved so well, or hated so fiercely as Sitting Bull. But now, on December 17, the day of his burial, his friends had fled, his enemies—and especially the relatives of the dead policemen—were strong and bitter, and the lukewarm made haste to mount the bandwagon of the victorious faction.

This is not the place to tell how the brave policemen (many of them once Sitting Bull's boys, whom he had trained to the warpath) buried their fallen comrades with military honors and all the pomp which Standing Rock's little church and state could afford. They deserved honor for their courage in attempting his arrest, and the granite shaft above their common tomb in the Roman Catholic cemetery at Standing Rock will long keep their memory in the minds of men. It is said that the funeral cortege of these valiant men extended all the way from the Dead House to the cemetery, and the photographs of the burial would seem to bear out the story.

Sitting Bull was so hated by the mourners that they would not consent to have him laid away with their dead. So great was the excitement, the uncertainty, that, as Father Bernard puts it, "It was deemed unwise to give the chief a public funeral." Sitting Bull was not a Catholic nor a Christian of any recognized sect; his body was in the hands of the military; he was buried in one corner of the Post Cemetery at Fort Yates.

J. F. Waggoner, then a soldier at the post detailed for work in the carpenter shop, made the box for Sitting Bull. For nobody troubled to go to Mandan and buy a coffin for the Chief. He made the box 2 by 2 by 6 feet 4 inches, and while he was working at it, the soldiers kept coming in, each of them driving a nail in the Chief's coffin. Private Waggoner, who knew Sitting Bull well, said he did not think such an act was much of an honor, any more than if it had been the coffin of any other major general. "For he was surely a fighter, a thinker, a chief, and a gentleman. He had eaten many a meal in my house, and I cannot but speak well of Sitting Bull."

Mr. Waggoner goes on, "There were no police in my shop while I was working, and no officers there to give orders—for a wonder." When the box was finished, he took it to the Dead House, and they put the body into it. Says he: "We buried him just as he came in, wrapped in a blanket frozen stiff with blood. He was not scalped. He had seven bullet wounds in his body, and his jaw was around under his left ear. He was a big man; he filled that box chock-a-block. They had to sit on the lid to close it. The lid was not nailed down."

There were present at the time the hospital steward, Saddler, J. F. Waggoner, the carpenter, Johnny Hughes, teamster, Lieutenant P. G. Wood, Twelfth Infantry, and Guy Wood, the officer's son. They loaded the long box upon a two-wheeled cart, and an old army mule named Caesar drew the cart down the slope to the Post Cemetery. The grave was already dug. It was the middle of the afternoon.

They soon reached the open grave. Then Waggoner and another man held up the lid while "five gallons of chloride of lime were poured into the box, and on top of that a suitable amount of muriatic acid." Then the lid was nailed down, the box lowered, and the grave filled. The fumes rose up in a fog between the loose earth and the walls of the grave, even before it was half full. And so Sitting Bull was buried—in quicklime—like a felon!

Said Waggoner: "We laid the noble old Chief away without a hymn or a prayer or a sprinkle of earth. Quicklime was used instead. It made me angry. I had always admired the Chief for his courage and his generalship. He was a *man!*"

Indeed, the triumphant party at Standing Rock misjudged the temper of the whole American public; they were a little too blatant in their intense satisfaction, and soon had the press attacking them from all sides. One of the first dispatches sent to the press from Standing Rock (December 16) begins: "That the Government authorities, civil as well as military, from President Harrison and General Miles down, preferred the death of the famous old savage to capture whole-skinned, few persons here, Indian or white, have a doubt." There was some apparent basis for this supposition at the time: General Miles had been the man to seek an arrest by the military, and President Harrison, when interviewed for the *New York Herald,* said "that he had regarded Sitting Bull as the great disturbing element in his tribe, and now that he was out of the way he hoped that a settlement of the difficulties could be reached without further bloodshed."

But a man of Sitting Bull's character and fame could not be shot down and buried hugger-mugger without some recoil upon those responsible for the business. Too many able men knew him, too many of them admired him, too many sympathized with his stand against the abuses and outrages perpetrated upon his people by officers and citizens of the United States. Suddenly McLaughlin found himself beset with stinging implications and accusations. The *Chicago Tribune* spoke of "the assassination of Sitting Bull"; attention was called to the "fact" that "the chief had not one friend among the police sent to arrest him." Terms like "cold-blooded, premeditated murder" were freely bandied about; the public could believe anything about an official of the old Indian Bureau. W. H. H. "Adirondack" Murray, who had known Sitting Bull in Canada, and other public men who admired the Chief, printed eloquent defenses of his life, and poured objurgations upon those who had ordered his arrest. In one of the (deleted) chapters of his book, McLaughlin complains, "It was charged that he had been unjustifiably killed—and the charge was made generally by the people and papers that had been clamoring all summer for the extinction of the old mischief-maker." To add to these troubles, General Miles made difficulties, there was a threat of legislative investigation in Dakota, and the various philanthropic associations over the country, such as the Indian Rights Association, took up the cudgels and made inquiries. The agent's defense against these accusations has been repeatedly printed, in his book, in his report to the Commissioner, 1891, already referred to, and elsewhere. For a time it seemed as though he was rid of Sitting Bull only to be driven out himself: it was out of the frying pan into the fire. But the military men who knew him held up his hands, the Catholic church was loyal to its able son, the Dakota settlers stood by him manfully, the politicians fell into line with their constituents, and McLaughlin was confidentially informed that "the new Commissioner is a dandy; he will care for his own." McLaughlin's action was approved by his superiors, and in due time he was promoted.

But meanwhile he had a bad time. By the irony of fate it was a newspaper story which caused all the anxiety, and a newspaper story started in Bismarck, where the yarns about Mrs. Weldon had been printed, a story followed up by the National Indian Defense Association which she had represented. What's sauce for the goose is sauce for the gander.

The story went that Sitting Bull's coffin was empty when buried, that his body had "been taken to a dissecting room," and that a Bismarck merchant had offered one thousand dollars for the remains. Dr. Bland, head of Mrs. Weldon's society, immediately wrote to the Commissioner of Indian Affairs, demanding punishment of "any parties, whether Government officials or not, who may be found guilty of such desecration of the dead chief's body." For, he explains, "the reasonable supposition is that it is the intention of the parties in charge to make his bones a subject of speculation, and perhaps his skin also."

A long array of official denials followed, with statements made and endorsed by the post surgeon and Colonel Drum to the effect that "it was not mutilated or disfigured in any manner . . . sewed up in canvas, put in a coffin . . . and afterward buried in the northwest corner of the post cemetery in a grave about eight feet deep." A number of persons claim to have been present at this interment. J. F. Waggoner says most of these claims are false.

Among the papers of the late Major McLaughlin is a small package containing a lock of hair. It is labeled, in the Major's handwriting, "Sitting Bull's hair." Apart from this memento, there is no evidence to show that anything of Sitting Bull was left above ground, after his burial.

Had the reports mentioned that the body was buried in quicklime, they might easily have disposed of the legend. For, as is well known, quicklime desiccates a body, and often preserves it, since water is the great agent of decay. This, it appears, is what occurred in the case of Sitting Bull. Some years ago his grave was secretly opened.

At that time the Fort Yates Commercial Club erected the cairn of stones which stood at the foot of the grave. This labor made necessary some disturbance of the surface soil. I have excellent authority for the statement that one night, while these improvements were being made, a man whose name was withheld from me, and who was anxious to know the truth of these legends, opened the grave with the help of a friend. He found the complete skeleton there, skull and all, well enough preserved to show the horrible mutilation of the head. This excavation, secret as it was, must dispose finally of the yarns about Sitting Bull's bones having been put on show. After the inspection, the two men replaced everything as before, filled the grave, and tamped in the soil and turf, leaving no sign of the disturbance.

One would like to know why Sitting Bull was buried in quicklime. Was it to hide the mutilation of his body, or to prevent someone from obtaining his bones, or simply to show contempt for the man? One would have more faith in the reported impeccable behavior of officials, both Indian and white, who opposed him while alive, if they had not treated his helpless body so after he was dead.

Feeling at Standing Rock after those burials was intense. Sitting Bull's relatives and friends, their women and children, had no wish to remain in that district, and nearly all their property was stolen while they were held at Fort Yates under guard. Said One Bull: "We lost all our household goods. Everything, trunks, boxes, and provisions in Sitting Bull's house were taken, his cattle—all that he had—all disappeared. Some of the horses were also missing. We were overwhelmed with grief. Sitting Bull's children, Jumping Bull's children, all of them moved away to Red Cloud [Pine Ridge] Agency. They all lived down there, and died there; my uncle has a few grandchildren living there still. I also hated to remain here where we had suffered so much, but here where Uncle Sitting Bull had chosen a place for me, I remained; I respected his wishes." One Bull alone remained on the Standing Rock Reservation, and succeeded to the chieftaincy of the band on Grand River, left vacant by Sitting Bull's death.

Peace settled once more upon Grand River. But up at the Standing Rock Agency, there was some dissatisfaction, some fear. For nearly forty years, people avoided the old commissary building after dark. For, they say, every night the dead policemen, whose families were in want because the promised pensions had not been paid, came knocking at the door to draw their rations. If you were inside the building, you could hear those lurking shadows enter, hear their moccasins shuffle on the rough board floor, a restless moving about of those dead men, whose widows and orphans were left without protectors.

For nearly forty years they walked by night, until the Sioux were enfranchised, and Congress approved the recommendations of the Bureau and the War Department. Now they walk no more.

The site of Sitting Bull's cabin has been made a public park, and very wisely left unimproved. Near by you may find some Sioux, who —for a proper fee—will show you about the place, point out the sites of the cabins, the spot where each man fell, the grave of the seven men who died with Sitting Bull, and tell you the grim story of that battle in the dark.

And so, on that slope facing the sunset, the old captain was laid to rest, wedged into the box they had made for him, side by side with the white soldiers. That, one may believe, was a more fitting tomb than the Catholic cemetery up the hill a mile away, where he would have been huddled among the men who shot him down. For Sitting Bull had no hatred of the white men, only distrust; and if that distrust persisted and increased, was it his fault? He, at least, did not think so: Job himself was not more confident of his own blamelessness than Sitting Bull.

Years after, when Fort Yates was dismantled, even those soldier dead were taken away, and Sitting Bull was left alone on the bare hillside, overlooking the flats where he had camped so often, bracing his wavering people to defend their birthright.

For a long time there was only a wooden marker at the grave, bearing the simple inscription:

Sitting Bull
Died Dec. 15, 1890

This wooden marker was regularly replaced, as tourists as regularly whittled it away for souvenirs. Later a cairn of stones was raised, and the grave was secretly decorated from time to time. And after official malice had been weakened by death and time, there was an iron railing, a cement slab, a modest marble tombstone with the words:

SITTING BULL
Died
Dec. 15, 1890
Chief of the
Hunkpapa
Sioux

More recently, his bones have been removed and reburied in a more imposing and—we may hope—a permanent tomb.

BIG FOOT'S BAND AT CHEYENNE RIVER, AUGUST, 1890

(National Archives)

GHOST DANCER IN A TRANCE
(*Bureau of American Ethnology*)

SIOUX GHOST SHIRT
(*Smithsonian Institution*)

These successive markers are all signs of the change in public feeling toward the Chief, steps toward that monument which, some day, the state or nation will erect to one of the greatest of her sons. The white man's hatred for Sitting Bull has fallen from him, even as the soldiers who once hemmed in his grave have been removed.

Good cause for that. We Americans owe a great debt to our old enemy.

Because it is not the smooth path, but the rough trail, which makes us strong; it is not our friends, but our foes, who commonly have most to do with forging our characters. Consider what the history of these states would be had there been no native peoples on this continent—a dull chronicle of plodding clodhoppers, placidly moving each year a little farther into the vacant lands, carrying along their petty, outworn European ideas and institutions, their bastard European culture, unchanged and unchanging—so many rubber stamps!

But as it was, thank God, we had a Frontier, and, as historians are forever reminding us, that Frontier shaped America, moulded a nation unlike any other. That Frontier formed these states, made us what we are—and the Indian made the Frontier.

Sitting Bull, leader of the largest Indian nation on the continent, the strongest, boldest, most stubborn opponent of European influence, was the very heart and soul of that Frontier. When the true history of the New World is written, he will receive his chapter. For Sitting Bull was one of the Makers of America.

Appendix

Sitting Bull's Hieroglyphic Autobiography

Or War Record In Pictures Drawn By Himself

THESE DRAWINGS depict thirty-two of the sixty-three warlike exploits performed by Sitting Bull before 1870, when the drawings fell into the hands of a white man. The drawings are here numbered and arranged chronologically, not as in the original series, which contained numerous pictures of the exploits of Sitting Bull's brother Jumping Bull. In each picture Sitting Bull is identified by a pictograph of his name (a seated buffalo bull) connected with his mouth by a line, in the usual Sioux fashion.

Fig. 1. 1846. On Red Water. The boy Sitting Bull, as yet an unfledged warrior, is shown on horseback, charging an enemy whom he strikes with a *coup* stick. On his blue shield a black bird is painted, and four black-tipped eagle feathers flutter from the edges of the shield.

Fig. 2. 1853(?). Sitting Bull unhorses a Crow warrior with his lance. The story is well known, but no eye-witnesses now live, and the date and place are uncertain.

Fig. 3. 1856. On Yellowstone River. Sitting Bull counts *coup* with his lance on a mounted Crow warrior who carries a shield and a gun. As required by the obligations belonging to his shield, Sitting Bull wears his hair in a knot like a horn on his forehead.

Fig. 4. 1856. On Porcupine Creek. Sitting Bull, shown wearing his Strong Heart bonnet and sash, crouches behind his shield and shoots a Crow chief through the belly, at the same time being wounded in the foot. Flame and smoke pour from the guns, and the wounds bleed freely. Sitting Bull's black war horse awaits its master in the background.

Fig. 5. 1857. On the Missouri River. Winter. Sitting Bull, armed with a gun and wearing his Strong Heart bonnet and white blanket coat, strikes with his lance the Hohe lad whom he is to save and to adopt as his brother, named Jumping Bull, or Little Assiniboin.

Fig. 6. 1858. Near Rainy Butte. Sitting Bull lances and kills a Crow warrior, the slayer of his father in that very fight.

Fig. 7. 1858. Rainy Butte. This picture commemorates the capture of three Crow women, at the time when Sitting Bull's father was killed. Sitting Bull carries the lance made for him by his parents, and wears a bonnet with horns and a long trail of eagle feathers. A Crow warrior is represented as trying to arrest his charge.

Fig. 8. 1859. Near Fort Berthold. A Ree enemy grabs the bridle of Sitting Bull's horse. Sitting Bull kills him, and takes his gun and bow.

Fig. 9. 1859–60. Wearing his Strong Heart bonnet, Sitting Bull runs off seven Crow ponies: two white, two black, one bay, one buckskin, and one mouse-colored.

Fig. 10. 1860. Sitting Bull counts *coup* on a Crow woman riding a mule. She turns to fend off his lance as he strikes at her. This happened when the Sioux encountered Crow hunters among the buffalo herds and Makes-the-Enemy killed two Crow women.

Fig. 11. 1860. Amid a shower of bullets, which fill the air, Sitting Bull, riding his famous war horse Blackie, runs off two animals from a Crow camp. One of them is a branded Army mule, picked up or stolen by the Crows. These animals Sitting Bull gave for Brown Eyes, the girl who became his fourth wife.

Fig. 12. 1861. Sitting Bull, amid a hail of enemy bullets, wounds a Crow warrior with his lance, then drops it and strikes him over the head with the heavy notched wooden handle of his quirt, which is decorated with a dangling kit-fox skin—the insignia of his Warrior Society. The Crow carries a quiver, and bleeds freely.

Fig. 13. 1862. Sitting Bull runs off a bunch of Crow ponies. Sitting Bull was such a noted horse-stealer that the old men said nobody could remember all his raids. Chief Charging Thunder stated that to his own knowledge Sitting Bull took horses from the Crows twenty times, sometimes as many as thirty head at a time.

Fig. 14. 1863, June. The skirmish with General H. H. Sibley's wagon train on the Missouri River, near the mouth of Apple Creek. Sitting Bull, facing a heavy fire, as shown by flying bullets, charges a mule-skinner armed with a blacksnake whip, counts *coup* on him, and makes off with a saddled mule.

Fig. 15. 1863. Near Fort Totten, in the Devil's Lake country. Sitting Bull, wearing a red blanket, chases a mounted white man in a fringed buckskin coat, and shoots him between the shoulders. This was Sitting Bull's first white victim.

Fig. 16. 1863–64 (winter). Sitting Bull brings home nine Crow ponies: five bays, two blacks, one buckskin mule, and a little white mare. The mare he presented to his favorite sister, Good Feather.

Fig. 17. 1864. Under fire, Sitting Bull takes from the soldiers a chestnut and a buckskin horse. The buckskin he trained to run buffalo, and then gave it to his sister. These horses were captured in the Badlands from General Sully's troops.

Fig. 18. 1864. Near White Butte, on the Little Missouri River. Under heavy fire, Sitting Bull charges a white soldier. Though transfixed by an arrow from behind, and bleeding copiously from mouth and wounds, the brave soldier turns and shoots Sitting Bull through the buttocks, causing great loss of blood.

Fig. 19. 1865. North of the Black Hills. In a skirmish with the troops under Colonel N. Cole, of the Powder River Expedition, Sitting Bull runs off a slow pack-mule.

Fig. 20. 1865. On the Montana Trail. Under heavy fire from the soldiers, Sitting Bull captures a buckskin mare. He afterward gave her to his sister.

Fig. 21. 1865. On the Montana Trail. Sitting Bull steals a fast buckskin war horse. He gave it to his adopted brother, Jumping Bull.

Fig. 22. 1865. Wearing beaded leggins and a fur cap with ear-flaps, Sitting Bull runs off a horse belonging to the Powder River Expedition.

Fig. 23. 1866. On the Montana Trail. Sitting Bull takes a horse with a split ear from white men.

Fig. 24. 1866. Wearing his Strong Heart bonnet, and riding Blackie, Sitting Bull captures three Crow ponies: one bay, one black, one mouse-colored.

Fig. 25. 1867. On the Niobrara River near the Missouri. Sitting Bull shoots a white man armed with a sawed-off shotgun. Sitting Bull carries a revolver, and is riding a rawhide saddle, made by his uncle.

Fig. 26. 1867. On the Montana Trail. Sitting Bull overtakes a white man wearing an overcoat and armed with a rifle. Sitting Bull carries only a quirt, with which he strikes the fugitive. On his head Sitting Bull wears a bandana taken from some enemy.

Fig. 27. November 6, 1867. Fort Buford. In an attack on the wood-cutters from the post, one soldier was killed, one wounded. Sitting Bull captures a fine brown Army mule with a black spot on the withers, off side. He gave the mule to his sister.

Fig. 28. 1867–68 (winter). On the Montana Trail. Sitting Bull counts *coup* on a white man. In this affair Sitting Bull counted nine *coups*. This picture (No. 14 in the original series) was followed by eight others showing the other *coups* struck. But as the drawings differ only in the details of the dress and persons of the white men, they have not been given here. Several of the white men were represented as having hair on their bodies—a thing considered loathsome by the Sioux.

Fig. 29. 1868. In a skirmish with white men Sitting Bull rescues his unhorsed companion Jumping Bull, takes him up behind, and charges a white man armed with a rifle. Jumping Bull, being armed with a long lance, is able to strike the white man first. Sitting Bull has to be content with the second *coup*.

Fig. 30. 1868. Sitting Bull strikes a white man. This happened on the same warpath as the deed recorded in Fig. 29. Circling Hawk was leader of this war party.

Fig. 31. 1869. Near the Big Dry. An incident of the battle in which the thirty Crows were killed. Sitting Bull, wearing a horned bonnet and beaded leggins, charges the rocky barrier (indicated by the circle), and counts *coup* upon a Crow, who fires in his face, but misses. The air is full of flying lead.

Fig. 32. This, the last of the series, is incomplete, and lacks the picture of the seated buffalo, which should identify Sitting Bull. However, the shield is enough to serve that purpose. Sitting Bull himself explained that this unfinished sketch represented a fight with the Crows in which he killed one and counted *coup* on two others, who ran from him disgracefully. The date and place of this fight are unknown.

These thirty-two drawings, with the eight (omitted) described under Fig. 28 above, represent forty of the sixty-three exploits accredited to Sitting Bull in 1870. Chief Four Horns, from whose copies of Sitting Bull's originals our reproductions are made, failed to complete the new set. Probably most of the missing drawings depicted Sitting Bull's rescues of comrades in distress (*e.g.* Standing Elk, Kicks-Snow, Cloud Man, etc.), as he is known to have saved a number of men in battle, and such deeds are usually placed last of all in Hunkpapa war records.

> (These pictures are reproduced by courtesy of the Bureau of American Ethnology.)

Bibliographical Essay

I NASMUCH AS THE memories and records of old Indians are almost the only sources of reliable information for the first fifty years of Sitting Bull's life, no very extensive bibliography, properly speaking, is possible. However, in addition to the sources mentioned in the Introduction, and those included in the separate volume *New Sources of Indian History*, also mentioned there, we may add a few others, published and unpublished:

Norman Fergus Black's *History of Saskatchewan and the Old Northwest* (Regina, Sask., 1913) gives vivid portraits of some of the figures involved in obtaining Sitting Bull's surrender. Chief Luther Standing Bear's *My People the Sioux* (Boston, 1928) is a fine interpretation of that nation. One of the most intimate, accurate, and valuable books is the *Life and Adventures of Frank Grouard*, by Joe De-Barthe (St. Joseph, Mo., 1894), for Grouard was captured and adopted by Sitting Bull, and remained a member of his household for some years thereafter. Grouard's statements about the chief tally closely with those of my Indian informants; in fact, it was impossible to make them believe that he was not an Indian.

Miss Frances Densmore's *Teton Sioux Music* (*Bulletin 61*, Bureau of American Ethnology) contains a number of Sitting Bull's songs, both words and music. A more complete collection with original text and translations of his songs appeared in the *Southwest Review*, Vol. XIX, No. 3 (April, 1934), under the title "The Works of Sitting Bull, Real and Imaginary," by Stanley Vestal; in this the real songs or poems of the chief were contrasted with an amusing hoax entitled *The Works of Sitting Bull* perpetrated by one R. D. Clarke (Chicago,

1878), which ran into a second (revised) edition. In that curious volume Sitting Bull was presented as the author of verses in Greek, Latin and French, and a college graduate! My article has been reprinted in my book *Professional Writing* (New York, 1938).

For the wars of the Sioux and their allies, we have, in addition to the annual reports of the Secretary of War, the *Record of Engagements with Hostile Indians Within the Military Division of the Missouri, from 1868 to 1882, Lieutenant General P. H. Sheridan Commanding,* compiled at headquarters, Military Division of the Missouri, from official records (Washington, Government Printing Office, 1882). This is a digest of military reports, boiled down almost to bare statistics, but helpful. John F. Finerty's *Warpath and Bivouac* (Chicago, 1890) gives some account of Sitting Bull in Canada and of certain battles in a more judicious and unprejudiced way than most journalists of that day aspired to. The following year John W. Fletcher published his sensational and unreliable book—or rather compilation—*The Red Record of the Sioux, Life of Sitting Bull and History of the War of 1890–91* (Edgewood Publishing Company, 1891). His own apology for this book is quoted above in my introduction. For the Cheyenne part in Sioux warfare, see that classic of the Plains, George Bird Grinnell's *The Fighting Cheyennes,* reprinted in 1956 by the University of Oklahoma Press. It is interesting to note that all of the authors who have been most successful in gaining the confidence and accounts of old Plains Indians—Grinnell, W. S. Nye, Alice Marriott—are now published by this press. For further details on some of Sitting Bull's battles and family affairs, consult my *Warpath, the True Story of the Sioux Wars, Told in a Biography of Chief White Bull* (Boston, 1934).

This book contains a topical index covering both *Warpath* and *Sitting Bull,* so arranged as to provide ready reference for a study of Indian warfare, its tactics and strategy, matters little understood by white historians. It also contains a Sioux winter count or calendar, 1781–1932.

For an understanding of the Ghost Dance, see James Mooney, "The Ghost Dance Religion and the Sioux Outbreak of 1890," *Four-*

teenth Annual Report of the Bureau of American Ethnology, 1892–93, Part II (Washington, 1896). Insofar as Sitting Bull and the affair at Wounded Knee are concerned, Mooney is unreliable; the Indians would not talk, and all he could gather was the propaganda of officials of the Indian Bureau and the War Department.

The Clover Leaf for October, 1930, published some account of the fight in which Sitting Bull was killed, entitled "The Battle of Standing Rock."

Narrative of My Captivity Among the Sioux (Hartford, 1891) was written or published by Fanny Kelly, whom Sitting Bull rescued and returned to her white friends. I have discussed this in the text.

Personal Recollections and Observations of General Nelson A. Miles, Embracing a Brief View of the Civil War; or From New England to the Golden Gate, and the Story of his Indian Campaigns, with comments on the exploration, development and progress of our great western empire; illus. by Frederic Remington and others (Chicago, 1896). Insofar as this book concerns Sitting Bull, I have discussed it in the text. See also the reports of the Commissioner of Indian Affairs, especially that of 1872. So much for published sources.

Those unpublished provided much that was helpful and significant: to begin with—"Buffalo Bill's Scrapbook of Press Clippings." This threw much light upon Sitting Bull's year with Buffalo Bill's Wild West Show, both in the States and Canada. For photostats of this record I am indebted to Richard J. Walsh, author of *The Making of Buffalo Bill.*

Sitting Bull's own records of his exploits: "Hieroglyphic Autobiography of Sitting Bull," No. 1929 in the archives of the Bureau of American Ethnology, Washington, D.C. This is the copy made by Four Horns of Sitting Bull's incomplete pictographic record of his warlike exploits made in 1870. For Sitting Bull's own interpretation of these drawings, given in 1885, I am indebted to the late Seth C. Jones, formerly secretary, Municipal Art Commission, Rochester, New York. Reference to these drawings is made in the text.

Other pictorial records of his exploits made by Sitting Bull have since been published by Matthew W. Stirling, "Three Pictographic

Autobiographies of Sitting Bull," *Smithsonian Miscellaneous Collections*, Vol. 97, No. 5 (Washington, D.C., 1938), and by Alexis A Praus, "A New Pictographic Autobiography of Sitting Bull" (with seven plates), *Smithsonian Miscellaneous Collections*, Vol. 123, No. 6 (Washington, D.C., 1955). The interpretations of some of these exploits so recorded do not tally with the information given me by Indians who were present in the fights portrayed.

The foreign artist Cronau, who visited the chief while a prisoner of war, taught him to paint horses in European style and to dapple them!

An important record, the "Journal of the Expedition to Powder River, Kept by Major Charles Galpin," is our best account of the peace made with Sitting Bull by Father Pierre-Jean De Smet, 1868, now in the archives of St. Louis University, St. Louis, Missouri. For access to this I am indebted to Father G. J. Garraghan, S.J., who has since published it as "Father De Smet's Sioux Peace Mission of 1868 and the Journal of Charles Galpin," in *Mid-America, An Historical Review*, Vol. XIII, New Series, Vol. II, No. 2. (October, 1930), 141–63.

For the use of McLaughlin's "Orders for Sitting Bull's Arrest," in English and in Sioux, I am indebted to A. B. Welch.

One of the best and most understanding accounts of Sitting Bull while at the agency will be found in "Mary Collins Tells of the Dances of the Sioux and the Influence Held by Sitting Bull; a Short Autobiography," now in the files of the Department of History, state of South Dakota, Pierre.

Finally I must refer to three documents prepared by Indians: First, the records of Chief White Bull, Sitting Bull's elder nephew, who adopted me. These were written in Sioux when he was still a young man, and illustrated with pictures of his exploits. On the odd-numbered pages of his book, he recorded year by year the rosters of war parties, their casualties and *coups*, and on the pages opposite his personal and family history. Copies of these were made for me. Second, a Sioux text: "White Bull's History of Sitting Bull's Life" (1864–1876). Third, a Sioux text entitled "One Bull's Narrative: Sitting Bull's History from the Custer fight until his death" (1876–1890). These were given me by the authors.

Index

[*Note*—Where the same name is applied to two personages among the Indians, they are here differentiated by (a) and (b) when not otherwise identified.]

Acorn: 274
Adam, Silas, scout with Gen. Miles: 134
Adventists, mentioned: 275
Afraid-of-Bear: *see* Bullhead
Afraid-of-Soldier (Warrior-Fear-Him), killed in fight over Sitting Bull's arrest: 302
After-the-Bugs, wounded in fight with Crows: 115
Ahern, Maj. George P., quoted: 237, 248
Alice in Wonderland, Trial Scene in, mentioned: 239
Allen, Col. Alvaren, exhibits Sitting Bull as "slayer of Gen. Custer": 250
Allison, E. H. "Fish": scout, 224; prepares to claim credit for Sitting Bull's surrender, 233
All Over Black, accompanies Father De Smet on peace mission: 99
American Horse: *see* Iron Shield
American Legion, Sioux veterans: 59, 60
Ammunition, hard to get among Indians: 146
Andrew Fox, Sitting Bull's son-in-law, helps him with letter to Indian Agent: 282ff., 304
Animal People, provide customs for Sioux: 8

Appearing-Bear, in Battle of the Rosebud: 153
Arapahos, chiefs at installation of Sitting Bull as head chief: 91
Arm Strong (Broken Arm), killed in fight over Sitting Bull's arrest: 305
Arrow (O'Fallon) Creek: 126
Ash Creek: *see* Reno Creek
Ash Hollow: 142, 228
Assiniboin: *see* Ho'he

Bad, wounded in fight with Crows: 115
Bad Faces: 92
Badger, eager to kill trespassers on Sioux lands: 120
Badger society: 94
Bad Horse, stays to fight Flatheads: 123
Bad Juice, identifies dead troops as Custer's, and finds his body on battlefield: 172
Bad-Light-Hair, killed in Custer fight: 180
Bad Soup: 134
Baker, Johnny: 280, 282
Bakiula: *see* Looks-for-Home
Baldwin, 1st Lt. F. D., strikes at Sitting Bull: 206
Barbour, Asst. Adjt. Gen. M., issues order for arrest of Sitting Bull: 286
Bark Creek: 206n.
Barry, D. F., photographer: 109
Bates, Col. Charles Francis: 175n.
Battle of Fort Phil Kearny: 17

325

INDEX

Sacred Pole of the Sioux: 151

Saddler, John (?), hospital steward, at burial of Sitting Bull: 309

St. Paul, Minn.: 250

Sand Creek: 68, 142, 228

Sans Arcs: seek life of Bear Ribs (b), 50; ask Sitting Bull's help in fighting soldiers, 58; chiefs at installation of Sitting Bull as head chief, 91

Santees: perpetrate Minnesota Massacre, join Sitting Bull's camp, 51; many killed as snipers, 53

Sash-wearers, privileges and vow: 27

Scarlet Point: see Inkpaduta

Scarlet Whirlwind, One Bull's wife: 304

Scarlet Woman, Sitting Bull's first wife: 36

Scatters-Them, counts *coup* on Crow warrior: 30

Secretary of War, report for 1867: 97

Sex among Sioux: 6

Sha, "red" in Sioux tongue: 31

Shakers, mentioned: 275

Shaman of Sioux: prophesies, 26f.; firearms put strain on his art, 30f.

Shave Bear, conducts Ghost Dance: 287, 290ff.

Shave Head: 288; ordered to arrest Sitting Bull, prophesies his own death, 274; arrests Sitting Bull, 294ff.; killed, 301, 304

Shell-Ear-Ring, counts *coup* on Reno's men: 173

Sheridan, Gen. Philip H., bent on establishing army post in Black Hills: 132f.

Sherman, Gen. W. T., authorizes Father De Smet to seek peace with hostile Sioux: 98

Shield: with Sitting Bull in Canada, 207; one of his bodyguard, 289

Shoots-the-Bear: 63

Shoots-Walking: counts *coup* on Crow warrior, 47; in Custer battle, 165

Short Bull (a), killed in fight with Crows: 115

Short Bull (b), leader of Ghost Dancers at Pine Ridge, invites Sitting Bull to greet coming Messiah: 282, 283

Shoshoni: transfer stolen horses, 26; hunting grounds coveted by Sioux, 32

Shot-Through-the-Hand: 188

Sibley, Lt. F. W., escapes trap in Big Horn Mountains: 183

Sibley, Gen. H. H., attacks Sitting Bull's hunting party: 51

Side-of-Bear: see Bear Ribs (b)

Silent Eaters, dinner club organized by Strong Hearts: 96, 261f., 283

Sioux: greatest nation in world to boy Sitting Bull, 4; fight and defeat Iroquois at first meeting, 6

Sioux bird: see Meadowlark

Sioux chiefs escorting Mrs. Eubanks to Fort Laramie hanged by soldiers: 69

Sioux City Journal, story of Mrs. Weldon: 266

Sioux customs borrowed from Animal People: 81

"Sitting Bull," one of the names Sitting Bull's father heard uttered by the Buffalo God: 16

Sitting Bull: begins life with nickname "Slow," 3; his first pony, 4; follows war party, gets *coup*-stick from father, 8f.; counts first *coup*, 12; father dubs him Ta-tan'ka I-yo-ta'ke (Sitting Bull), 13; origin of his name, 16; studies the buffalo for emulation, 17f.; warned by yellowhammer and plays possum to grizzly bear, 20; song of gratitude to yellowhammer, 21; popularity with women, 22f.; saves prostitute from burning alive, 24; promoted to be sash-wearer of Strong Hearts, 27; accompanies Hunkpapa on warpath for horses, 26–28; sings Strong Heart song in fight with Crow chief and kills him, 29; made leader of Midnight Strong Hearts, 30; command of Strong Hearts makes him responsible for tribal hunting, 31f.; smokes war pipe for raid on Ho'he, 34; saves Ho'he boy from death,

INDEX

Crow surprise attack, 45; takes part in installation of Sitting Bull as head chief, 92; decoy to trespassers on Sioux lands, 120

Two Kettles, chiefs present at inauguration of Sitting Bull as head chief: 91

Two Moon (a): 140, 143, 145, 151

Two Moon (b): 173; opinion of Sitting Bull, 145

Use-Him-as-Charger, decoy to trespassers on Sioux lands: 120

Ute John, helps soldiers scalp Indian dead at Slim Buttes: 187

Utes, transfer stolen horses: 26

Van Solen, Mrs. Marie Louise: 265

Vest, George, of Senate committee to investigate condition of Indian tribes: 238ff.

Victoria, Queen: *see* Grandmother

Wade, F. C.: 225

Waggoner, J. F.: 312; made coffin for Sitting Bull, speaks well of him, 309ff.

Waggoner, Mrs. Josephine: 274

Wakan'Tanka, the Great Mysterious: 31, 33, 158; appealed to by Sitting Bull for help in stealing horses, 135; invoked by him to pity his people, 148; his vision of promise, 149

Walker, Col. Samuel: 70, 76

Walks-in-Red-Clothing: *see* Gall

Walsh, Maj. "Long Lance": 224; summons Sitting Bull to conference with U. S. commission, 214

War bonnet to crown Sitting Bull: 94

War Department: 233; wrangles with Indian Bureau, 71; violates clause of "Treaty of Laramie," 110; declares war on Sitting Bull, 139; reports, 206

Warrior orders: 59

Warriors-Fear-Him: *see* Afraid-of-Soldier

Washita River: 110

Water Carrier, claims Crow woman captive: 48

Weasel Bear: 305; picked to arrest Sitting Bull, 273; at his arrest, 293ff.

Welcome: *see* Makes-Room

Weldon, Mrs. Catherine S. (Woman-Walking-Ahead): 261; goes to help Sitting Bull, 264ff.; offers to meet Kicking Bear in debate, 274; mentioned in letter, 278; her portrait of Sitting Bull found in one of his cabins, 306

West Point, mentioned: 170, 179

Wet Hand, one of escort returning Fanny Kelly: 66

Whirlwind Bear, before U. S. commission with Sitting Bull: 215

White Antelope, leader of Cheyennes massacred by Col. Chivington and his soldiers: 68

White Beard: *see* Harney, Gen. William S.

White Bird (a): arrested for horse-stealing, 211; reinstated after punishment, 212

White Bird (b): 288, 295, 297f., 307; picked to arrest Sitting Bull, 273; badge saves his life, 302

White Blackbird, counts *coup* on two Crow women: 47f.

White-Bordered-Tail, counts *coup* on Crow warrior: 47

White-Buffalo-Chief: counts *coup* on Crow woman, 47; wrestles with soldier he pulls off horse, but is beaten, 62f.

White Buffalo Maiden: 100

White Buffalo Woman, wife of One Bull: 134

White Bull (a) (Big-in-the-Center): 116; sings song of futility, 119; fights Flathead single-handed, counts 30th *coup*, 121; gets Flathead scalp, 124; smokes pipe in hail of bullets, 128f., 148; in Battle of the Rosebud, 153; in the fight against Custer, 162–72; kills Custer, 170f.; shot in fight with Col. Otis' men, 190; reports Sitting Bull's conferences with Gen. Miles, 194ff.; watches chief

345